ABOUT THE AUTHOR

Throughout four decades at the pointy end of electronic music, the Secret DJ has experienced it all, from the first stirrings of the Acid House revolution, fame and adulation as a superstar DJ and producer, losing it all through a combination of bad luck and bad choices, and scraping back into the game once more.

The first book, the at-times hilarious, at others harrowing, *The Secret DJ: From Ibiza to the Norfolk Broads* tells the brutally honest story of that dizzying rise to fame as a DJ, producer and short-lived pop star – and an even quicker descent into illness and isolation, when eventually the bill became due and it looked like all was lost.

Throughout it all the Secret DJ never lost their wry sense of humour, dedication to the central mission of championing the real heroes of club culture, or belief in the power of dance music as a force for positive change and unity.

Rising again as a performer, artist, promoter, columnist for dance music bible *Mixmag* and fearless truth-teller and activist, for many the Secret DJ represents the awkward conscience of a subculture. One that's grown from a youth movement set on changing the world to a multi-billion pound industry that all too often puts profit ahead of people, spectacle ahead of substance, and cash ahead of creativity.

First published by Velocity Press 2020

velocitypress.uk

Copyright © The Secret DJ 2020

Cover photo
Photo of the Secret DJ taken by Victor Spinelli
Make-up by Sheena O'Brien - musemakeupibiza.com
Colourisations and preliminary design by Ed Coward
Final design by Bodie Cameron - @curse273
Concept and art direction by The Secret DJ

Cover design
Banana Gun Creative

Typesetting
Paul Baillie-Lane
pblpublishing.co.uk

The Secret DJ has asserted his right under the Copyright, Designs and Patents Act 1988 to be identified as the author of this work

All rights reserved. No part of this publication may be reproduced, in any form or by any means, without permission from the publisher

ISBN: 9781913231057

PRAISE FOR THE SECRET DJ

"It's rare for a writer to capture the excitement and absurdity of dance music culture at the same time, but the Secret DJ did that to great effect in the first book. This latest chapter in the story promises to be every bit as exhilarating, providing an important critical voice at a time when 'the society of the spectacle' threatens to suck the life out of those clinging to the acid house dream." **Justin Robertson**

"I once spent a fine and wonky evening at Claridge's Hotel with this Secret DJ fellow and a less secret, ultra famous superstar DJ type, who you'd think would be the centre of attention. But no, it was Mr Secret that kept us very amused and highly illuminated with his many tales, theories, and a steady supply of vodka and tonic. If his second book contains a tenth of the wild imaginings and brain expanding possibilities that he told us that night, it'll be a solid gold winner." **Richard Norris**

"The first book is a raw, effective and bizarrely emotional tale of 'the life'. Superbly true and direct. I can hardly wait to hear the tale of the music movement being told by The Secret DJ in Book Two!" **Miguel Campbell**

"The Secret DJ returns to once again pull back the curtain on the world of dance music and the sometimes harsh, but always hilarious, realities of what lurks behind it. Get ready for a second descent into the far(cical) side." **Neville Watson**

"Really enjoyed the first book, both hilarious debauchery and insightful commentary on a world usually kept behind the curtain. I'm looking forward to the next instalment, hoping for a lot more righteous anger within." **Posthuman**

"I loved The Secret DJ - some all-too familiar characters mixed with the highs and lows of what this industry can throw at you. Excited and intrigued to read the second instalment...how much more extreme can it get?!" **Denney**

"I never read books about electronic music, why would I? But I guess The Secret DJ is more an anarchist handbook for shattered dreamers than a manual on how to make it big on the scene. Can't wait for his new adventures." **Ivan Smagghe**

"We all have war stories, us jobbing night-lifers. From having sets ended by soldiers with automatic weapons in Juarez to coming-round in Glasgow city centre suddenly best pals with a gangster who's most affectionate nickname was 'Wolf'. I've bagged a couple over the years. And yours are undoubtedly more vivid, funnier or more ludicrous than mine. The Secret DJ's are better still." **Ewan Pearson**

"I loved book one, waiting to live the DJ life vicariously again thru book two!" **Arthur Baker**

"The Secret DJ's first book managed to do something very different to the existing dance music memoirs (and I should know as I have read them all). It functioned not only as a hilarious jaunt through the insanity of the glory years of dance music – i.e. when there was still money in music - but as a harrowing portrayal of the emotionally, physically and mentally taxing straits an international DJ will find themselves in. Anyone with even a passing curiosity about 'the industry' should read it and await its follow up, especially if they have any frankly dangerous notions of joining up professionally, which I cannot in all good conscience recommend." **Manu Ekanayake (music and culture journalist)**

"Every participant in the music industry will wince at the thought of falling under the glance of the Secret DJ's withering pen, but still find themselves avidly leafing through his pages for the merest mention." **Carl Puttnam (Cud)**

THE SECRET DJ
BOOK TWO

CONTENTS

Preface	1
Chapter 1: Decades Of Dickheads	5
Chapter 2: It Was Right Grim Blah Blah Blah...	11
Chapter 3: Epiphany Pie	25
Chapter 4: The Lunatics Reach A Short-term Rental Agreement With The Asylum	32
Interlude: Showgirls II	42
Chapter 5: Don't Touch That Dial. Or That. Don't Touch That Either. Just Don't Touch Anything, OK?	44
Interlude: Be The Freak	60
Chapter 6: I'm Just Going Outside And I May Be Some Time	62
Chapter 7: Event Horizons	69
Chapter 8: You Know The Honeymoon Is Over When...	81
Interlude: Brighton Rocks	88
Chapter 9: The Crack Of Doom	93
Interlude: Fudd 'n' Bugs	100
Chapter 10: Resident Evils	107
Chapter 11: There's Actually Loads Of Businesses Like Showbusiness...	115
Chapter 12: Uninvited Guests	125
Interlude: Here Endeth the Lesson	135

Chapter 13: The Pyramid Scheme	138
Interlude: The Shit Chauffeur	150
Chapter 14: Bad Eggs	155
Chapter 15: 'Slebz 'n' Schlubs	160
Chapter 16: Espionage, Sabotage, And Triage	167
Chapter 17: More Endless Claptrap About Playing Other People's Records	182
Chapter 18: Throttling It To Death With Love	198
Interlude: Lost Like A Fox	209
Chapter 19: Old Man Yells At Cloud	212
Chapter 20: Not Something To Joke About	220
Chapter 21: Don't Call Us, We'll Call You	229
Chapter 22: Chasing The Dopamine	239
Chapter 23: The Promised Land (Members-Only)	246
Interlude: Still Here	251
Chapter 24: My 0.004 Cents	258
Acknowledgements	272
Glossary of Terms	274

PREFACE

Come on in. Come into the club. Let's call it 'Klub Glurge' for ease. Pre-pandemic of course, and thanks to the wonders of globalisation, there's a club like this in every major city of the First World. Come in quick, because this place is getting a bit of a reputation, and while its presence in this formerly run-down part of town was a major boon for property letting agents when the only people interested were students and artists looking for a district that was mainly cheap and a bit stabby, it seems like overnight the cranes and flammable cladding sprang up everywhere. Once these streets are *100%* poorly-finished and vastly overpriced studio flats, the Caymans-registered landlord of this place is unlikely to want to deal with the inevitable noise complaints, not when there is fat developer money on the table.

No time for dancing right now (who dances anymore anyway? *sweaty* is so very off-brand darling), we need to get backstage, where we find the support DJ, a resolutely underground ex-model with a huge and enthusiastic Instagram following. Leaning against the wall in her trademark monochrome, she's multitasking; smoking a cigarette, approving a tweet from her PR in support of trans rights in the comic book industry and speaking to her agent, who's just signed her up for large money at a festival in a country that last week stoned several dissidents and non-binary people to death. She's possibly not aware that the agency has several other (and far less in-demand) DJs they'll be able to offload on the event as a job-lot contingent on her commitment, but the money is like really *really* good and as one of the shockingly few female DJs on the line-up, her name will be victoriously high on the bill.

Eyeing her lazily through the door crack of the dressing room opposite is the headliner, a paunchy pub-faced lizard. A confirmed 'ladies man' dressed in streetwear he's at least 30 years too old for and his own Twitter feed is full of borrowed bants 'n' rants, peppered with conflicts with strangers about political correctness gone mad. Though nothing has been proven (yet), most of the club's underpaid female bar staff and stage runners have been warned informally to trust what their instincts and his long-standing reputation are screaming at them and not to go anywhere alone with him. Absent-mindedly he dismisses the other DJ as too high profile, and his lazy gaze moves on, scanning for easier prey. His driver is already getting the Rohypnol ready, and the manager and his lawyer can quietly deal with the fallout afterwards, as usual.

Tonight's promoter is a perma-tanned, veteran 27-year-old in a tastefully frayed grey T-shirt, painfully American teeth and religiously trimmed stubble. He is babbling some anodyne praise about the headliner's latest lazy release, even though he'd literally never heard of the ancient DJ until last week. The track was created, the headliner vaguely recollects, by an aspiring teen producer using pirated software in a high rise suburb of a nameless city in Russia, so the standard verbal shower is a tad more irritating than usual.

The speaker pauses for a brief second to accept a sponsored energy drink from his fellow promoter, another nondescript faux-Bohemian whose entire experience of the world so far is a gap-year and *very* nice holidays. The pair can date their relationship all the way back to their impossibly expensive boarding school. The stakes are low tonight, even after the embarrassingly large fees paid to the DJs the numbers are unlikely to dent the capital they've built up from a little dabbling in property development and, let's be frank, a pair of very healthy trust funds. They did put a lot of thought into these bookings though, combing social media to see whose numbers were biggest and favouring name recognition, and ideally, a little controversy. One of them is even mildly curious to know what music to expect later and makes a mental note to ask someone 'what sort' is being played.

There's a small gaggle of honking human geese in one corner that is almost an entire third of what is left of the music industry. They aren't interested in anything anyone plays tonight either, the owners of the various business they work for told them to come tonight 'or else', having all received calls from one of the promoter's Dads, a man so obscenely powerful just his name appearing on your phone can make you sweat. Over in the corner near the main booth is a small herd of old men in coats who only come out two or three times a year to hear certain approved old names and to check out a younger one that might make muster. They are pals with some of the remnants of the biz and have come on the free list of the support DJ. They never pay to get in, and yet loudly complain about the prices once inside, and everything else, all year, until the next annual visit.

These are the endangered Balearic Silverbacks or 'Workwear Jedwards'. North of 40 or even 50 years old. Their main purpose is to tell each other they invented everything, nothing is any good anymore and the venue, staff, punters, drugs and DJs are all absolutely *awful*.

A couple of times a year they migrate as a large group known as 'Dad's Army' or 'The Chelsea Pensioners' to see DJ Harvey, whom they worship as a minor deity. Then stand in groups and tell each other he is rubbish while writing down what records he plays. Later they will go back to their home set-up and pay a small fortune on the internet to find all his records. Once a month Balearic Silverbacks try to forget they don't have a nice house, secure job, lovely family etc. and pretend to be DJs. They will play Harvey's records to a tiny half-empty pub, or around a pool in Ibiza to a small gathering of other Balearic Silverbacks, who will all roundly agree it is all absolutely *awful*.

Indeed the silver-haired DJ playing the warm-up set tonight is a prime example. 90 minutes of strictly vinyl-only, post-Balearic yawn. He is something of an anomaly, not merely by dint of being twice the age of nearly everyone else here, and musically completely inappropriate. He volunteered to pay all his own costs and waived any fee for the opportunity to impress colleagues at his corporate graphic design consultancy with his tales of DJing at the weekend. Possible clients are here too, he suddenly realises mid-track, surreptitiously taking out his iPhone to make a note to ask his accountant if this comes under 'business entertaining'. He likes to do nice festivals if the weather is good, and twice a year he loses a shitload of money to import an obscure elderly DJ from Chicago to perform for his big-coated mates in the upstairs room of the cool pub one of them owns, toasty-warm in the knowledge that he, and he alone, is keeping the true spirit alive.

Back 'front-of-house' now, let's grab a drink at the bar; perhaps the spirit megabrand whose generous sponsorship of 'dance culture' overseas has helped an entire generation of third world ravers know which 40% proof alcohol best encapsulates that authentic European club vibe. Never mind the music, grab a shot for Instagram at the visual sweet spot designed for just that purpose, chosen with all the care someone no longer employed used to take over the audio sweet spot. The place is packed now, and approximately 90% of the paying customers are primarily there to take a picture or video with their phone, ideally with the model DJ in the frame. If they don't get it, there's always a chance the DJ will do/say/wear something dead wrong and there will be shiny digital currency in that too. Whatever happens tonight, it will happen via their phone and they are ready. The other 10% have their phone out also, with Shazam in the holster, an obscurity loaded in the chamber.

Not that any of this matters if the rumours about the imminent closure are true. The freshly-imported, well-heeled residents will not want to hear a peep of any of that 'vibrancy' that sold them on the purchase and are petrified of the 'local colour' they were promised in the egregious promotional real estate video. If, indeed, they ever arrive through the entrances that are specifically segregated between rich and poor, depending upon if the block was even required to provide affordable housing. The oil-rich owners are more than prepared to sell Klub Glurge, it was, after all, the plan since day one. They own a lot more around here than just the disco.

Not a soul in the place wonders for a second whether Klub Glurge is what the Acid House movement was really hoping for all those years ago. Back when we, yes, even me, crumbly old Secret DJ; spectre at the feast, raven on the bust and grand onion in the custard, thought that we might end up changing the world...

CHAPTER 1
DECADES OF DICKHEADS

At the end of every decade two things always spring to mind for me. How Antoine de Caunes, the extremely French presenter of the legendary Eurotrash TV show, used to deliberately pronounce decade as 'dickhead', and how silly decades are anyway. I've been a DJ over a period stretching across four dickheads now, even if 2000-2010 doesn't feel like one at all. I'd just like to make a point right here about DJs claiming in their biographies that they've been 'playing for 20 years' when they are clearly not even yet 30 years old. You start counting from when you became a professional. Not when your Dad let you play on his stereo as a toddler. The day someone *pays* you for your skills is the day you graduate. Sorry and all that. I don't make the rules.

Balearic Silverbacks will often tell you that the 80s were bare wicked. Maybe it was for a handful of them in persistently wealthy London. I thought the 80s were pretty shitty myself. What was certainly stand-out about the period, however, was that culturally things felt fresh, futuristic and unique. As if that which came before was in black and white. No, I mean it really *was* monochrome, we had a black and white telly for the beginning of our childhood and nearly everything we read in terms of books, mags and comics had very little colour. Most of all, there was an energy that bleak governmental polices, try as they might, simply could not diminish. We fought, quite literally, for the right to party.

It's debatable that we won the 80s. We *defo* won the 90s though. The 90s were just silly. The Labour Government changeover in the UK in 1997, finally, was a nation-wide party and it truly felt like anything was possible. If you want to imagine what 90s clubland was like, just look at the USA doing EDM now. In the 90s we were fizzy, optimistic, completely off our tits and almost entirely devoid of seriousness. There was daft money everywhere for equally daft things. It was a daft decade and not a moment passes where I wouldn't go back there.

Don't get me wrong, if, for example, the 1970s were peak creative freedom for the film industry; similarly the 90s were the absolute peak for electronica, and arguably for music as a whole. Let's be frank here, streaming changed things so much that many insiders believe the late 90s and early 00s was the last time there was a recognisable music business. The 90s were particularly the time electronic music was recklessly handed over to people outside the control of the industry. Independent of expensive recording studios and major label offices. We saw the likes of Massive Attack, Portishead, Leftfield, Björk, Aphex Twin, The Prodigy, Daft Punk... the list is massive. All genre-bending, fresh and utterly unique. Nearly all of these names made their start on home-made set-ups. Major labels were getting excited by this new vibe, and crucially, not really understanding it at all, or where it came from. The absolute apex of any creative industry requires that the money men do not understand it. They give, and the artists make. It's only when the failed artists start to work inside the big machine that this ideal relationship sours from a plumptious peach into a bad raisin. Labels hiring 'kids who get it' immediately find themselves being steered by Gatekeepers who immediately put padlocks on everything. It's far, far better when the industry is ignorant, rather than clued-up. If you ever wonder why films and music are currently so incredibly bland and uniform, this is one of the main reasons. People who think they know everything suddenly taking the wheel, crippling those actually at the grindstone, all the while everyone petrified of taking any kind of risk, or worst of all, offending the internet. The greatest periods in art were entirely about risk and offence. Sure there is great stuff about now if you know where to look. But it's tiny. Niche. Don't make me say the word 'artisanal' or I'll need a wash.

The millennium? Well. That was a hell of a party. Short, sweet and also the fulcrum upon which everything suddenly tipped over. It went weird, *fast*. The superclub era was over, and their own greed did for them. The loopy wages being charged on the millennium (and we were seeing things like private jets for DJs for the first time) meant an economic bubble burst. Ironically it wasn't the rich fat cat DJs who paid the price (the rich never do), but the middle tier. Promoters just looked at

CHAPTER 1

the stupid money going out of the door to DJs and simply started doing it personally. This period spawned hundreds of promoters appointing themselves as fresh residents who'd never DJ'd a day in their lives before. Or more reasonably, their unknown mates who were pretty good DJs started to get work for very low wages. DJ Giant Fat Cat and Co still got paid if they sold tickets. Not much changed for them. There was a massive purge of mid-range DJs who, to be fair, probably *did* get paid too much without bringing enough people through the door. And the board was set for what we see a lot of today. Cheap support and the same overpriced big names as headliners, everywhere, all the time. Money talks.

During this very odd dickhead, the no-mans-land between 2000 and 2010, the landscape started to shift in a very subtle but ultimately seismic way. The fun times were over. The cash spigot was turned resolutely OFF. A lot of those quite annoyed, suddenly unemployed, mid-range DJs started to look for jobs behind the scenes and we began to see a rise in very *very* serious people who took themselves very *very* seriously frowning most bumptiously upon anyone having fun, and consequently, the era of discos-as-artform really started to take shape. I'd even go so far as to say some of these types were extremely pissed-off and used their new power to enact revenge on the scene that rejected them. Conjecture, sure, but I stand by it. Personally, I had about as much fun as anyone else during the first half of this time, which wasn't much. Thank God music started to get really good outside the Minimal bubble I was getting trapped in, and what started as 'Electroclash' morphed into basically 'New Music'. Plus there was the wee magazine-generated 'Nu Rave' blip that came along full of colour and kicked the arse out of all the boring.

Then almost as quickly as things got interesting, things started to wilt and die-off. Clubs were empty. In 2010 The Conservatives were back with a vengeance and everyone was soon skint again thanks to the bizarre 'austerity' programme. This time found the grey men (sorry, always heterosexual men, always the blandest grey in hair and soul) who kept trying to tell us spangly discos were minimalist art galleries had their final victory in sight. Few young people were interested in discos. Nothing was enjoyable, anywhere. Everyone abandoned the fun and sun of Ibiza and moved to Berlin to declare they were now modern artists, which is about the most telling aspect of this period. Articles started to appear in major publications asking if it was the end. Had our scene finally died?

One thing illuminated this period very strongly for me. I was playing just before a very large legend on the former Space Terrace around this time of great flux. I was over the moon. He was a hero to me. I was playing very much stuff the Terrace was not used to. The current stuff. Fresh that season. Darker, more German and more Techno than the happiness, handclaps, flamenco guitars and bongos that was becoming, frankly a bit of a cliche. The crowd went wild, which was a hell of a relief 'cos it was risky. Daytime. New vibes perhaps not suited to it in terms of what came before. I turned to the legend to hand the roaring crowd over to him, pleased as punch, and he looked like a man who'd lost a tenner and found a fiver. Sour and despondent. He turned and pointed to the last record that was still turning and said: "*that* shit is why I am retiring". I was devastated. Only the following decade and his subsequent retirement-as-promised would prove the change in sound would endure, rather than him. No one's trousers are too big to be pressed by the steamroller of time.

By Enya's ambient alarm clock! I honestly never thought I would say this, but two things properly rode-in and saved the day. Day-glo American arrivistes, who knew very little about anything we were doing, and very young Europeans who knew quite a lot, because they were raised on it. Deep House, new Techno and EDM saved us. Say it loud. It's the truth. From 2010 onwards there was a wave of youthful energy that washed over everything, cleaning out the old, grey misery guts and re-invigorating everything, everywhere. Thank God for them. I salute you all. To think that this thing has been going so strong for so long is truly amazing and a great, *great* privilege to be part of. Long may it reign.

While the dance music industry has undoubtedly grown to almost obscene proportions, the spirit that first conceived it has suffered greatly. I had a grandstand view of this process. This book seeks to celebrate the good and warn about the bad. COVID-19 might even perhaps become an opportunity to reset things and get back to the spirit of the founders. I

CHAPTER 1

will chart this thing from my first experiences of it to its current form as a personal journey. There is no escaping the theme that Acid House has been brutalised by capitalism. Some might call this simply progress. You may argue the inevitability. Capitalism eats everything. It *must*. And this is capitalism through the prism of post-war propaganda, co-opted from the highly efficient Nazi machine over to America via people like Edward Bernays. His skill was to utilise his uncle's thinking, one Sigmund Freud, and replace dry advertising such as "buy this thing, it is jolly hard-wearing and most reasonably priced" with emotive messaging that appealed not to common sense, but aimed directly at our hidden, basic, highly Freudian emotions. Such as "Psst! Hey, kid! In order to feel good, you MUST buy this thing". Sound familiar? Smells a bit like this new 'emotion over reason' thing our politicians are all doing nowadays, right?

'House is a feeling' is the mantra of the pioneers who helped start the whole thing. However, we now live in an age where reason is completely paved-over with random feels, in order to coldly manipulate. Bernays monetised feelings. In order to exist, capitalism must engage with you. Feelings are engagement. Have the feelings behind our disco thing been hijacked too? The cry I hear most often from those generally in favour of capitalism is that all progress is good. Things used to be pretty bad, even in my short lifetime I can remember true poverty and national economic disaster. Things are not quite so randomly violent on the streets nowadays, and people are slightly more prosperous; ergo, everything is just fine thanks. No. It's way too complex a thing to polarise and simplify like that.

Gentrification is a case in point. On the surface surely a district that used to be poor is 'better' when property is higher value, therefore 'nicer' people live there. What is wrong with that? It's this kind of non-logic that is everywhere currently. From the deeply stupid 'all lives matter' (which is like saying to a suffragette "votes for everyone!") to the equally dense "when is international men's day?".

The 'feeling' and 'positivity' of the situation being 'better' and therefore highly advantageous simply steamrollers over every single inconvenient detail, objection, warning, consequence, difficulty and human life in the way. Here we see fake Americanised positivity and advancing technology working hand-in-hand with capitalism and The New Stupid. Modern life in a nutshell. Don't get in the way of our sunshine, progress and good vibes or we will pave you over. Plough you into the earth and salt the ground. Even the pleasant-sounding term 'gentrification' is a trick, sounds nice, right? It is not. It is the war cry of the rich. This is their world now. Entirely.

I give you this potted history above so you can track the changes to our biz in macro form, in preparation to look at it in more detail. Clearly the disco follows society. As society experiences political and economic change, so do we. I'm not harking back, just thinking aloud. I accept change. I've spent a very long time trying to push the future. It would be hypocritical of me to stop now. I'm merely suggesting that we learn from the past. Don't make my mistakes. Understanding the trade is as important as having the skills. Bypassing either will lead to a very short career indeed.

All any writer, journalist or author can ever do is somehow report from where they are at. No matter how fanciful, colourful or dull, it's about making a connect, just like the emotional bridges we seek on the dancefloor. A book is just a bosun's chair, suspended between two ships in a storm.

CHAPTER 2
IT WAS RIGHT GRIM
BLAH BLAH BLAH...

There are plenty of excellent books with who did what and when in Dance Music. I tend to find once you start to debate the history it very quickly descends into 'who did it first?' supremacism, which is utterly ridiculous. European electronica, Industrial, New Beat and Disco productions had as much to do with our cultural development as anything that happened in New York and Chicago. And when does anyone mention that every single piece of equipment of note that provided the foundations came from Japan? It's a fruitless argument when it is all about ownership. No one owns love and unity. Everyone worked hard on what we enjoy today, all over the world. Is there a continually ongoing process to whitewash all the colour and diversity out of things? Oh, without doubt! But that is a story for later. What I want to do is try and express the experience. Dates, stats and origin stories do not convey impact. Information is not experience. And believe me, Acid House was ALL about impact.

First, you have to understand what it was like before: 'B.C.', meaning 'Before Clubs'. There were various scenes in various countries all over the world but the tide changed in the 1980s. For sure Disco was dominant in the 1970s but it became a dirty word after racists and homophobes worked so hard to demonise it. Soon Disco was dust in the breeze. Being deemed 'uncool' is the driest of wastelands, the harshest of banishments. No one is saying nobody gathered to enjoy music together before the 80s, of course not, but it was a very different thing. If it wasn't a disco (by now dying out), it was versions of the rock model. The band. The stage. The setlist.

The late 70s and early 80s were particularly filthy. A time of global downturn, unemployment, crime, violence and corruption. To come out of state school at that time was to arrive into a large nothing. A debutante at a glacial ball celebrating sub-zero opportunity. Only the rich had prospects, and the wealthy were a lot fewer in number than today. Culturally these times can become strong, however. It's a loose rule that I just made up but the ratio for cultural strength is directly proportional to the degree of economic hardship. The worse things are, the harder we try to improve how we feel about it with escape, distraction and artistic beauty. Capitalism, as we knew it then, was failing around 99% of the global population dismally, and still is. So you made your own fun; knit, weave, sing and paint your good times for yourself. 'Cos for sure, no one else was going to do it for you.

With art, timing is everything, and something few can lay claim to. Right place is all you can manage, right time is an accident of birth. In the postwar years in America, for example, there was great uncertainty throughout the nation as to whether peace was real, what was ahead and who the enemy now was. This was reflected in its more credible art, such as jazz and abstract painting. They matched the mood with a spiky weirdness and apparent lack of form. Mainstream US culture did the opposite and produced high cheese as a form of comfort to salve the lack of security people felt. The 1950s were simultaneously an artistic era of great experimentation, and also great conservatism. The mid-to-late 1970s were similarly a period of great uncertainty in the United Kingdom. A tiny Dark Age.

'New Wave' amongst others rose to prominence as this time came to a close. Post-punk. Slightly more polished than its predecessor but still raw and energised. Still very guitar. Still quite shouty. Still very much about the crowd idolising the individual or small group. Trying hard to be 'indie' and 'underground', if not in appearance only, but in truth very much controlled by a still vast and powerful major label music industry. A slight change in look, but to many, not a huge difference in the business. Still 'rock 'n' roll'. Still mainly blues chords and progressions, fancy hair and tiny trousers. Still prospects and hopefuls aping their idols in the hope being elevated from the blood and dust of the arena by the hand of Caesar. Clambering over the fallen to be blessed with the vast riches and adulation they are conditioned to dream of.

CHAPTER 2

In basements and bedrooms, outhouses and garages all over the world something else was happening, however. A cold war against normality was growing. A discontent with poster boys and Barbie girls, the studied cool, the achievable evils, the inevitable 'stardom', the cash you'll never have. The word was leaking out that it might not be all it was cracked up to be. Not the jolly lark advertised. Often fatal, frequently misery-inducing. For the perpetrators as well as the observer. Jesus, Pink Floyd made entire concept albums about how awful and empty it all was. Frank Zappa spent a lifetime satirising the hollow mummery of the beast. There's a 'something's got to give' aspect about fin de siècle society, and it happens way more often than every hundred years. Mainstream culture equally as derelict as the surroundings. A bag of rotten mince about to burst. Even the arch but slightly more approachable stars of New Wave were still thin, pretty and talented. Still 'stars' and way WAY out of your league, loser. The styles were old, however. Dry. Overdone.

People in highly distressed post-industrial towns like Dusseldorf, Detroit, Sheffield and Manchester felt the loss especially hard. Once they'd had everything. Relevance. Purpose. Wages. Now they were an empty ruin. Abandoned even by their very own nations. Some cut adrift for decades. Entire generations were born into a yawning void. Looking up at parents made destitute and powerless. Gazing out of a window into the endless grey. Perpetually bored. Utterly unchallenged. And nothing annoys someone in prison more acutely than stories of prosperity and glamour. What relevance did ANYTHING culture had to offer mean to someone frozen in this second Ice Age? What use are sharp pop songs and cool shades worn at a jaunty angle to someone trapped in a block of frozen water? Sure, many still clung. Started new bands and new sounds to perpetuate the rock beast. Fresh versions thought of as new, but really not novel at all. Technology, however, once the beating heart of these abandoned cities, was always in the blood of the citizens of nowhere. Still is. Even now. I should know, I am one. Technology was the engine of the industries that drove these cities to greatness. Makes sense that it would be again. My own journey was mapped directly to the shiny rise of Tech, and remains so to this day.

All I can do is tell you about what I've seen and been around. It's all I've got. I wouldn't dream of calling myself a historian. I was there, though. Since the start. 'Start' is a relative term depending on how batshit-crackers you are about being the first about everything. I was definitely there at the start of my own journey into sound, be weird if I wasn't. This was England in the mid 1980s. Sure we all played in dreadful bands. Sure we all followed some weird trends and wore some bizarre trousers that seem hilarious now. Who didn't? To comprehend the impact of Acid House you have to understand the scenario before it came along. It was nigh-on impossible to make a record of any quality without equipment, infrastructure and property that totalled up to gazillions of paper pounds. To have the connections to even be *considered* for recording was utterly fanciful. The means of production, pun very much intended, were in the hands of industrialists. Music industrialists. Sure there were small versions of the big machine, and many a strong independent sub-movement came from them. But the methods and music were very similar, top to bottom. All the attitude, contrary stances, tight pants or massive hairdos in the world couldn't change the simple process of write, rehearse, gig, get spotted, get a deal, release records, tour, maaaaaybe chart. Repeat. It was the same process for every morbid Mancunian pub band or sun-drenched LA supergroup.

Around this time I helped make flight cases and manage a recording and rehearsal studio. Sounds grand but I basically laboured for the boss for peanuts and filled-in when he wasn't there. Which was a lot of the time. The place was, like most of its kind back then, a dismal and damp hellhole held together with gaffer tape and layers of black paint so thick they looked and felt like rubber. Random misshapes of foam and sprayed insulation made the place look like H.R. Giger's nasty sex dungeon. Like many studios it was a very badly made wooden building built inside a vast brick basement. So everything from corridors to door frames was wonky, ill-fitting and strangely small. Like a two-by-four padded submarine built by a simpleton. It stank, of course. Everything that is entirely populated by men ends up stinking fairly fast. Give it years and it reeks. Something to do with men's noses switching-off after a certain time without women, possibly, I'm not a zoologist. You can maybe say you've earned your spurs when you've built an entire set of flight cases for a rock band during the days of a week, then spent every night carrying amplifiers through a smelly wooden labyrinth, continually assaulted by muffled sound at great volume, listening to spotty nerds complain about everything from the crisps to the soldering. It was like spending years inside the organ of a bad giant, wandering its rotten spleen, a damp forgotten duct.

BUT, and that is a big but, what we did have there was a small recording studio. That was everything. That was why I was there. Everyone with even a whiff of music in their lives will know what it means to get anywhere near a recording studio, even a terrible one that stank of man-foot, paint thinners, burnt plastic and Goth hairspray.

I would walk the three miles there and three miles back in the pitch dark across parks that were a no-mans-land when the sun went down. Passageways populated with upright animals. Junctions with options that contained either Skinhead boot boys or wildly random gluesniffers. One walkway had warning markers of cricket stumps with dead hedgehogs covered in melted seven inch singles like some sort of Lord of the Flies ritual portal. In these dark parks I once saw someone beaten to death with a tennis racket, apparently for the crime of trying to play tennis. Gatekeepers of the Acid House narrative will tell you the 1980s were all Ibiza sunshine, orbital raves, dungarees and bandanas, smiley T-shirts and loadsamoney. It really wasn't like that at all. Not even for them. It was mostly a new regime of hard right western governments brutalising the globe for profit. Capital cities enjoyed this at everyone else's expense. Quite literally.

Part of this political drive was to centralise power. Regions were abandoned and even actively defunded, capitals raked in what was left of the power and money, so the Acid Dads of London are forgiven for being parochial in their view. Visiting football stadiums is not living outside the capital. How could they possibly know what life was like out in the wastelands many of them unwittingly voted to destroy? Making 99% of the rest of the country irrelevant was the entire point.

In the same way that the 1960s didn't really extend all that much further than Carnaby Street, Haight-Ashbury and a few thousand kids out of many, many millions, so the Acid House story has been compressed into a tale about a handful of people going to Ibiza and coming back to London. Or a couple of venues in New York and Chicago inventing a new sound. The truth about this thing based around electronic music is way WAY more complex than those who profit greatly from the simplified stories we are allowed to tell. The fact is that everyone who has been involved in this thing has their own very personal story. I worked in studios making very basic electronic music for nearly a decade before I'd even met anyone else doing it. Let alone knew of a scene that didn't exist yet. Lordy, I would have made a human sacrifice and prayed daily to a multi-snake-headed, goat-arsed deity for a scene! I'd been at it like a monk for what felt like a lifetime before I'd even heard a House record from America. I was heavily into Einstürzende Neubauten, Giorgio Moroder, Dub Reggae, Cabaret Voltaire, Kraftwerk, Joy Division, The Young Gods, Finitribe, Can, Front 242... I'm just telling you that it is perfectly possible to have your own journey and for it to have nothing at all to do with the accepted narrative. It's OK to not be in the gang. It's fine to stand apart. The truth is more important. I wasn't cool. I wasn't special. I didn't invent shit. But I was there, knee deep in cables since day dot. I was trying to work out how to use one of the early sequencers with a manual that only came in Japanese when most people were into Rare Groove and were still surprised by digital watches. I didn't change the world or even make so much as a ripple, but I lived for the pointy end of music. Myself and thousands of others, naturally. However, it was, and remains, my entire life.

Now around this time I dabbled very poorly with all sorts of instruments but the one thing I could claim with any veracity was that I could play the drums. Not brilliantly, but I could pass for one in most bands bar a few high-end jazzers. Imagine ten years of gigging, lugging, humping, driving, scrimping, thumping and generally lumbering.

Then some fucker invents the drum machine.

Like most drummers I was always an early adopter of tech. There's something about not having much to do and the rest of the band ignoring you most of the time that leads to an interest in the technical side of things. At first, like most kids who'd literally spent their entire life trying to get the kit together, I found the concept of being replaced in seconds by a tiny machine at first hilarious, then abhorrent, then unlikely, then the slow process of realisation started to kick in. As with most tech, the personal opinion of an individual has very little impact on its progress. One day you wake up and it is normalised. A wee while later and people have forgotten what the original thing it replaced was even for. So at first, tech wasn't sequenced. That is to say it did not loop or run in a programmed fashion very often. They were merely electronic instruments. When you hit the pad it went "bud-ooo" like a camp plastic pigeon. It did not go "bud-ooo" a second time unless you told it to by hitting it. Giving it some digital breadcrumbs to follow was a long way off. It sounded pretty rubbish, but on the plus side, it still needed someone with a modicum of skill to get a performance out of it. The trouble started in earnest when sequencing arrived more widely.

Drummers are often the person in the band who ends up doing the sound effects on the concept album, or the tape loops. They are forever edged out of melody but are sometimes allowed to venture into sonics as long as it doesn't detract too much from the singer's ego and the guitarist's envy/love of the singer. You'll find a lot of dance music producers were drummers, bassists and keyboard players, and the reason it is nearly always drummers, bassists and keyboard players is because this was the first ego-free youth culture to have emerged truly intact. Supposedly. I will spare you any more tales from the stool, and suffice to say that suddenly I realised drummers weren't the butt of the jokes any more or the de facto beast of burden, but the one most likely to embrace engineering and production. Then the day comes when you start to understand that for the first time since Tubular Bells, you don't need any daft strutting peacocks around at all to make music. In fact, you don't need anyone. You're not the bottom of the pile anymore, the pile is all yours. Tech gives, and Tech takes away.

At the same time, and contrasting with all this futurism, Northern Soul was a big influence. I'm not old enough to have been one of the true faithful, it was the domain of our older siblings. But the attitude shone through across generations. It was the thing we looked up to, which often has far more impact on you than your own, current obsessions. It was slightly out-of-reach. Relentlessly omnipresent and inevitable.

It was some years later when I realised that the words 'Northern Soul' meant a type of music, rather than a pithy description of who we were. Most of all it was uniquely the scene that didn't need a thing from anyone. Meaning it had a finite amount of records available, so had no need of new 'product'. It was all old music, ideally music completely forgotten or ridiculously obscure, so required no expansion into new areas. It was a closed loop and completely independent of the music industry at-large, and no matter how hard that industry tried, it could never co-opt it. This has never left me. A celebratory working-class culture utterly focussed on music for dancing. Absolutely everything that followed for me came from this. Sure, there was Disco, always there is the Disco, but my personal mecca was an actual Mecca. Discos were for people with money. Northern Soul was for the workers. In a sense, I'm still on the train with the older kids, trying to pass as legit, and failing. Being knocked back and waiting outside until the last train back. Fascinated by what might be going on in there. Never quite passing the threshold. There's quite a few of us who came up this way, although I only discovered that much, much later. I was just one of thousands. Doesn't everyone spend those early years totally convinced that they are the only lonely kid in the world?

This was the difference and also the connection between the studio and the dancehall. I had an obsession not only with the tunes and how they were made, but how they were *received*. To me, the immediacy of a huge ballroom full of people enjoying music alongside you was everything. Had no interest in TV, sport was strictly for Normals, certainly didn't want to be a pop star. I was still engaged in the real. Still a member of a living human community. Alternate realities online were mere science fiction back then. It was all about the now. Even the drugs were about enhancing the reality of where you were. Amphetamines. Businesslike stimulants that, like an athlete, were strictly for physical performance. Giving a cold, steely edge and if anything, the opposite of a trip. In Northern Soul, the music and the crowd was the high.

Quite a time passed between being a grubby, ham-faced urchin, pressed against the window, messing with tapes with my mates, to eventually working in a studio. But the connection never left me. While perfectly au-fait with whatever the musical flavours were of the time, and having a strong understanding of what went before, *The Funk* was becoming everything. An obsession with making people react had taken hold. It starts on the drum stool. There's nothing more immediate than starting off a song with a groove and seeing everyone react, including the rest of the band. This *functionality* if you like, was a laser-precision revelation. Sure people wrote nice things. Melody and song construction were all very well but there was a huge pull for me to engage the primitive. Almost all great art understands this simplicity.

Who knows what the psychology of it all is? Something to do with youngsters wanting agency? Early sexuality? Being heard and more importantly, felt? Forgive me if this rambles but, in short, I'm trying to say that my earlier experiences not only of forbidden rituals in casinos but also things like ceilidhs, which were my first exposure to music and its impact on surroundings, were all hibernating in me waiting to burst forth later when music was being made. I never just made music only for myself, I made it for the room too. I won't bore you with my childhood music lessons, tin whistles, violins, bodhrans and pianos. Lots of kids had these in their lives. Thanks to the encouragement of good parents, it got room to breathe, grow and become important. Maybe that is another story for another book. Suffice to say I was now pottering about seeing just how much could be achieved solo with a room full of fairly basic technology, aching to connect with dancers. It felt like I had got as far as was humanly possible and was barely shaving. Already stalled, encrusted in a prehistoric wasteland where nothing was possible and everything was elsewhere.

Then the revolution happened.

To understand Acid House you have to understand how it arrived, and what it arrived into. Impact is everything. All that dark satanic mill shit above is to show you how dismal and monochrome everything was until this explosion of light happened. To some, perhaps in London or New York, these things are their entitlement. Just more fun and fashion. Their inheritance. Their birthright. To the rest of us, something way more. Something significant. It was unity. It was action. Finally.

This new thing was never about the DJ. Not for a moment. My first DJ 'gigs' took place in a cupboard with a large slit in the door, ostensibly so the dancers could shout requests at you. You DJ'ed in a completely different room to the dancefloor. That is how important you were. Slightly less than the glass collectors but maybe one up from the cleaner, as at least you had a slightly bigger cupboard that only smelt of poppers rather than bleach. Our purpose at other times was to warm up for bands and maybe play a few tunes afterwards too. The idea that a record was somehow a superior experience to seeing a group play live was loopy.

Now I'm not saying clubs didn't exist until Acid House. Oh Lordy no. All over the UK there were venues that went on as late as TWO O'CLOCK IN THE MORNING and as such, were considered thoroughly debauched hellholes. One of things that may help clarify the great impact of Acid House was that the entire United Kingdom shut down completely at 11pm, weekends included, and midweek the streets were pretty much empty from 7pm onwards. The TV stopped at midnight. Because who on earth is awake after then? Murderers? Plotters? The criminally insane? As a member of several bands, I'd drive all over the island to perform gigs that often started at 7.30pm. Getting home from distant ones you might be on the road after midnight and literally never see another vehicle for hundreds of miles. There were attempts at 'nightclubs' but, as usual, Britain did what it always does and slavishly copied America in as beige and weak a fashion as was humanly possible. Could there be anything less glamorous than mock glamour? It is so very English. 'Sophistication' as simply a khaki-coloured word, instead of an assembly of almost unreachably excellent attitudes. Protest music made by Gay, Black and Latinx Americans played to endlessly white, untroubled little Englanders was never going to work for youngsters barred at the gate. Anyway, we weren't demanding entrance, we were giving them a five-minute bomb warning to get out. The DJ did exist, but flapped

CHAPTER 2

and blathered non-stop over commercial music, once more proving that inserting a giant throbbing ego into the middle of a unity ritual was bordering on the obscene.

Of course, as kids, we found these old discos massively hilarious. We'd go dressed like 'Normals' and then start spitting and pogoing like punks to the slow dances. Do the new 'breakdancing' to inappropriate tunes and frequently, as was the fashion back then, get into fistfights. Because back then there wasn't much in the way of subcultural 'tribes'. They existed. But outside of a very large city, there were merely Normals who were 99% of the population, and 1% of 'Freaks'. Freaks might consist of all sorts. I knew ageing Punks, Reggae Boys, Goths-that-did-not-know-the-word-'Goth'-yet. I knew Jazz Funkateers and Soul Boys and Soul Girls. Skinheads that didn't know they were supposed to be racist. Yardies and fey, mop-topped New Wavers. 'Mods' that suddenly appeared back from the 1960s, and that until I saw *Quadrophenia* years later, seemed oddly incongruous but familiar at the same time, refugees from the ballrooms with chalked floors. Every single one of them could be of several sexual or racial orientations. One thing we all had in common was quite simply that we weren't Normals. Normals were everywhere. And by this, I mean people our own age as well as adults. They liked football, had money and jobs and liked to get smashed on 12 pints and fight anything slow enough to catch or, at a pinch, each other.

Once the pubs finally kicked them out, if a Freak was unlucky enough to be anywhere in the vicinity, they paid for their very existence in blood. This is one of the things people cannot comprehend currently. That to choose your vibe you did so at great peril. I will not be over-egging the mix by saying you could die for it. I am by no means saying violence against difference no longer exists, it's just back then it was so commonplace it was as inevitable as the weather. The hardest of rain. I wasn't kidding when I said I saw someone killed simply for playing tennis. Imagine, every time you stepped out of the door looking anything at all but the 'correct' shade of bang-average could be your last day on earth. If you find that hard to swallow just be thankful we did it so you no longer have to. Don't get me wrong, we may have been vastly outnumbered but we were nobody's prey. Where I come from you could quite easily end up regretting your decision and end up in hospital after being beaten very badly by someone in eyeliner and lipstick. I've toured with bands who looked like the New York Dolls but were all working class lads who had to fight every day to be that way. Physically fight. Every. Single. Day. Granted, there was a lot less to do back then.

All insanely hostile and violent pubs aside, even after the Second Summer of Love, many venues around the UK held onto that dangerous vibe. Things rarely change overnight in the real world. If you are watching a dramatisation of the 1980s and everyone is driving around in pristine 1980s cars and wearing the most current 1980s fashions you know immediately you are dealing with those who have no idea what it was really like. More than half of what you saw in the 80s came from the 70s, and even 60s and earlier. No one immediately ditched their old car and bought a new one. No one burned their bell bottoms on Dec 31st 1979 in preparation for the new dawn. Things take time. Borders are blurred. It took a while for the spiky hardness to be blunted from clubbing. Acid House was a revelation for some of us, far more people initially ignored it at best, ridiculed it at worst.

It was a lottery if you could find somewhere safe to party in the 80s and even well into the 90s, so something had to give. For example, if you went to the very legendary Orbit in Morley, you were in a highly legit proper Techno zone. Raving with genuine pioneers. However, if you went to the host venue 'After Dark' on any another night of the week it could be touch and go if you walked out unaided. It is quite easy to enjoy liberal cosmopolitan ideas and relaxed jovial atmospheres of the capital cities of the world, where civilised zones have been agreed upon by money. It takes a good while to permeate the rest of the planet.

'PSV' in Manchester's Hulme was sometimes really loved-up and friendly and other times teeming with proper whizzed-up maniacs glaring at you like you were lunch, and absolutely everyone in there was very much a long-term stranger to breakfast. 'The Kitchen', not far from PSV was another very interesting hellhole. As rough as a sandpaper suppository, but every visit was a properly legit adventure for us curious bumpkins with less brain cells than balls. There was a regular rave in Bradford Mills that only ever seemed to play music that was always just a bit too fast, no girls at all, and regularly had a moshpit. Scary scenes. Club UK in Wandsworth, some years later; again, you could easily have a legit good night in there or get killed outside with a machete. It was peak UK machete time around when Club UK got closed prematurely. Or maturely, depending upon how much you love big swords.

The Thomas A Becket on Old Kent Road was an original. A pub that turns into a club at 11pm. Original proper gangster boxing gym upstairs and dense singularity for maniacs. It is still going, is the Thomas A Becket. You can literally stand outside it at 6am on a Sunday and not hear a peep. Looks shut. Just knock and a wave of steam comes out and deafening Garage vibes. It was 'a late drink' but also a place you might never leave if you weren't very careful back in the day. If you are especially lucky, and not dead yet, you might get accepted enough to be shown the basement. Which is not a euphemism. It's their version of the VIP area. A rambling underground treasure-trove of old odds and ends, sofas and boxing memorabilia and the scene of much shady doings.

There was a place I used to work in Swansea. Rough town. I may be wrong but I am pretty sure the police used to cordon-off the high street and just patrol the border. Like *Escape from New York* or something. In fact, coincidentally, the club may have been The Escape, but don't quote me, was ages ago. Had one of those portholes at eye height I the front door. I rocked up there once and the big doors were shut and when I knocked the wee window opened and the security explained they had to wait for the fight outside to finish. Grappling intently behind me were a topless chubby kid wearing dress trousers, cummerbund and polished shoes, and his opponent wearing jacket, ruffled shirt and bowtie but nothing else. Presumably a fight to the death over the only tuxedo in Wales.

Pre-Acid House, some of the only all-night spots you could go to after The Queen told you to go to bed were 'Blues'. Jamaican and/or gangster-owned illegal after-hours that were basically domestic houses in rough areas. On entering, however, you'd find out it wasn't one house but several all knocked-through. A labyrinth of danger and promise. 'Sonny's' was a case-in-point. A Blues in Chapeltown, Leeds. Could be a laugh, could be a murder. Then off to The Gaiety, which was rough, but not nearly as dangerous and featured quite possibly the UK's first and only drive-through drug dealers. Or maybe we'd plump for 'Upstairs/Downstairs' over Armley way. A district famous for its brutal prison and not much else. Decisions, decisions!

There was one in Sheffield, I forget the name, it was a most excellent hellhole. It used to be owned by a consortium of gangsters that had a few clubs around The North. One fellow we dealt with was quite avuncular, a ruddy-faced killer called 'Don John'. I asked his ever-present minion once "Why the nickname? Is it Don as in Don Juan?"

He went: "No kid, Don John as in Chuck-The-Body-In-The-Don-John." The Don being the local river.

For the win though, I think, pound for pound, the place that was technically a disco that I had the most fights in was Leeds Irish Centre. A very memorable night there once with my highly sophisticated European cousin dancing with the wrong girl and finding out the very hard way just how unsophisticated England was back then, and apparently, as far as foreign visitors are concerned, still is. Even my Mum got in the fight. Good on her.

The journey of culture follows society-at-large to the letter. We used to gather in grim and dismal places because that is all we had. Relics of a bygone age. Working Men's Clubs. Pubs. 'Discos' that were for white people who couldn't dance. The only spots with any kind of cultural power and potential impact were often quite deliberately made illegal. If you wanted something off-the-menu, out of hours, or God forbid something from your own culture, you quite literally could be killed for it. Before alternate realities and virtual communities, all we had was the night. It was our internet. It was the place we made our own. Away from it all, whatever it may be.

Why mention all this? Clearly we needed change. Powerful and lasting change. It certainly wasn't going to manifest magically, if we wanted something different, we'd have to make it happen.

CHAPTER 3
EPIPHANY PIE

The first rave I went to was purely accidental. Prior to them I was a participant of Warehouse Parties (we simply called them 'The Parties', not having the pithy skills of marketeers) which were fairly common across the UK, and the music was varied, both current and older. Some cooler spaces that resembled the clubs we have now were starting to open, but still every town in the UK closed at 11pm, and the couple of hours after that were the province of chrome and carpet hellholes that wanted no part of Freaks. They were strictly knocking shops for Normals. The music dire, and the evening very much about the sweaty ego of the wacky DJ. There was a peak at this time of 'personality' radio DJs making moves into TV. Most chrome and carpet DJs had their sights set firmly on a new kind of stardom which had nothing at all to do with music.

Many varieties of excellent dancing music were represented at The Parties, however, especially Funk, Reggae and Rare Groove. The Blackburn area was particularly rife with venues, being especially blessed/cursed with limitless empty industrial spaces. At the time there was a strong connection between 'Rock' and any kind of live event. Many of us who played in bands and were part of the wider music scene would also work casually backstage for theatres, nightclubs and TV studios. Being adept with tools, knowing how to wind a cable correctly and not being entirely unfamiliar with a flight case could easily lead to all sorts of adventures. One of the links between the various strands of events and my own personal bridge into Acid House was, once again, all about the technology. Quite simply, we had access to the equipment the parties needed.

Discontent, and there was a lot of it in the 80s, was in contemporary protest songs and their lyrics. In pop and rock interviews. Sometimes even within concerts. There was an awful lot to be annoyed about. But for the first time it felt like people were *gathering*. Not to listen to an idol speak, or sing on their behalf, but simply to be with each other at

The Rave. Shoulder to shoulder against the cold. It was strange at first. Being at a big gathering that played all sorts of familiar and very danceable music and then suddenly this odd, repetitive and almost childlike rattle came on. Sure we had electronic records but they were still made in a 'musical' manner. They had structure and modulation. Chords and choruses. I myself was experimenting with it but it was still thinking very much within the strictures of making records in a 'proper' studio in order to buy them in a shop and take home to listen to.

The idea of a song that started and didn't really go anywhere was unheard of. I mean there were experimental things, and indeed ones we embraced. But experimental had no place at a *party*. Good Lord, no! The furore that surrounded 'O Superman' by Laurie Anderson was something to behold when it bothered the charts. And by no means as relentless as a Techno record, it had modulation, lyrics and structure. No coincidence perhaps that she ended up married to the author of 'Metal Machine Music'. Phillip Glass and Steve Reich were 'classical' and therefore exempt from criticism, but this new music we were hearing now and then was clearly made by the street. And let's not beat about the bush here. 'The Street' means mainly Black and Latinx, wherever the address. To me, repetition *is* The Blues. It is the first time it made sense to me, and to this day, I see House and Techno simply as their latest incarnation.

Still, this new vibe crashed into other more traditional dancing music and stuck out like an uncle at the kid's table. We'd be rigging the lights or sitting by the sound desk and look at each other with a dubious glance when these tunes came on. What were they thinking? This stuff is awful! Sounds like it was made in someone's bedroom. If it resembled anything, it was a vibe akin to Hi-NRG, the weapon of choice in the LGBTQ+ community at the time, with a slight connect to the Northern Soul crowd. Of course, I could try and pretend, like many of my peers, that I arrived fully formed, proper and correct, dressed 'just-so' and 100% cool and bang into this scene... but as I've said before, it is a lie that things happen overnight. Most of all, what was to come wasn't purely a musical revolution. It was cultural. The music didn't make a lot of sense on its own, and neither did the drugs. Did anyone take ecstasy before Acid

CHAPTER 3

House? I did. It was pretty weird. Being used only to occasional LSD, you fully expected it to be similar. Without context it was strange. Without a bunch of others on it with you too, also rather odd. It all needed to come together to give the full effect. And one day it did.

Friends were a big part of it. I absolutely was dragged kicking and screaming into it. I wouldn't have got it otherwise. I was fairly solitary much of the time, especially working mainly at night. Still am. Once, however, my crew heard of a big party going on not too far away, and crucially, one of our own was providing the equipment once more. This always meant easy access, and maybe even some free beer. It was a weekend, no work for a change. I confess I really was not interested in what little I knew thus far. I was curious about everything under the sun at that age. I wasn't *actually* pulled-in protesting, but you could colour me 'highly reluctant' none-the-less.

Walking in, something was immediately different. The buzz among the kids outside was obvious before I'd even crossed the threshold. Everyone seemed wide-eyed, boggled and giddy as kippers, happy to just mill about. Outside a huge metal roller shutter with steam pouring out a small door in it, like Vulcan's very own furnace was hard at work. Bass throbbing and reflecting off every surface for half a mile, too muddy to make out anything else over the thunder. Only car headlights for illumination outside, guerrilla vibes. The inside was pretty dark as well. A single light sometimes flashing. A single laser. A single strobe. Sometimes none were operating, sometimes all three. It was disorienting enough while still fresh and sober. Stumbling over concrete sills and uneven floors, getting lost. No idea who was there, or what the music was, or even really where it came from. The overall experience was absolutely fresh and unique. An audio ghost train, foxing and jinxing. Nobody faced the front or sought out the decks. Quite the opposite. There was no front. You'd arrive and you and your pals would form a little unit on the periphery and barely move from it. On this occasion we felt brave and pushed into the middle a bit. After all, we were into sound. We even attempted to find the audio sweet spot like proper muso nerds, arguing whether the racket was in mono or stereo. As if it mattered.

This time the music was not varieties of funk and soul, but very electronic. Not completely unfamiliar. Shades of Moroder could be heard. You could tell no one was going to play any Trouble Funk. The Amen Break was not going to feature tonight. It felt way tougher. Very new. Frankly not my thing in large doses, and especially at a party. Then someone asked if I had a tenner. Ten pounds was a lot of money then, but still only half the price of the chunky pill on offer. There were four of us. It would be some years before I fully came into my own as a dreadful beast. All it took was a cheeky half. It wasn't my first experience of MDMA, so I was sophisto enough to advise caution. It was still very early days.

It creeps up on you. It's not like a flash of lightning or a cartoon bulb over your head. It creeps. You start smiling. Then you notice you are smiling for no real reason, which is funny. You laugh at yourself. You go a bit queasy. You might be sick. Might not. Then your face goes cold. Then hot. You notice you've not been bobbing about in your usual deeply uncool, slightly detached and somehow also highly self-conscious manner. No. Rocking back and forth like you mean it. Actually *into* it. You lock eyes with your mates. Same. They feel it too. They are me. Ah, we are all the same. Not just our quartet but the whole place. We are the same. A revelation as wide and deep as it is obvious and inevitable. Simple. Clean.

Now electronic drums were nothing new. In fact it could be argued they were what I was best at. The tempo and patterns were nothing earth-shattering. What was making my guts flutter was the frankly daft bass-impersonator, the Roland 303. The sometimes chunky, friendly burble would warp slowly into a more aggressive, sinister monster. A sci-fi silver-foiled sandwich. A full multi-frequency assault. Isaac Asimov 'avin' it in Adidas. For the first time we weren't listening to a performance or an assemblage of virtuosity. We were buzzing solely off the sonics. Most of the records were not just entirely electronic, they were produced in a very amateur fashion, but what that also meant was that they were often relatively dry of overall effects and processing, so the range of frequency was accidentally much bolder and drier than traditionally recorded music. More immediate. Raw. It simply sounded like the future, towards the end of a decade that was utterly obsessed by it. Those who don't get it can hear nothing but the relentlessness of the drums. Those of us who do never hear them, we just feel. It was like a second language. If you don't speak it, all you hear is dull babble. When you are fluent, it's lyrical and exotic.

I want to tell you something funny happened. I want to paint a picture. To be frank, I can't. I remember the falling into it fairly clearly. The rest was a soup of smiles, butterflies in the stomach and visual blurs. Then it was the next day. I don't recollect drinking anything at all. A huge occurrence for a weekend night, perhaps a first of not being fighting drunk. Feeling a bit special. Very different. Most of all, *getting it.* I walked away a different person and never truly returned to normality.

Folks might read that last part and attribute it all to the drugs. Yes, there are people who literally believe that if you have a half of an 'e' it can change you permanently. They are that petrified. You'll never be able to make them understand the whole experience. How revolutionary it was, and how needed. Things were so dire in 90% of the United Kingdom sometimes I think it could have been anything that made the transition. The right sandwich might have changed my life.

I was entirely a fresh convert to the burgeoning culture, I confess it took me a while to really get fully into the music. It wasn't easy to come by in shops, and regardless, something I preferred to experience in its natural habitat. Something to this day I think is significant. For me, the music, the crowd and the vibe from that particular substance are forever intertwined. One of the three always seems to somehow be missing lately. If not in the event, then in me.

Notice what is missing from the recipe? Yeah. The DJ. Who cares? The DJ is as totally irrelevant now as they were then. It's just no one has told them. The DJ is by far the worst problem dance music has. A chronic disease.

Music is an ongoing and never-ending evolution. Perpetually eating its young and birthing new beasts almost daily. The first thing you do when you make music is try and take the latest thing in a new direction. I mean, if you are serious about it that is all you ever try to do. Chase the horizon. Tech is always there as part of the push forward. "Oh, so the machine can do *that*? Well then surely it can also do *this*?" One of the first things we did was try and add what we experienced in our lives into what we were currently working on artistically. A sort of 'proto indie' started to emerge with bands I knew with a traditional rock set-up using tech a lot more. What was bizarre was that there were already people being retro about 1988 in 1989! The thing was that the experience was fully cultural, so people became extremely reverent of it immediately. There is no more zealous a convert than those who perceive themselves as first. Lines were drawn. Gangs formed. Uniforms agreed upon. No one told me, naturally. I was far too reclusive to hang out at cool spots and gather intel on fashions. I spent all my time making music, sometimes playing it, working all night and most weekends. A lonely mole. Albino-like and squinting, uncomfortable with the rare appearances above ground during the day.

My musical epiphany was a little later, and, as usual, not very cool. We'd dropped acid one time for some strange, uncalled-for midweek reason. Wandering the faded Victorian streets after midnight with all the synapses fizzing but not a clue where to put them, one of us said:

"Let's go to Z's house. He's a writer and a massive speed freak. He never sleeps and loves it when things get weird."

Oddly I'd never met him before, but he was almost famous in our wee backwater. Then again, it didn't take much to be well-known when you lived nowhere. Odder was that you apparently had to enter this ever-open oasis of random hospitality by climbing over its very tall back wall and tapping on a window lightly with a thin stick. Everything is odd on acid, though. I learned later that this was because he took so much amphetamine he was permanently on-edge and jumped out of his skin if the phone or doorbell rang.

For someone so delicate he sure loved some harsh and loud sounds. It was one of those moments we all have. We were sat highly receptive and minds so open it may as well have been trepanation in front of someone who knew a lot more than us. And wasn't mean with it. Over the next six hours or so until the sun came up he played all sorts of cosmic wonders. Some I'd never even heard of existing, but truly mind-blowing, especially for a mind looking to be blown. Important factor, that.

CHAPTER 3

Then a slightly cunning look crossed his face.

"You lads are on acid," he observed.

We couldn't deny it and just laughed hysterically. It seemed to him like he'd made a discovery he was most pleased with. With a flourish he reached behind his armchair, a throne you got the impression he rarely rose from, and produced a record with an extremely garish cover of TV-like distortion. He put on 'Stakker Humanoid'. I doubt a single person reading this has never heard it. Imagine hearing it for the first time, when prior to it very little came close to sounding that way. For me, it was a major event because here were those sounds from the warehouses being used for the first time in a way that I recognised. The epiphany of 'Voodoo Ray' would come soon too, in more appropriate surroundings. One of the things that blew my tiny mind was that the vocals on this new music were meaningless at best, hilariously fatuous at worst. My mate, who played guitar in one of our bands, used to be delighted that all Jazzie B appeared to do was say: "Oh Yeah" and he would beam with joy whenever he heard it. There was something almost outrageously bold about doing almost nothing, but it still being beautiful.

Every single style and genre has its rough pioneers, and then someone comes along and adds real musical ability to it. Even something like Grunge, which I'd seen a fair bit of and was mostly awful, would potter around dirtily for a few years and then suddenly there was Nirvana. I'm not trying to be cool, clearly. Few would call this the road to Damascus, or at least rustle up a more obscure and fitting fake baptism. Something clicked in me though with 'Humanoid'. It didn't burble or meander, it *rocked*. I understood rock. The possibilities were suddenly endless.

CHAPTER 4
THE LUNATICS REACH A SHORT-TERM RENTAL AGREEMENT WITH THE ASYLUM

From warehouse, mill and field, we came to dance. Free for all at the point of entry. That did not last long. I'd like to catalogue the detailed decline into cashing-in but I'd have to confess I was more than happy to finally get paid. No one paid us at all to play music for a very long time. A solid decade working for free. Then we got lucky and we got paid very little. Barely enough to cover getting there and back. As the 90s arrived it was almost as if you woke up one morning and it wasn't on the sidelines anymore, it was abso-flippin-lutely EVERYWHERE...

There we were one night, just raving. Yorkshire. Filthy place as usual. Cracking vibe. Suddenly the police were at every exit and entrance. Some working lights came on. They were trying to get to the DJ. Bass Terrorist was playing. In the melee he ran back up to the decks, grabbed the mic and screamed:

"Fight the fucking pigs!" at the top of his lungs and attempted to lead locking them out.

Naturally, this did not endear him to them one bit. He was promptly arrested and we discovered later that he was the first person ever to be jailed under 'The Criminal Justice Act' which had been bumbling around as 'The Bright Act' for some time now after one particularly zealous Conservative made it his personal ambition to end fun. If only they'd stopped there. We later discovered, as did the Travellers first-hand, that it was developed to attack far more than just pop-up discos. There were hundreds of police everywhere you looked. It was several thousand per cent more effort than they had made with us previously. Something was afoot. This meant three months indoors with Her Majesty for Bass Terrorist, the Jesus of our scene, or possibly John the Baptist. The burning, lidless eye of Sauron was now glaring at us, and we were defo going to lose the blinking contest.

Being everywhere and also outside of the wider system of society was *not on*. Against the rules, dear old thing. *Not cricket*. Simply will not do. New laws needed to be passed and be quick about it. Those pesky Travellers were always host to seditious types, but finding comradeship alongside an entire generation of very pissed-off and bored youth? *Cannot* happen. Must *never* happen! The police started in on us. We weren't going to go away quietly.

* * *

An organic and genuine grassroots protest movement was quelled almost as soon as it was born. Legislated against, brutalised, attacked, demonised and then before you could say 'u-turn' was suddenly all over the TV, in the charts, record shops and, most crucially, driven indoors and roundly *monetised*. The first nail in the coffin hammered smartly and firmly home barely two years into its life. And most of us were absolutely fine about it. Let's admit it, few lamented what happened to the Crusties. Fewer cared if we had to pay for things now, there was so much interest it was purely a seller's market. If you put on a rave at this point one of the hardest things you had to do was try and make sure it wasn't oversubscribed. This was the point, however. For every supremacist saying it was all over before it began, there was a new national unity, closely followed by a bonafide international youth movement. Suddenly it wasn't an inclusive church for all. It was now the exclusive territory of little gangs claiming it was theirs. You all know a crew like this. Every town had one. These agile purists, so acrobatic in their logic, roundly condemning everyone who enjoyed the new cultural wave, while simultaneously pocketing as much money as they possibly could from the same people they said had ruined it. Some still do to this day. Taking the cash with one hand and mocking the other that had just paid them. Eternally too good for it all, dismissive and superior, yet always on-call for cash. Sure, things were changing-up quick. Smart businessmen and a handful of pioneering women were taking the thing by the neck and dragging it into the 90s whether it wanted to go or not. Suddenly the larger music industry started to notice. It had to have it. All of it. And we called the shots. The larger music biz did not understand this emergent new music one bit. No clue what it was or where it came from. They simply fell over each other to give anyone wearing the right clothes and saying the right things lots of money.

Acid House thrust a generation of deeply unready Freaks into positions of cultural influence and enforced entrepreneurship almost overnight. The lunatics took over the asylum for a short while, completely. We were everywhere, like a rash. It was more than music and dancing. We were the chosen enemy of the state. Not something to be taken lightly. A brand-new industry emerged and was helmed by people who didn't have a clue, were often utterly deranged and spent quite a lot of time out of their minds. Smelt a little like revolution. Didn't take long for the whiff to subside, however.

Myself, I was alternating between band gigs and DJing. By this point, I'd served an almost entirely unpaid apprenticeship of a decade of playing every night of the week. Yep. Every. Single. Night. In student towns there were gigs where it was 10p a pint. TEN PENCE! It was mayhem. Tell me you are a DJ when you've played to 1000 paralytic students who literally throw 1000 pints of liquid in the air when you play a tune they like, and throw 1000 pint glasses much more accurately if you play a tune they don't like. Monday you are playing 'Indie Dance'. Tuesday; 'Rock'. Wednesday; 'Funk 'n' Soul'. Thursday; 'Hip Hop and R&B'. Friday is booze-day and anything goes. Saturday is House and Techno. Sunday you want to die. It's a rough number but performing every night for around ten years is what? 3,600 gigs with a few Christmases and sick days off? Sometimes more than once a night. Sometimes you are playing records to help out mates in a band, sometimes playing in the band too. Sometimes between brutal shifts of manual labour. You transport and set up sound systems. You take them down again. It's entirely possible to get trapped in these situations for life. The trick is to travel. If you seriously think the music industry is coming to rescue you from your cross-eyed bumpkinhole you've been watching way too much TV. When you get in a rut, get out of the rut. Fast. Get on a train. A bus. Get on a plane. Go where the action is. Trust me. It will not come to you.

CHAPTER 4

I guess for the sake of this narrative these are still the years when no one was trying to fleece anyone too hard. I mean, we were completely indistinguishable from today's Hipsters but the striking difference was that we wouldn't think for one minute it would be OK to charge 20 euros for a bang-average burger served on a bearded spade in a burned-out skip. It just wasn't there yet, morally. Sure, the 80s and 90s were pretty gung-ho economically but the counterculture still existed and most importantly, still had the 'counter' bit intact. The greed was still very centralised. Very, very much still a minority religion. You could live on nearly nothing quite happily and no one wanted all that much than they already had anyway. I know we didn't. Even the extravagant 90s were relatively cheap to exist in if you wanted to. Maybe it's all in my mind because these were peak years of an age when you really don't give two fucks about anything much. You'd literally only spend any time where you lived to sleep. And not all that often to boot. You'd wake up, leave to find something to eat and not return until you were paralytic or exhausted. And at that age, being exhausted might take several days and nights to happen. I look back in pure bewilderment at this time of wide, panoramic plenty. Perpetually awake, forever wandering around the capital with boundless energy. Why? Looking for something, I guess.

Regular readers of my columns and the previous book will know my constant foil, erratic wingman, part-time nemesis, and full-time drug-addled henchperson, the famous 'Tour Manager'. Named as such for the one and only time he was employed to do that job and promptly arrived two hours late for the flight on his first and last day. He was wearing a newly made T-shirt that said "Sack The Fucking Tour Manager" in large friendly letters rather hugely on the front. Naturally, I obliged him immediately.

Tour Manager, rather amazingly, also owned a club. But not for long. Soon it blundered out of his fingers and into the grasp of some, quite astoundingly, even more clumsy than his own. He stayed on as one of the managers, out of sentimentality more than anything, and thereby cemented his own doom by working out of love for the last piece of his empire, for people who couldn't love the place if they tried. For a pittance.

If this club was a car, it would be a clown's car. One of the first things the new owners did was change its already completely awesome name. Surefire indicator of what was to come if ever there was. The original name was so completely ridiculous that once I was outside there, out of hours, and a taxi pulled up and simply idled outside for a few moments. I wandered over near the car and overheard a proud-voiced, moon-faced child report:

"See! I told you there was a club called that!"

While his cohorts gawped, took pictures, and then promptly drove off. I can't say what the name was, but if we call it 'Spunky's Muff' it wouldn't be far off. The ludicrous sentence "Are you off to Spunky's Muff?" was a staple of the region. The name was so good/bad that basically no one, especially the staff, called it by the vanilla, generic new brand the new owners gave it. They even answered the phone "hello, Spunky's?" until it eventually closed down. What chance has a place got that doesn't even know its own name? The fact a bar opened attached to it called 'Dickheads Prohibited' only confirmed its status as a total wrong-hole. No. Really.

To give you an idea of how doomed it was; they had no ice machine. This might seem trivial but if you know just how much ice a bar uses in a night, how many glasses, or straws, or ten pence pieces... well, then you will know how a club works. There were four bars, each open for about eight hours. That's a lot of ice. So as well as having all the demanding and sometimes dramatic issues of any club, Tour Manager had to run around town for a couple of hours before The Muff opened, blagging huge amounts of ice from every friendly venue in town. You know, the ones that all had ice machines as standard. Like a proper venue. Only some of the ice made into anyone's drinks intact, much of it ending up being a sad little lukewarm boot puddle in TM's car. The new owners didn't think an ice machine was important. This happened every single time it opened. For about ten years.

The toilets would flood constantly. And by flood I don't mean nice clean drinking water. One of these Old Testament happenstances led to Tour Manager sending me the best text message I've ever got. I queried:

"Hello you raging nitwit, how's it going?"

Which, when he eventually noticed his phone and might be on his 'up' cycle, could result in a thousand words by way of reply. Instead it simply read:

CHAPTER 4

"Can't talk, knee-deep in raw sewage."

He really was apparently. The brown derby did not stop there.

During a grand event early-on in its history, something of a coup was scored by getting the extremely elusive Laurent Garnier to appear. An act of brilliance matched only by the French star discovering a large pile of dog shit in the booth, unfortunately mainly using his feet. This was not to be the first time the booth was full of dog shit either. The grandness of this event was eclipsed however by the massive firework display that was, to put it bluntly, assembled almost entire indoors but 'aimed' at the sky. Not much of the display displayed. It merely roasted the unfortunates tasked with the touch paper within the enclosed space and filled the entire place with dense, acrid smoke. This baptism of smog was tellingly appropriate for the rest of the venue's life. The erratic venue was across several levels connected by a glass lift that simply never worked. Periodically there would be a sighting of it, trapped between floors, entombing some vital stock, equipment, staff... even sometimes a less-than-essential DJ, drooping down from the ceiling like a sad cave formation. Encased in crystal. For all to see. A tragic chandelier of shame.

If this was Rome burning, our Nero fiddled like Billy-o. When not, for reasons completely undiscovered, randomly painting garden gnomes bright purple and placing them around the venue in odd nooks, Tour Manager liked to spend the most crucial moments of crisis at home with his pond. There he celebrated his naval ancestry by making model boats and staging mock battles with his top off, sweating bollocks whilst ripped to his tits on cheap wiz. Most memorably buying an ornamental bridge for it that did not fit, shrugging and leaving it floating amidst one of his tiny Airfix sea battles with a sign saying simply 'A Bridge Too Short'.

Back at the venue, I'd sit for hours with Tour Manager while we watched the CCTV footage of one calamity after another. A personal fave was watching replay after replay of him managing to fall off a three-legged stool while attempting to change a bulb, managing somehow for the stool to flip over on the way down and impaling himself upon and between the legs upon landing. None-more-fun was had than watching Quag Allurgie, another rare freak inexplicably thrust into the limelight by Acid House. We see him in blurry night-vision spending the best part of eight solid hours on his own with a coat hanger and a bit of reversed gaffer tape, going madly at the letterbox-esque cast-iron drug safe. Resembling some sort of Victorian backstreet abortionist or real-life purple gnome forced to fight a baby tank with a big paperclip. Hours could be fast-forwarded or rewound as he gamely tried and failed to scoop up confiscated shit pub gak, pills that contained very little pill and a couple of Bic lighters. It was like a drugged-up version of the amusement arcade crane grab. We'd 'oo' and 'aah' as he'd get close, then pull out nothing. It was like watching snooker, only even more boring and a thousand times weirder. We loved every moment.

Believe me, Quag has had the upper hand with me more times than I can count. Life is a perpetual competition to him. He's cunning too. If he can't beat you at one thing, he'll just change the game until he does. Instinctively knowing that defeat is defeat for his opponents, no matter what the game is. Quag had the skills of Trump long before they were used on the planet to keep us all enraged and confused. Once, back when pills were almost pure MDMA he handed me one, then stood back as I looked around for a drink. They used to be vile things, impossible to swallow without retching when at their most powerful. I spied a champagne bottle and took a huge swig. The whole room went dead silent.

"*Holy shit...* you just drank Quag's piss," said someone in reverent tones.

Apparently, there had been someone stealing drinks from the backstage area at every opportunity. So Quag laid a trap of pissing in loads of fancy bottles and leaving them lying around. Arguably, Quag's piss was so potent and drug-laden it qualified as some sort of new and highly mutated intoxicant of its own. Somehow I got large kudos from this, as I took it in my stride and did not drop dead immediately or change into a lickable trippy tree frog.

Lots of daft things have happened to me in the last 35 years, but I pale in comparison next to the mighty Quag Allurgie. Like Tour Manager he was effortlessly surrounded by drama and intrigue. Unlike T-Man he was adept at manipulating any ensuing chaos to his advantage. As we've seen with modern politics, keeping everyone totally confused, never telling the truth, obfuscating with clowning and nonsense... these skills can lead to success if you are the one orchestrating the confusion. Who could be a stronger avatar for the Acid House loons suddenly being in charge than Quag?

I first met him in a Goth clothes shop in about 1985. I wandered in there and I think The Cramps were playing, or something very like them, at a volume that was so oppressive that a cynic might think they didn't want anyone to come in the shop. Quag has always been what you might call a dedicated follower of fashion, whatever it is at the time. He was lurking around at the back like a bat. Goth as you like. I went to try a jumper. The intense volume lowered for a second and a voice said:

"Yul nevuh gerrin thad faddeh."

Which was Quag for "you'll never get in that, fatty". Somehow I understood him from the get-go, and always would. Often wishing intently that I couldn't.

"Dun cray, av sum wuzzeh wattah ah kid."

He was offering me what was a rare sight in 1985, a bottle of mineral water. 'Whizzy-water' was basically water and amphetamines. It was lunchtime on a Saturday. Over the years, I would cross paths with him, always keeping my distance, out of self-preservation more than anything. Hilariously, early-on, Quag was actually the tour manager for a band I worked with. You'd see him on TV sometimes, scuttling about trying to fix something that wasn't broken to be in front of the camera for a second. Goth band roadie eventually became tour manager.

If it was possible for a worse tour manager to exist than Tour Manager, Quag was it. He'd have to be woken up by the band in the morning, whom he called 'The Celebrity Squares'. The band would give him the day's itinerary and the merchandise sales report from the previous gig and drive him to the next one. He'd come alive for the gig and spend it leaping about on the mic shouting out incomprehensible things to people who didn't even speak English, let alone speak Quag.

Long before he was winging it as a dance music promoter, he was always around the rock scene, as was I. His disastrous term as tour manager culminated in the band's soon-to-be homecoming gig. This was to take place, ironically, in the venue he would later come to be a successful promoter in. The plan was that, as usual, rather than do anything as boring as work, Quag would dress up as the pope. Then at the highlight of the gig, be swung over the crowd and stage. 'Pope on a rope' right. Geddit?

All the gear was hired from a climbing shop not too far away, the idea being that Quag could stand on rail on the unused part above the balcony and jump out above the crowd, and then swing triumphantly across the space. Ropes were attached to the apex of the venue. All went to plan to begin with. Band on stage below DJ booth, Quag up on railing, arms out, place packed. Crowd on floor below looking up, and when he jumped they all cowered, as the ropes weren't obvious with all the smoke and lights. Anyhow, that bit worked, but none of us had thought it through. How to get him back again when he stopped swinging, and hung suspended at a comical angle in the middle of the hole in the gallery. It took two people, one pushing him with a mop, the other trying to get him to grab one end of a broom being waved at him. Took an endless five minutes to sort and somewhat detracted from the big homecoming gig. It was very Quag. In a sense this sums him up. A world famous band finishing a global tour triumphantly in their hometown, and yet somehow, impossibly, it becomes all about him.

I won't apologise, this is simply how it was. This is the life. Idiotic as it seems. You are forgiven for wondering what the hell this has to do with the music biz. This is what it is like to be perpetually trapped outside of normality. Endlessly sentenced to live in a 1950s British kid's comic. One of rude words, arrested development and practical jokes. If you have lived the life you will understand that this very much comes with the territory. Even if you don't live it full-time as I did, you will see it at weekends on the road. The permanent childishness. The never-ending daft. You will have read about the stars of rock from the 1970s who did this sort of thing but with considerably more money. This is one of the effects of the Acid House revolution. An entire generation of rock 'n' rollers emerged, not just a tiny percentage of the population, but a large proportion of it. People didn't need obscene amounts of cash to burn to have fun and be truly outrageous. It is so very rare working class people are given access to anything. It must be taken.

For a time the Acid House revolution genuinely elevated those utterly excluded to positions almost resembling power. We had magazines that reached out to the world. People who were never supposed to leave the factories were suddenly drifting around the planet like spores. We exported our culture to every corner. A voice rang out that could be heard clearly, and spoke to others just like us, everywhere. It's very different now. You've seen with your own eyes working class kids mincing around with wheeled luggage, toy dogs, false teeth and steroid bodies. Not reaching out in the name of change, or fighting the power. Now they are hungry for it. Too dainty and special to do things like carry stuff, engage in inconvenience, endure the slightest discomfort or even have time or the inclination to believe in things they do not wish to. But underneath all the tattoos, teeth and plastic fish-faces they are as dull as dishwater. Basic. Terminally ordinary. Devoid of personality. Mercifully free of substance. Blessed with the dimmest of comprehension of life's complexities. Conversely, if you are reading this most resignedly, eye-rolling and thinking aloud 'what an idiot'... well, you are absolutely correct. Seriously, and I'm not being faux-modest here, DON'T DO WHAT I DID. If there is one purpose to any of my words, it is this; Just don't. I am an idiot. Stop reading now. It's only going to get worse.

This previous era of excess was our heyday. And at the peak of any art form its successful artists are lauded not only in the 'workplace' but are encouraged to be extreme examples of humanity at all times. Possibly without any of the humanity part. We expect and even demand our exemplars to be excessive and ridiculous. We get annoyed if they are not, then deride them when they are. Dance, monkey! *Dance!*

It's less of 'a thing' now, expecting our artists to be excessive. Now we merely insist they are excessively healthy, pretty, and as bland and unthreatening as humanly possible, like English cheese. I think that perhaps back when we were unexpectedly thrust into positions of power it forced us to up our game with how we got noticed. The world was watching, so all we could do was rise to the occasion by being as chronically odd as possible.

INTERLUDE
SHOWGIRLS II

For some reason, probably to do with colossal amounts of narcotics, Tour Manager would undress a lot. The cupboard he occupied under his venue was blisteringly hot, containing as it did everything in the place that produced heat, and nothing at all like an ice machine. Frankly I'm amazed he didn't go off. He spent his many, many hours there, doing things that were necessary only to him and the drugs he'd taken, mostly on his own. His solo missions were endlessly complex and urgently essential, to him. Utterly pointless to the outside observer. This is a common feature of the drug life.

Finding TM lurching about wearing very little was a hideous lottery. But in summer those odds leapt at your face and went for your eyes. The upcoming weekend was a gig in Brighton and then Moscow, followed by Jakarta. As per, I was doing most of the actual management of the tour, like picking him up, instead of the other way around.

I arrived at his empty club at the early evening rush hour, on one of the hottest days of the year. It was dark and unpleasant inside. The heat making some of those 'club smells' a little more overpowering than usual. A light at the end of the tunnel was the doors leading to the 'garden' being wide open. Just at that moment, a piercing cry, and a familiar:

"Fucking holy hell!" drifted to my ears. I emerged blinking into the dazzling sunshine just in time it would seem, as a dripping wet T-Man was hurriedly putting his underpants on. I felt some sort of greeting was in order to gloss over this trauma.

"That was lucky, I could have been scarred for life a moment earlier. Nice of you to dress. Glad to see you made an effort too. Did you hear me coming? It's not like you to notice something like that..."

"Are you simple man? It's not you, you crud! it's THEM!"

He screeched, gesticulating upwards.

The venue, like many in the UK, was part of the Victorian rail system's many archways across city centres. Being fairly cheap (until gentrification arrives of course, then suddenly the rent quadruples), badly maintained, away from residential, and frequently unused. I looked up to see a packed train of sweating commuters, looking like a row of meerkats in suits, trapped on a carriage, stuck waiting for signals. They'd just enjoyed the unique spectacle of a naked Tour Manager spraying himself with a hose like some sort of negative, satanic version of an American fizzy pop commercial. Where his skin was usually translucent, it was scarlet red from embarrassment. It was quite hard to embarrass him.

"Time to go to Brighton."

"Anything to get the fuck out of here." He marched past me.

"Are you putting clothes on? I really hope you are..."

"FUCK OFF," came the standard reply.

"Why were you hosing yourself down?"

"I went on a date last night, when I got there she got in the fucking back seat. Thought I was the taxi driver!"

"So the hose is... penance?"

"No you fool! I was hot!"

"OK".

CHAPTER 5
DON'T TOUCH THAT DIAL. OR THAT. DON'T TOUCH THAT EITHER. JUST DON'T TOUCH ANYTHING, OK?

As the Dance Music explosion began to legitimise, we began to see true electronic experiments happen in the music itself. New genres seemed to appear almost monthly. The drive was always to push forward. Still, and no idea why, the Gatekeepers were trying to look backwards. It might be something to do with the past being easier to dominate than the future. They were (and still are) engaged in a constant battle with anyone trying anything new in a genre that is supposed to be about the sound of science fiction. Youngsters were regularly vilified for daring to participate, with the dusty old dogs getting in stronger and stronger positions of power. Myself included. You think I don't know I'm a Gatekeeper too? The greyest Silverback of them all? Pfft. 'Course I am.

My first 'proper' job in this burgeoning new industry came as the 90s were peaking. I was still living in London at the time and through a friend heard that a major commercial radio station was franchising across the UK, or at least trying to. I watched with horror as they steamed into a very major city and got it quite horrifically wrong for a while, for a start not employing a single Black or Asian person on-air in a city that was famous for its diversity. Forcing their trademark, "it's a Laaandon fing innit" on a fiercely independent and deeply rival city. I quickly got involved with gaining the licences for more stations.

All I knew was this: I knew dance music intimately, and I knew the geographic areas they wanted to move into as a native. I was certain they'd need the latter and was beginning to worry they needed the former sometimes, as their daytime playlist was moving quite clearly away from playing anything resembling what I considered Dance Music. This was merely the opinion of a complete idiot of course, one with zero experience. Don't get me wrong, I was no thrusting Young Conservative or budding captain of industry. I was genuinely appalled by the clumsiness of the move and did not want it to happen twice. I'd had some good times in London but it felt a bit like it was time to take what I had learned back home. Call me a hypocrite if you want but there wasn't a raver anywhere by now who wasn't trying to make a go of the newly formed (fanfare please) DANCE MUSIC INDUSTRY... ta dahhh. I thangyew.

It all seemed to happen so organically that for a long while I genuinely mooned around thinking we'd all won the revolution and we were taking over the world. Getting justice at last. The meek were inheriting, finally. I even talked myself out of a decent wage after they offered me a job (or rather I told them they needed to employ me, that is how you get work, no one offers you shit). I'd effectively won the licence to broadcast for them by going to every regional player I knew, which was all of them of note and getting them to write fulsome letters of praise in support of the bid. Local Pirate Radio hoping to go legit didn't stand a chance. Not because we had more money, and yeah we did have more by the bucket, but that we knew exactly how to play the thing. They did not. At all.

I was no executive. Never sat at a desk in my life. Didn't even own a suit jacket never mind the bottom half. Lost that in Wales. But I was sharp enough to make myself invaluable. I straight-up told them they had fucked it up in one city and I wasn't going to let them do it twice. I reeled-off a dozen local players, genres and DJs and explained quite frankly that more than half of them were Black and a couple Asian. Part of the remit of gaining a licence to broadcast stipulates explicitly that you must represent the area and its diversity. A broadcast licence has a lot of criteria, actually. I was so thick and inexperienced I actually even thought the rules mattered. I was the only one at management level who did, I discovered later.

I built that radio thing as a labour of love from the ground up. Literally, a shell of a building was an ultra-modern station within a year. I wasn't paid, or given an official title until the opening broadcast date started to loom. Eventually, I was given the sop of 'Specialist Music Producer'. This cleverly avoided any kind of real authority in the boardroom and avoided any potential clash with the Head of Specialist over at the other place (who I rarely met, but discovered later was a most excellent fellow, ironically struggling just as hard as I was, with equally tied hands).

However on the plus side 'specialist music' was literally the entire output minus daytime prime. 7am to 7pm was 'presenters' rather than DJs as I knew them (some of these unknown presenters, who at the time knew exactly zero about dance music, are now considered radio and TV royalty). Prime was news, weather, automated playlists and lots and lots of advertising. It was radio. 'Office hours'. It was the time Normals ruled the earth. The rest was all mine, including the entire weekend. The Freak Zone. My people. I was on-air every weeknight too for four hours. 10pm 'til 2am. Can you imagine? I worked there literally every moment I was awake, round the clock, and got paid less than half in a week than the average labourer earned in a day. I didn't care. I was a kid. I loved every minute.

I personally made every drop, bed, ident and piece of audio they needed to launch in my growing home studio. I didn't just find and hire every single legit DJ, I found our breakfast show presenter, cleaners and even the receptionist. I was utterly obsessed with my new baby. I then went to work on what is known as the Test Transmission Tape. A loop of about eight hours played constantly via the main transmission tower to check the equipment and tweak the broadcast range. We were later to discover the signal stretched from Scotland to the South, owing to our transmitter being almost exactly in the centre of the geographic UK and one of the tallest in the world. This was not an accident. It is almost impossible to get a national licence. Easy as pie to get a media monopoly for newspapers and TV if you are a billionaire. Less so for radio. Something to do with it being essential in national emergencies. The only solution to dominate the nation's airwaves was for several local licences to join up into a de facto national network. It had never been done before in the UK, or at least achieved by any commercial stations. Again, I had no idea this was the endgame at the time. There was one commercial station given a nationwide license but it played entirely safe and popular classical hits for the dusty middle classes, and this was no accident. They passed an entire new law specifically targeting and opposing my people, no chance we were getting heard across the land unless we sneaked it. Some of this move was a response to the state-owned BBC networks head-hunting most of our brightest and best. Stealing our sound and hosting it on their channels. We had to beat them at their own game. I was too naive to think what any of this might mean long-term. I just wanted to play new music and tell the world how great it was. I was smart enough to navigate the corporate corridors, but way too cheerful and young to be a predator. It just isn't in my nature. I want everyone to succeed, not just me. Always have, always will.

Much of this will be hilarious and/or confusing for people raised on the internet. The internet simply did not exist at this time outside of a couple of labs. It's very simple to empathise with, however. Just imagine radio used to be the internet. It was where we went to get info, send messages and reach out to each other over huge distances. It was in every home, vehicle, commercial premises, hospital, shop, method of public transport and government office. It entertained and informed, dictated styles and fashions and made us laugh and cry. It also made a lot of money but was free to experience. Wherever there were people, there was radio. And wherever there is access to people, rapacious advertisers smell blood from miles away.

You know when you are getting something right in the commercial field by the companies and brands who want to work with you. You think a Berlin club is cool? You should see how hard it is to get Coca-Cola to want a piece of your action. They go to you if you are doing something right, not you to them. Every time. Levi's? You couldn't get them on the phone if you wanted to. Mercedes? Forget it. Prestige brands are BIG money. Some of the highest-paid people in marketing are the ones who can make those connections. Amazingly, we had brands falling over each other to speak to our advertising department. We had their ads on the Test Transmission Tape before we even started to broadcast. They were paying us before we even opened the doors. Making plans over years, worth millions. Me? I didn't see a penny, of course. I was a company director's dream. Absolutely oblivious to anything except making things cool as fuck. And cool as fuck is what *everyone* wants a piece of. Wish I'd known that understanding your own value is absolutely EVERYTHING in a capitalist society.

Because 'value' doesn't mean money. It has in fact long surpassed something so pedestrian as cash. Our betters understand this fully. This is how the 1% operate. They understand the *true* value of things, while we piss about thinking banknotes and plastic cards are money. It works two ways naturally, knowing what is worthless is a skill in itself. If you think some things don't have value, or even crazier, are above being evaluated, you've clearly not seen how stocks in Tinder/Match Group performed, or how short-selling happens.

Now don't get wrong. Old Me, not to be confused with Current Me, who is also not young... Old Me hated all that corporate McGuffin. With a deep passion. Applied with all the faux-purity and lofty arrogance of youth. They had to bully me just to mention the station's name on-air. Ads were just a break to gather my thoughts for the next bit. I mention all this to make you understand what was at stake. To help you understand value. Because if you are contributing to the revenue of an employer, especially significantly, you *must* value your input. No one else will. Literally. My bosses must have actually been rolling around laughing at how little cost to them I helped launched that multi-billion network for. Trebles all round, that kid is doing the work of ten for the wage of 0.5.

I bet you weren't expecting this nonsense when you finished book one? I wasn't always a stumbling, honking, drug-addled moron, you know. I only got good at that later.

What is important to note in terms of the wider music industry and our co-opting by it, is that our newly formed Dance Music Industry was so very young. Not merely newborn, but entirely populated by youth. At the start, even our biggest dogs were only a few years older than our youngest pups. This continued for some time. So yes, easy pickings for the older, wiser, fatter, slyer, Music Biz. Obviously. When new things come along there is always a huge panic in the industry at large. It's taking away from them as far as they are concerned. Not just money, money is meaningless. We made noise. Anyone can make money, not everyone has the balls to make a ruckus. Money follows noise. Every time. Noise was what we did, in every sense of the word. This is why the money flocked to us. This is why we were beating off brands with a shitty stick and shunning the grubby advances of the major labels. Also, back when radio really mattered, we weren't just being aggressively absorbed by the wider music biz, we were also fighting another archaic system. Radio itself. Let me give you an example: launch day.

I had two immediate bosses. One I quite liked who was running the new station we were in currently, or at least would be if I wasn't doing most of it for him. We got on fine apart from his obsession with R&B. I'm not against the genre, I'd made a couple of R&B tunes on the side, was a huge fan of the adventurous production values. He was just dead-set on it being the future, and wanted it as the drive of the primetime sound at the expense of every other genre. Apart from this one 'agree-to-disagree' topic, and a rather mild one at that, we got on famously. He knew if he left me alone I'd drive myself into the ground to work for the place for peanuts, I knew that if I didn't trouble him too much he'd happily stay in his cubicle all day on the phone. Sometimes he'd take me aside and gently school me in what was 'Radio' and what was not. To say something was 'Radio' was like an actor pontificating about 'theatre darling'. 'Radio' was to suggest something ancient and untouchable. Legit. You were either 'radio people' or on the outside. You were 'Radio' or you were a civilian. I was resolutely not radio. At all. It was why things were working so well. Both of us had an immediate boss, Le Grande Fromage. He was the polar opposite. Where my boss was relaxed, listened and guided... the top dog was bombastic, deaf and unctuous. Most delightful was that he was in the possession of the most 'Radio' voice you could imagine. Deep, sonorous and oozing insincerity. He strode and boomed wherever he went. He was 'old radio' and found every single one of us annoying, inexperienced and disrespectful. Sure, some of it was the old 'bad cop, worse cop' routine with these two. As I didn't have to deal with either of them much, I barely noticed until it was crunch time.

Not really knowing anything about 'radio' but knowing a fair bit about music didn't help me. Thinking music has anything to do with radio is like believing virtuosity has anything to do with a career as a musician. Or thinking being an actor has anything to do with how good you are at acting. Sure, one helps the other but really... doesn't matter. It's way more complex. Sadly at this time, I did not know this. In my simple state, I minced around smugly thinking making the output extremely awesome was all that was required.

So part of this happy ignorance was my populating the place with rabid Freaks. Top to bottom. The receptionist I hired would gossip perpetually with callers on the phone and openly criticise the staff with complete strangers. One of the cleaners was a kleptomaniac. Half the DJs were raging drug addicts. It wasn't entirely stupidity on my part. All that matters in art is authenticity. Even cynical and ironic work must be authentically arch. So I staffed the place with real. Optimism was part of the scene, pragmatism was old and boring. Most of all, I needed the best music and that meant the best DJs. Didn't matter if that DJ was certifiable, I had to have them. If you wanted the best DJs in this barrio, it meant having to go through Quag Allurgie. Yeah. Him.

Quag didn't own much, he just thought he did. And in a sense, if you believe hard enough it can manifest a little in the minds of others. This went for the DJs who sometimes played at his event. It also included every visiting DJ and visiting dignitary. Didn't matter that they were world famous. If they appeared anywhere in what Quag considered 'his' territory, they belonged to him. Territorialism is one of the things you encounter most often on the journey through this industry. Or any. Regions, markets, districts... call it what you will. There are many gates and doors, all with many key holders. Borders are purely an agreement between people. They do not exist otherwise. All you have to do is decide not to agree, but you must understand the consequences. I understood Quag very well. Best to make him feel part of things. A lot easier than fighting. And let's be clear, the best music around was centred around Quag's vast, rotating ego. He made sure of it. It would benefit him greatly if 'his' DJs were being beamed all over the country. It was a no-brainer. If this meant him taking credit at every turn, so be it. A good leader understands humility. If you have to win at all costs and on top of that be seen to win, one will eat away at the other. I knew who was running the radio station. All I needed was for it to succeed. Keeping people happy was part of it.

Dealing with the vitriolic fallout from the unlucky, those left out of the loop... that was also part of the job. It wasn't Quag who would have to deal with the other, volcanically furious 99% of promoters and DJs not being offered spots. He didn't know I'd sat down with nearly everyone of note prior to him. I even arranged for the after-party of the launch to be held at his current venue. I was at peak useful. And if you are useful, Quag LOVES you. If you have fame, Quag is charm personified. Spookily so. It's rather like 'The Special Relationship' between America and the UK. Which I understand to be that the United Kingdom does whatever the US demands quicksticks, and without complaint, and in return, the UK gets absolutely nothing but the two words 'special' and 'relationship'. Suffice to say, with people like Quag, and the industry is full of them, it's entirely a one-way street. If you understand that, it will never be a problem.

As launch day loomed closer, I was spending day after day coaching the DJs. Few of whom had ever visited a professional radio environment. Some had pirate radio experience, some had guested playing records. None had hosted in a modern studio. Neither had I. But I'd had a year to get up to speed. News of the coaching got back to Quag. As was his usual trick, he called me into his office on a pretence, and once there behaved as if he was my boss and asked why he didn't have a radio show too. I patiently explained that it was 90% about playing records, something he did not do. He countered that he knew everyone in the biz (he did) and could bring a lot to the table. It was possible there could be a 'chat' show based on the industry. It was new but not beyond the realms of possibility. A few years later I'd help teach him how to DJ. Another story. For now, another bit of tuition was needed.

I'd have to get a demo together to sell him. A pilot. I arranged for him to go into a studio with a mutual friend. Selling DJs to my bosses in the boardroom hadn't been necessary thus far. But at this late stage convincing them of a more talk-based concept at the 11th hour was going to need approval. I'd already used up a lot of juice convincing them a 'radio presenter' for peak time breakfast show from London was a terrible idea and they should use a raw local girl. A black girl. Something that took months of shady backstage tricks on my part. Upstairs were not exactly all-ears to more unconventional manoeuvres from me, not by now. I'd used up my tricks. I'd spent years trying to make my interests look like ideas upstairs had had, and they were smart enough to let me believe that.

Our mutual friend, something of an authority and safe pair of hands whom I'd also secured as the main Sunday DJ on the schedule, called from his studio. Quag was not taking to the demo. Or maybe was taking too much. Take after take after take, in fact. After what seemed a very long time it was abandoned. Quag wasn't happy. OK, I'll set up a meeting at head office with Le Grande Fromage. Quag's supernatural charm and spooky hypnotism would win the day and let me off the hook.

I drove him there, made the introductions and left them to talk. I knew not only would Quag probably secure the deal for himself he'd probably convince the big boss to allow Quag to take over the whole station. Quag could do that quite easily. His powers of persuasion were legendary. Through the glass I could see them chatting animatedly. Quag only did animatedly. Never once seen him 'off'. Permanently switched-on is the curse of all of us born this way.

The high pow-wow was over. Part of Quag's skill was theatre too. He knew that getting his potential future boss, me, to act as butler for this occasion and sit waiting outside like his driver, showed power. Le Grande Fromage and Quag came out of the boardroom all smiles and handshakes and bonhomie.

"Thungyuzz ullalud, loogunz furwurdz tuidz!" said Quag.

"Can I have quick word?" boomed the syrup at me.

"Won't be a minute Quag, wait in the car?" I said.

We stepped back into the impressive boardroom. The whiff of rich walnut, polish and savage ambition reached my nostrils. We didn't even sit down as he practically grabbed me and hissed in his perfect tones:

"Are you deranged? This is RAY-DEE-OH. Radio! A VO-CAL medium. You literally just sent me someone whom I did not understand

CHAPTER 5

one word of. My face hurts from smiling and nodding. The. Man. Cannot. Talk!"

I just looked perplexed. For some reason I always understood Quag perfectly. I just forgot, frequently, that no one else did. The drive back was not easy. Later Quag Allurgie would break a record, appearing on television as the first person speaking English to require English subtitles.

However, compared to the grand opening day, this diversion with Quag was a jolly picnic. A solid year of preparation and the day was finally here. Amongst many other epic things, it was the first time everyone involved was in the same space. I'd been the bridge between 'Radio' and 'Dance Music' the whole time. Shuttling between each faction. Training up each side in the habits of the other. I was about to learn the difference between preparation and reality. Straight off the bat, I noticed two of my DJs had not turned up. This was important in many ways, not least of which the group photo planned that had to include everyone. Due to the 24/7 nature of radio, it was also unlikely everyone would all be in one room ever again. This absenteeism was an ongoing problem. 'Real' DJs often looked down on radio. Radio was mainstream and they were 'underground'. Didn't matter that we were trying to bring the two together. Snobbery is always a problem.

Once DJ Son of God turned up at Tour Manager's venue with an equally cool support DJ. It was the first time I'd ever encountered DJ royalty completely off duty. He was nice enough, but when I asked them politely if they might consider popping on-air at some time in the future, they simply laughed, called me 'Radio DJ' and then asked me to carry their record boxes for them. I put down some of the no-shows at the big launch to this disdain. Also drew a small list mentally of imminent firings and subsequent hirings. Then I started the angry phone calls. Call one I discovered the root. Last night was Quag's birthday. Shit.

I was plain with them. Turn up in under 20 minutes or never turn up at all. One was contrite and already on his way. The other was, worryingly, not just still unaccounted for but last seen in the company of a legendary producer who was famous for two things. Co-writing and producing one of the earliest bonafide top pioneer records of our scene, and mad for the smack. Other drugs you might be excused for, or be able to wing it on an important day in a big crowd. If my missing horse was mounted, he wasn't going anywhere. Then, just as I'd given up and started to think up excuses, Le Grande Fromage simply said it was time for the photo and anyone not there was fired. I've still got the photo somewhere. There everyone is, and at the side is the blurry figure of missing DJ lurching into frame. Making it by seconds with me staring daggers at him. Captured forever.

Thinking back, it would have been better if he'd not arrived. Nowadays he's not only fully sober but an utterly delightful human. Back then, not many of us could manage delightful. To be fair, of everyone involved, he was my biggest worry but also my favourite to listen to. Not just musically. He was naturally hilarious and engaging, but a constant liability. The grand opening became a Molière farce instantly now he was here. My crowning glory was reduced to running interference between Le Grande Fromage, my difficult protege, and his heroin-loving sidekick. Both clearly out of their minds in the middle of the day, still awake from the night before, if not longer. At one point I was literally running across rooms, weaving through champagne and canapés to physically separate the ambassadors of Freakville from the Kings of Normal. Sometimes deftly, often desperately. Sweating profusely. Eventually, I managed to convince the problem kids to, quite simply, fuck the fuck off.

"It was just me mate's birthday!" he whined as I packed him off into the dusk with the combination of promise and threat it usually takes to deal with someone off their tits. Just a sample of what was in store for me for years to come. Relief washed over me. Nearly lost my day-old job before getting paid. After working free for a whole year!

The stentorian tones of Le Grande Fromage boomed over the assembled, now all indoors. He was about to engage in his God-given function. His raison d'être: talking at people for ages. He began to ooze, preach and declare. Champagne flute in hand he stood on a chair in front of the huge darkening windows and addressed the assembled throng. Olympic-level pontificating ensued. He WAS radio. And radio was talking in his highly radio voice. I wasn't listening however as my recently ejected protege,

CHAPTER 5

DJ Batman and his smackhead Robin, were looming into frame outside in the car park, right behind Le Grande Fromage. I prayed silently as, equally silently, they clocked the light inside, saw everyone in the studios looking outward, and began to caper and gesticulate rudely. Literally, the only two people who could have sacked them were the sole people not facing in their direction. Then, as fate would have it, in his deeply, deeply professionally sincere and therefore utterly insincere radio voice... Le Grande Fromage reached his booming climax:

"Radio is a privilege. It's not a job, it's an honour to address the public. A calling. Now I'm no monster. This is the music biz yeah? I get it. There are 'characters' here. Well. Let me tell you 'characters' this. Only two things mean INSTANT dismissal There are two crimes I do not tolerate. ONE! DEAD AIR (didn't matter no one knew what this meant, which is if radio says nothing. Goes quiet for more than a breath. He assumed he was addressing 'radio people').

TWO!

(dramatic pause)

DRUGS!

I. Will. Not. Tolerate. Them. ANYONE intoxicated on these premises will never...drone, drone waffle waffle..."

I'd stopped listening. I had to. DJ Batman was at that moment pressed against the window behind his head. Well. Part of him was pressed against the window. Winking like one of the alien face huggers from the films. Robin next to him, doubled up with laughter. A pink sack full of drugs stuck to the window behind King Radio. His brown starfish quacking almost in time to the words of our new overlord, inches behind his head. If anything at all described the next few years as a metaphor, it was this opening party. An entire generation giggling and trying to hide it, whilst mocking our imaginary bosses from prehistory. Blindly thinking they were running the show while we pressed our arses against the window behind them, counting time until the days were ours.

With great ceremony and seriousness, somebody went on-air and we were live. Finally. I went to have a small heart attack and a lie-down in a darkened room with some thinly-sliced cucumber. Wishing only to be disturbed by nothing more challenging to the ear than silverware touching fine china.

The next few years are another story. I think we've nearly done radio haven't we? Want to know a few factoids? I bet you do.

First of all, nearly every moment of radio you have ever loved is prerecorded. The stars send in their links (the chat between tunes) from home or office and may never even have heard the tune played before, or after, their voice is parachuted into the mix. Or will likely hear them ever again. All those authorities that bestride the world like colossi? Half of them have absolutely no idea how their own radio show is made. Or who made it for them. Those hour-long mixes? Never went anywhere near them. Wherever there is money, there is fear of losing it. This is the conservative drive at the heart of the engine of capitalism. Fear means nothing is left to chance. No surprises. No improvisation. No art. If you think this is a shocker, imagine, this was 1997. It's got way worse since. In those days the digital system was called SADIE, and everything you heard was loaded onto it way WAY in advance and simply played like a tape.

Except, that is, on my watch.

For a couple of years, every bit of specialist output was myself and my crew doing it entirely live. And it was glorious anarchy. It wasn't merely rebellion, I also had no idea how to use their system. I used to have to do it wearing two gigantic pairs of headphones at once. Four cups, two ears, looking like Ming's brother. Pong the Pitiless. One set for the radio desk and the other for mixing. I had hundreds of guests, famous and obscure. Local and international. Our output had dedicated Drum & Bass, R&B, Reggae and Hip Hop shows with not a white face in sight, unique to us. I made damn sure of it. For a few years, we were red hot and we knew it. The chaos paid off in spades.

My immediate superior tried to hint at the future. Took me to one side and told me fairly emphatically that it might be a jolly good idea if I got some shares in the place. A letter was also sent to everyone along these lines. He looked at me earnestly and suggested it was very timely to do so. My response wasn't just my usual impenetrable density for subtlety. Imagine my amusement at the people who'd paid me almost nothing for years telling me to buy into something. With what? Unlike all the other DJs and presenters I didn't have a single moment free to capitalise on the thing. Do appearances, gigs and spin-off deals? Are you serious? I was live on-air every weeknight until 2am, lucky to be in bed by 5am and back in the office about 30 mins after I woke up. If anything at all went wrong, it was me who got the call at 5.30am. Or 5.30pm. Or any time at all. Seven days a week.

Anyone with experience in the corporate world will know what is coming. When something makes noise it attracts attention. Attention is money. It starts with denial. Of COURSE we are not being bought out! There will be serious penalties for anyone found spreading these terrible rumours. Don't be ridiculous, we're not selling-out to that horrible, vanilla chain of stations owned by a huge conglomerate. How very dare you! Etc. etc. Current Me would immediately hear these words and think "So we're being bought out imminently then? Best get ready". Old Me didn't have a clue. It was flattering. I was responsible for much of the success and the rumours of a buyout were just enjoyable gossip. The fact I'd almost outright been told to buy shares a few weeks previously was utterly lost on me.

Then, as in all takeovers, weeks of denial suddenly turn into a day when a troop of suited strangers file into the place, tell you that the key card system has been changed and can everyone hand in their fobs? We are your new bosses. I'd not seen Grande Fromage for a while, so he wasn't going to be missed. I'd seen my immediate boss not 12 hours earlier, loudly telling everyone there was no takeover. I never saw or heard from either again. I heard years later of the pair doing exactly the same to a station in another town, by now understanding that the couple were a professional duo of developers. They did this every few years all over the place. Buy-in, build, sell. Laugh all the way to the bank.

I asked the gaggle of *very* impertinent strangers if I could address my staff in private. I made some calls and for the second time, and the last, nearly everyone was in one room the following day.

"The rumours are true. We're no longer a dance music station. They told us all today that nothing is going to change. This is a lie. We all know they are a bog-standard commercial music-type outfit. I hired every single one of you here, and earlier I had to explain to these people why I run nearly everything but haven't even got a proper office. It is clear they didn't get it. I swear to you all, right here and now, not a single one of you will still be employed here in a year. We are not wanted. They will make you re-apply for your own job knowing full well they already have your replacement. They've only been here 24 hours and not one of them has done anything but lie to us. Now is the time for us to join hands. Together we have power. If we all stand together they will know we mean business...

so...

WHO IS WITH ME!?"

Long pause. Tumbleweed drifts across my face. Haunted silence. Nothing. I am Spartacunt.

The new bosses learned of this dramatic and highly pathetic moment almost immediately, likely from someone I'd given a nice career to. Next day I was informed my services were no longer required. I was proud of the small and limited measure of influence I had on the daytime mainstream output. What we call 'The A-list'. A constantly rotating number of plays for the most popular stuff, or music we think needs to be heard. Fairly recently I'd staged a coup and managed to get Thomas Bangalter from Daft Punk, and his new tune 'Spinal Scratch' on the A-list. Which meant hearing it at least three times an hour. The station's audio output is constantly on speakers in the offices. As I packed up my things and got escorted out, this slab of pure dance anarchy was playing on the speakers that operated within the building.

By the time I crossed the car park, switched my car's ignition on, (and the station was constantly tuned-into in my car) the cunts had Robbie fucking Williams playing. Took them less than five minutes to fuck up my life's work. And I got a free life lesson in value. I took where I was and what I had for granted. I did not value my place there. And if I did not value it properly, who the hell would?

Where do you go after that? I met with BBC Radio One, formerly our mainstream enemy and literally the only step up feasible while still in the same country. A far more brief meeting than when I first barged into radio, where this time my explaining where they were going wrong was somewhat less well received. No interest whatsoever in changing what they had. That was the end of my radio career. And the end of my interest in the corporate world. What else did I learn? Well. If you don't *own* shit, you don't own *shit*. To this day I will never let a hand come from above and take what is mine. Sure, if the deal is good, sell the hours of your life for cash. However, I've found that there isn't a sum invented that can buy my time now, not full-time. You can rent me, dear, but it'll cost you. I'd rather be skint and in-charge of my destiny every time. But that's not for everyone, I get it. By the way, I was spot-on. Every single person bar one was gone from that place within a year. Now it is a national network of beige, middle-of-the-road music held together with deeply cheesy adverts from brands no-one cares about. And everyone who built it is rich, except me. And it is *white* now. White as snow in complete contravention of the licence it is supposed to qualify for and in full betrayal of the community it is supposed to represent. It no longer serves that community in all its diversity, it serves the shareholders and the middle class white minority. Forget what happened to me, that was just me not knowing what I was doing. The crime here is the complete surgical excision of black culture and influence from the airwaves. Unquestioned and utterly unchallenged. Unnoticed. Utterly unforgivable. It was my first experience of Acid House as a tool of corporate speculation. I was watching the mobilisation of the energy of a generation for the benefit of the money men, and I was probably helping without even knowing it. It was a sign of things to come.

INTERLUDE
BE THE FREAK

Petrol stations feature very heavily in the life of any working DJ. For a while in South London the local petrol station was the epicentre of our universe. It was the only thing open when we were awake, which was night time. Ours was spanking new and could only be accessed on foot by an alleyway called 'Norman's Passage', which amused us all, greatly. At the time we were experiencing the fresh tidal wave of madness in the United Kingdom that was hybrid skunk. Saturdays were spent blacking out all the windows, getting absurdly high, and then loads of weirdos would start playing Acid Jazz really very badly. After this extended jam session of cosmic wonder, matters would culminate in the ritual known as 'Being the Freak'.

The Freak was one of those special types of individuals that if harassed enough would do almost anything to be left alone. Up to and including petty misdemeanours and light larceny. The ritual would commence as the sun went down and supplies ran low. The Freak was formerly known as 'The Battersea Starer' due to an unfortunate incident where he stumbled into the wrong house and bedroom, and subsequent hilarious local paper headline.

"Be The Freak", someone would begin. That was all it took. Then others would join in. He would be cornered, eyes darting madly left end right looking for an exit. And the chant would rise:

"BE THE FREAK"

"BE THE FREAK"

"BE THE FREAK"

Being The Freak involved sellotaping as many objects to his head as possible. Chicken carcasses. Telephones. Remote controlled cars. Lamps. Hats at impossible angles. Roller skates. Small sculptures of minimal value. Sometimes clear kitchen film would be applied to help construction. Many, many, many layers. Until his head was often a metre in diameter. Sometimes even more. Then he had to wear monster feet and a kaftan, go up Norman's Passage, press his giant head against the petrol station window with a gentle 'doink' and in the most sinister and tiny voice he could manage, ask for a 'Wispa' bar.

"Can I have a Wispa?" The Freak would whisper.

The man who worked there had seen The Freak at least four times that month. He was fairly nonplussed, usually. 'The Final Freak' was a month later when the colossal noggin staggered and shuffled up to the kiosk security glass like the world's largest lost toddler and the man behind the counter clicked on his microphone simply said straight off the bat:

"One of these days you're going to get stabbed many times right in your giant head with a very large knife…

Wispa, was it?"

CHAPTER 6
I'M JUST GOING OUTSIDE AND I MAY BE SOME TIME...

If we want to track the changes in the industry, a great barometer is festivals. Like the rest of our business, festivals used to be filthy, free, random and spontaneous. Now it is completely the opposite: pristine, expensive, regimented and a place politicians now go to address the middle class and youth vote. Ironically, the frankly frightening minds behind the Great Brexit Swindle planned, amongst many dirty tricks, to have the referendum vote to stay within, or leave the EU, during Glastonbury. Very shrewd. Again, you may see these changes as a vast improvement, depending very much upon how often you need to wash or use a mirror.

In the really early days, the only way for us to get to Glastonbury was a National Express coach. Free in. No fences. Nearly every band was an ageing version of prog-rock or metal. Some whizz, tepid lager and maybe a bit of 'shroom action and it was a laugh and a half. Other drugs didn't exist for us. No phones. No money! No way of getting any. You literally brought everything you would need with you. We'd look on in envy at fancy folks with cars and transit vans whom, granted, were covered in just as much shit as we were. There was only one backstage area and it was as badger-rough as everywhere else on site. There were no VIPs. Few people bothered to camp. We arrived the Tuesday before the weekend of the fest and the very idea of 'Glamping' was beyond comprehension. Indeed, we'd be hard-pushed to see a tent at all, because we'd stay awake for more than a week. Sometimes catch a couple of hours under a truck like the world's worst mechanic. Or curled up in a bass bin like a shrew in a haystack. No, really.

Then we started to go as a gang. It was before Acid House really took off and we all played in bands. But it was funk you heard wafting over the grassy knolls by now, not metal. We were the ones they told off for changing the comfy status-quo 30 years ago. We were the proto-hipsters

CHAPTER 6

- although no one had beards except one or two of the riggers and a couple of actual wizards. We were 'ruining it' for everyone. The hippies and other Gatekeepers loathed us. We brought speakers and electricity to the peripheries where it had never been before. We were mates with travelling sound systems like Spiral Tribe, DIY and Tonka and were the first people to rave there. Indeed, we got in big trouble for it. Everyone hated us 'cos we were skint, energetic and pretty. We were the Millennials of Acid House.

We were the first to play House and Techno there. I was one of the first DJs to play records on the sidelines and sometimes between the bands on the big stages, or at least to mix them together, and it's something I'll always be proud of. The Second Summer of Love didn't really dent Glastonbury, 'cos we were already knee-deep in what Acid House was just starting to do. We had a huge tin bath full of mushroom tea in an army surplus tented bar. We jammed for hours in our bands and between we played records. We gave the tea away. Because back then you really could go there without a penny. Loads of things were free, including being there.

A naked man with a long stick kept coming in our bar and demanding tea because he was 'A Dragon Slayer'. We told him he was a Pool Player. We told him there was a dragon needed slaying in the next field. He went off to check. Came back and every naked inch of him was drained of blood. He'd seen the new giant dragon sculpture for the first time whilst out of his mind. "*I'm definitely a Pool Player!*" he told us. Then he fell asleep on one of our benches, so myself and Private Pumper, former Royal Marine (and at the time the world's strongest transvestite) carried him like it was a stretcher from our peaceful periphery to the busiest drag and stood back to watch him wake up, teleported into Dante's Inferno.

Next time we saw The Dragon Slayer/Pool Player he had climbed to the top of one of the scaffolding towers at one of the first car-park raves and was wanking on the crowd. We thankfully never saw him again.

We were the first people to dress like idiots. One year there were some people from Torture Garden who came as latex wasps... and something started. A year later, I took my pristine referee's uniform and put it on, on day six, just as everyone was reaching peak skank and looking well rough. I minced about giving people yellow and red cards. There is something about a referee that transcends even police for a force to be reckoned with. I had hippies on their knees crying 'cos I wouldn't tell them why they got a red card.

We were wearing ball gowns and tuxedos dancing with gypsies in Lost Vagueness, hand-in-hand with gay lads and lesbians to House music 20 years before NYC Downlow et al.

Every generation thinks they are the first.

One year I played on the Radio One stage for 52 hours without pause. For two-and-a-half days and nights, I mixed records together. I arrived in an estate car full of records and CDs 'cos unlike the newbie DJs I knew how long things could go on for. Sets weren't two hours but 8, 16, 24. Back then, of course, you could get the amount of people who arrived with vinyl instead of guitars onto one bus. Instead of the other way around.

I have no sense of smell, so I once rescued a girl's wedding ring from the shit pit. Folks held my ankles and lowered me into the toilet trench. I've been helicoptered off site after my ancient hernia split and proud to have puked in the only clean toilets in the whole place at the medical centre.

We always met at the Tiny Tea Tent if we were lost. And we always asked for "some tiny tea please" in a teeny tiny voice. We even did the steam lodge properly. 'Cos it was literally the only place you could approach clean. We'd see how many could crush into 'Minuscule of Sound' for shits and giggles. For reference, the answer is 22 until one of the wall panels collapses.

"Beak! Beak! Beak!" – can still hear a Liverpool voice, selling cocaine back when it was strictly for celebrities. An amazing lift when it was nearly over and we had nothing left in the tank.

And no politicians, no matter how progressive, would ever consider attending to win us over. 'Cos we were scum. Not nice well-heeled voters. Every year I prayed for it to rain, not because I am a bad person, but because I had the most fun there when it did.

CHAPTER 6

We also made sure everything was spotlessly clean once it was over. The peripheries were pristine the whole 10 days. Don't see that so much anymore. We helped turn Glastonbury from a crusty mudfest to what you love now over a 15 year period and the organisers barely acknowledged we existed, and were happy to forget all about us when suddenly everyone wanted to go. We were the first to do many of these things that you now enjoy under threat of violence from both police and security. And you know what? Who cares!? First schmirst. Everyone going for the first time is just doing what we did. There was those before us too. There is *always,* always someone else you can find who did something before you. I'm sure there were gay metal fans there in the 80s. Everyone is convinced they are first.

And looking at it on the BBC from your sofa still has no more resemblance to what is happening there than watching a major sporting event does to being one of the players. Even as I reflect here on the page, I know that if I ever go there again, I will love every minute. And as ever, find something highly weird on the periphery and never see so much as a falafel, guitar or pop starlet.

Just like everything, it *definitely* isn't what it used to be... but then again, nothing is. It is safe, expensive and gentrified. But then again, what isn't? Shut up moaners. You are just jelly.

Because I also know that despite every awful middle-class 'pop-up', 1000 plastic DJs-for-a-day and badly chosen megastar, there are kids and workers there for the first time ever who, like me, will one day look back and say: "Those were some of the best days of my life." Ultimately, it's up to us all to make - and live - our own Summer of Love, every single year.

Yeah.

DJing at a festival is quite different than at a club. Sure, now there are basically big branded clubs doing their own festivals and franchised tent lineups, but most festival DJ gigs tend to be in fairly standard festival surroundings. For every Dekmantel or Sónar there are 50 small town, oldskool festivals.

I guess one of the main tenets of DJing is about whether or not people are actually there to hear *you.* There's absolutely nothing wrong with being the background music if it's a festival. A gig is a gig, and they all need to be taken seriously. When you are capable of treating a gig in a field pissing with rain being watched by a disinterested cow with the same gravitas you would headlining a serious club, then you can call yourself a DJ.

I honestly believe that if you go about things with a pure intention and try to match the vibe of where you are then people will feel it, and respond positively to you. When you are head-down boshing out completely inappropriate 2am genre music in the middle of a sunny field at lunchtime, you are a pain, not a pleasure. Despite the powerful volume at your fingertips, there is always an element of fitting-in with your surroundings. That can include anything from a highly credible club to a mate's house party, and every permutation in-between. Knowing your place in the vibe is no different from having the chops to do a good, solid and subtle warm-up set.

A bad warm-up can *literally* destroy a whole night, everyone knackered before midnight because DJ Swole demanded he spew out all his bangers immediately, like a confetti cannon full of rusty spanners, ego and dirty sausages. This applies even more stringently to festivals. They start *way* earlier and people have often been there a couple of days already with very little good rest. Few arrive early, especially those staying off-site. The daytime is for wandering around in a daze, checking out stalls and getting your bearings. Utterly failing to put your tent up properly. Scoring some plasticine off a man who mysteriously has no change. Those sort of things.

People will gravitate to your style if you match the overall vibe around you. Avoid you big time if you don't. If you are playing music that suits the weather and the feeling, they will come. Once you have a small gathering, the rest is basic DJ skills 101. Coaxing them into a groove, building an atmosphere. Then passers-by will see this and join in. DJing done correctly is always a subtle thing, even when your choice of weapons are quite blunt and macho. You always have to start cleverly or you will have nowhere to go. Reel them in, don't smash them over the head with a sock full of audio bricks.

Understanding your place in your surroundings is key. Being part of it, not the imagined focus, is the humility required to excel at the job.

CHAPTER 6

Because it is never better when you are all in it together, this is its *purpose*. This is what we are for. It's a party. A celebration. Not a concert. Once you start to think everyone is there for you, you are lost. You are there for everyone else. As is everyone in the place. We are all in the house, or tent, together.

An early memory I have of one of my first 'tents-in-a-field' was arriving to perform at an 'orbital' rave. So-called because they popped up around the major ring road that surrounds London. I'd worked at festivals like Reading and Glastonbury, but this was new. Absolutely everyone seemed out of their minds to me, and none more than the people running them. The 'security' were clearly gangsters. The organisers nowhere to be seen. In fact, there was no one to meet us at all. There appeared to be no backstage to the big top. We just walked around and around it in a ridiculous pantomime and it seemed closed on all sides except for one big flap. The giant gash belched steam, nutters and racket. There was nothing else for it. We'd have to plough through.

Carrying frankly too much equipment, we figured we'd have to just brave it and choose a random point to aim for. I was elected to be the prow. I heaved and squeezed and shouted and made very little progress through the throng. I turned around to my mate and shouted:

"WE WILL NEVER GET THROUGH! AND I DON'T KNOW WHICH DIRECTION!"

At this point, a small miracle happened. In front of us, like the biblical Red Sea, the heaving throng started to part. Perhaps it was my shouting. Perhaps it is my right because I am so very important. Perhaps someone was coming for us.

Someone *was* coming. Pelting towards us at sprinting pace was a horrific sight. A gurning raver had clearly chewed through her glowstick and it had exploded in her mouth and over her face. Correctly believing it to be highly toxic, and quite possibly highly radioactive, she was screeching and wailing at welding volume whilst pelting through the crowd, all under a strong ultra-violet light. I turned to laugh with my mates only to see them all turning and running like everyone else as the horrific screeching Day-Glo banshee shrieked past me through a perfectly empty valley. The looks on the faces of the ravers were almost as petrified as hers. It was a sign. I turned to join the rest of the band and we left. Pulled the eject cord. Never to return.

My 52 hour set at Glasto was for the Radio One stage, at the height of the minor culture war between the hippies and the ravers. I arrived very early to find a curfew had been imposed on the sound system because the 'racket' was spoiling the 'vibes' for the rest of the festival. I had to play for the next 12 hours officially (it was a different time, there weren't enough DJs drawing breath on the planet to have 20 of us doing half-hour sets) but there was strictly no dancing allowed until the sun went down. On pain of disconnection and expulsion by the organisers. After many hours of doing my best to be ambient, laid-back, old school or basically anything I could muster that wasn't danceable, I had about 500 people sat on the grass in front of me. It was a new thing. I really liked it. I'd managed to be inoffensive but not disappear. People stopped to listen. They got comfy. I should point out that it was by no means background music. People were listening. It felt like a very civilised concert in a park, possibly a twee bandstand. I liked it. Something was happening.

Completely by accident I put on 'Love Hangover' by Diana Ross. If not for any other reason that I was struggling to find more tunes that you couldn't dance to. As any fan will know, it has a very long, chilled-out and soulful first half. I'd almost forgotten that it morphs into a full-on disco tune. One-by-one the people started to stand up as the beat came in. A small cheer went up. I saw people start to run towards us from the further edges. The sun was just going down. Almost as if I'd meant it. It was genuinely magical. A moment I will never forget. I went on to play for the rest of the night, the next day and the following night non-stop. We had formed a unit, the people, the DJ, the workers. We'd lived through the 'crisis' of the curfew and knew what to do when it came around again. Everyone was happy, especially the organisers. We went from sitting down and listening to classical, ambient and vintage pop through disco and funk and eventually into House and Techno through the night, into the next day, through that following evening and once again going past dawn.

Together.

CHAPTER 7
EVENT HORIZONS

After a while you start to see patterns. After 40 years around DJing, I've inevitably developed my own classification system for gigs, like Charles Darwin on the Beagle, only with slightly less vivisection. At the top of the tree are your 'Premium Events'. Everyone is there to see *you* at a Premium Event, there is an agreement in the air that you are the boss and you could fart into a microphone and they'd love it. You don't have to be the headliner on the bill for it to be a Premium Gig, but you probably are. Here you can do 'the journey' and implement a planned crescendo or wandering safari of sound. You could take exactly the same set of records from a bad gig and put them in this situation and everyone would go crazy with adulation.

It's simply a form of mass hysteria when it goes this way. The hyperbole and sometimes sheer size of the thing means people bring the vibe with them. The top 1% of DJs operate at this level nearly all the time. They have bad gigs too, but they are rare. I tried to think of a dry, corporate title for these sort of gigs because they frequently can be corporate-funded. However, a brilliant underground club or impromptu rave can certainly be a Premium gig too if the hype is right. It's about the anticipation and the atmosphere more than anything logistic. The crowd decide long before they arrive that this gig is really going to be something, so it is. It is consensus. The DJ almost has nothing to do with it. You'll go insane pretty fast if you start to think you do.

After a couple decades at-it, a good gig is just one that goes without a hitch. A lot can go wrong with events dealing with large amounts of people. It's a good day when it just goes well without any hiccups. You can't expect all gigs to happen without a hitch. You will turn into a raging, frothing diva if you start to think that way. However, it's good for the soul to notch up the good times and aim for a standard of fuckup-free professionalism.

'Jobbing Gigs' are the next type. There are lots of them. Here the promoters know your name, and some of the more discerning customers too.

However, most people in the club don't care who you are. The 'agreement' that you can do whatever the hell you like is not in place here. You will have to do some work, which may even SHOCK HORROR include playing records you might not want to. Many upper-level DJs don't get this part. The 1% are lost in these situations and just do their inflexible thing and let it fail. It's easier for them to scuttle the supertanker, rather than turn it.

You could still be a headliner but the everyday Jobbing Gig has something missing that would elevate it. It may be parochial or on a bad date. A gig in the local disco turns into a Premium Event on New Year's Eve, for example. Dates matter. There is an element of the hunt in a Jobber, where you must try out several things to see if there is a reaction to anything you are playing and if there is, you leap on it like an elderly lion and do more of the same. A pro will always win-over a Jobbing Gig's crowd. They want to have a good time after all. Try not to let them down by being a dick. It's just a matter of flexibility. Big DJs tend to struggle here. They are generally, but not always, the most inflexible.

Next, there are Bad Gigs AKA The Hellish Nightmare. No one has any idea about you, what you do, or indeed any notion of music that you can comprehend. They are drunk and difficult and would happily storm the booth and plug in their phone if they could. You've been placed between two other acts who have no resemblance to you musically whatsoever. These are professional events that no matter what you do, you can't play your way out of the bad vibe. Your abilities are ineffective here, no matter what.

Bad Gigs are what separates the pro from the amateur. Amateurs always freak out, complain and kick against it. A pro just gets on with it. A pro gives it as much energy as a Premium Gig. Smiles and is gracious with the nightmare requester who will not leave it alone. Promoters also know when things are not going well, they most of all. Who do you think will form a strong and lasting professional relationship with them in a crisis? Someone freaking out or someone trying to help?

There's a small but important distinction between an 'Amateur Shambles' and a Bad Gig. You may even be getting paid, but everything about an Amateur Shambles is shocking. No crowd, no equipment. Bad sound.

No handling or repair of the situations as they unfold. It's nothing to do with bad luck or 'vibes', it's just plain mismanagement. It's fair enough to call out an amateur situation if you are a professional. You shouldn't be there. Something failed with the agent and a chancer got through the net. Try to be diplomatic about it if you can.

Don't get me wrong, there is nothing wrong with amateur gigs done well. 'Amateur' here refers to attitude. Some of the best situations you will ever work in will be house parties, impromptu raves, warehouses and beach gigs that may have been organised by a domestic cat with a crayon. So go figure. I'm not saying an Amateur Shambles is anything to do with money, it's just handled very poorly by people who've either never done it before or are consistently terrible. Bad Gigs can be just bad luck. Can happen to anyone. An Amateur Shambles is something someone has put together without care or attention and is doomed at the heart of it due to organisers just not giving a shit, or having no clue.

'The Underground'. Inevitably we arrive here. Now lots and lots of things will claim to be underground. In fact, I often put the word 'underground' in inverted commas because it's a highly relative term. Underground is tough to describe 'cos it can happen in very unlikely places. Admittedly most of what claims to be underground is merely supremacists trying to be better than everyone else before even so much as a mixer is plugged-in. For many, 'The Underground' is literally just a black T-shirt. Something to be thrown-on when it suits. All of the above gig types can be underground, as opposed to commercial. But many commercial events can be very underground and an awful lot of underground events are all about the money. If you are confused now, well that's fine. It's supposed to be confusing. Keeping people confused and flappy about what is cool is *very* important when you want to make money out of gullible fashionistas. There are, however, some people who are entirely about the underground in a very legitimate manner. Believe me, they are extremely rare. We live in a decaying capitalist structure, so it's very difficult to simply say The Underground is anti-commercial. It cannot be so within capitalism, even when pretending to. However, the true Underground retains an element of *protest*. That protest can be against poor quality. It can be simply against what is perceived as mainstream. It can be against the oppressive fashions of the time. It is contrary in nature but must strive not to be contrarian for the sake of it. Quite simply, The Underground poses a question of attitude and carries an unwaveringly high standard. I always say True Underground is a little like Love. If you have to ask… then it's probably not.

When you boldly go off to somewhere dead weird? These are 'Star Trek' gigs. They can be both brilliant or disastrous. They are always way off the radar. Usually, you play in a big city with at least the promoter, driver and crew speaking some form of English, as do many of the punters. Star Trek gigs often start where no one from the get-go has anything but their own language (which is fair enough in their own country, obviously!) but it can make the whole thing very strange and feel very distant and isolating. And you tend to find that if no one speaks any English at all, it's pretty out of the way. Consequently, much of the tech and set-up is unusual and sometimes a little out-of-date. Often these sort of gigs that can be the most rewarding, the people *really* into it and the surroundings interesting and new. Though the hellish nightmare potential is also *extremely* high, these outer space gigs are certainly a lottery but never, ever boring. The original Acid House feeling can be strong with these ones. Personally, I love these types most of all.

Pure Corporate gigs can tend to pop up if you start to do well. Ask any pro DJ with reasonable management if they do corporate and if they say 'no' you are talking to a liar. You know why I can be so bold? Because what is the difference to playing to a load of suits in a sterile box and playing to a festival crowd with the sponsors who make guns and bombs actually paying you? The only difference is that in a field you're rarely confronted with the awkward details. At least playing at some sort of dismal product launch you are fully aware of what is going on. The days of not selling-out are harder and harder to remember. Get to a certain level now and it's nailed-on that someone very nasty will be involved somewhere in the process. No, the response is not to shrug and say "what can you do about it?" and count the money. The job is to find out what bad jazz you are up to your neck in, and then do something about it.

CHAPTER 7

Industry-only gigs happen a lot. Everyone there is somehow connected to the biz. Industry gigs are often amazing because, frankly, professionals really know how to professionally party. Conversely, no crowd is colder than a hostile industry gathering. Bookings are very rare, however. You'll have to be around a very long time to get asked to do these. Imagine the egos involved in putting together a line-up to please the pros? A good industry gig can make a career. Break one too. I can't decide if the one I did where I got 200 scowling pros to play musical chairs was good or bad for me. I do know I will never forget watching them cheat, gouge and wrestle for the handful of seats at the end.

I omitted to put a category right at the top called 'Special' but these are the best we can hope for. Anything can make a special, one-off party. At any level in any circumstances. The Special is what we all strive for. But the factors are so varied it's almost impossible to pull off without a fair dose of luck. Some gift from above, some chink in the clouds lets in the light and things present more than the sum of their parts. There's a queue around the block that winds everyone who gets in the door up to fever-pitch. There's an amazing batch of pills going round. It stopped raining just at the right time. You arrived at a grotty and dank basement and it turned out to be 100% legit proper filth. There's a sound engineer who really gives a shit. There's a DJ who actually really thinks about what they are about to do instead of creak through the motions. And it's not in the eyes of the beholder, everyone agrees the next day, THAT was a special one.

Hey, it's not rocket science but you'd be amazed how many people mix these gigs up. You get amateurs who think they are premium. Premium events that are a hellish mess once they start. One of the worst things you can do professionally is to arrive at work and fail to understand where you are at. If you can't read a situation, you will be instantly lost in it. Almost every single in-situ DJ problem comes from failing to comprehend where you are, and matching what you do to it.

Magnitude isn't always a factor but in terms of genuine connection, generally the smaller the better for me. My biggest outdoor event personally was, without question, the UK Love Parade. A copy of the huge annual German event that had first launched in Berlin. I've done stadiums, I've done the main stages of festivals, but this was a different order of massive altogether.

As I've said, the bigger the gig, the less it matches the original intent of Acid House. Not so much in volume of people, but the economics and attitudes involved. This one was different, however. Less a stadium-sized rave-up than a city takeover built around a kind of rambling conveyor belt of trucks, like Rio's Carnival, and therefore perhaps more appropriate. Or that was the plan anyway. Sounded legit to me.

The UK Love Parade was to be held in a town that was very familiar. It was Tour Manager's town, Quagville. I was due to be the very first DJ to play and my band was the only live act to perform later in the evening. The entire city was buzzing with electricity several weeks prior to it. Every access road anywhere near the proposed site, a vast Victorian park just outside of the centre, was closed-off or jammed with traffic from breakfast time of the day itself. The event was due to start at midday. As was I.

Luckily as well as having a band, attendant tour bus, tour manager (a real one this time) and various items of equipment, we also knew the back roads to get on-site. The roadblock across the city was no issue whatsoever as we jinked, slid and chicaned through the gridlock. Managing, in fact, to get there at 10am. Literally the first artists, and ahead of some of the crew and organisers. We parked our bus by the main stage, something we didn't even realise the event had. And like good idiots, started drinking immediately. We had a solid posse with us and although weren't sure what to expect, we were feeling the buzz unfold.

A knock on the bus door opened to find a stressed-out looking organiser. You can tell the rank of a Festival Elf by how many pointless lanyards and bracelets they have. This one looked like the Lord Mayor of Paradeville. The Mr.T of plastic festoons. We recognised each other immediately from the 52 hours of madness at Glastonbury a year or so previous. It was the boss. He asked me to come up to the stage.

As we mounted, I could hear, or rather feel, a rumbling. As we got to the black serge curtains he said, simply:

"Have a look at that…"

CHAPTER 7

Two hours before the scheduled start and there were people stretching to the horizon. By no means 'full' yet, if it was possible to fill several dozen square miles, but after all these years I am pretty good at guessing numbers of attendees. It's a small superpower, like guessing how many sweeties in the jar. If you don't have this skill, you will get ripped off extremely easily if you intend to promote anything. I'd say there was about 10 to 15 thousand kids there already. Milling about. Getting settled. All facing an empty stage.

The bigger the gig the more potential for carnage, of course; some years prior I bumped into an old friend, an excellent fellow DJ who was touring the world at the time fronting his record label and accompanied by one of our industry's most notorious rock 'n' rollers. Ironically the hero of this particular story is no stranger to misbehaviour himself, but compared to his sidekick, he was a saint. Let's call our sensible friend 'DJ Dastardly' and his perpetually thirsty sidekick 'Muttley'.

The duo had just returned from a gig on the tour in a South American enormodrome. The event, as all were at that time in that region, was most heavily branded. The main sponsor was Durex, the famous prophylactic manufacturer. To this day, I'm not convinced that our craft suits these stupidly large EDM-style events. Back then? Even less so, having had to do a few myself. The thing about size is that, in a sense, that is the only thing going for it. When you take that away, nothing is left. In this instance our heroes arrived in a 30,000 capacity stadium, only to discover it only had about 400 people attending. All of them immediately in front of the ridiculously huge booth, essentially making the place look empty.

Those who had attended appeared to be basically local rival gangs. Gangs being very popular in this part of the continent, and somewhat essential to deal with in the area if you were a fan of breathing. DJ Dastardly, a good egg and professional, gamely launched into his set. The two gangs were somewhat apart. Not particularly dancing. In fact, he looked up at one point to see a row of them had formed in front of him to make pointy-point gestures at their ears regarding the music, then made slashy-slashy gestures at their throats and pointed at him repeatedly. Universal sign language for "this music is unpleasant to us, so we are going to kill you". Simultaneously the only people moving were out-of-work local dancers boinging around dressed as man-sized, sponsored spunk.

Now *that*, Dastardly explained, is a tough gig.

The tour with Dastardly and Muttley may as well have been cursed. Muttley was such a maniac that Dastardly had to hide his contact lenses on top of wardrobes as when he was in a frenzy, which was every day and every night, Muttley would drink *anything*. No, really. He would drink anything that might fuck him up. Up to and including clear and obvious poisons. Muttley was constantly on the verge of being arrested. At one point, asking directions at the hotel desk and not getting the answer he wanted, he poured a drink on the reception computer saying:

"Take that, Tron,"

and staggered off into the night.

The tour was long and arduous and also, on the times I bumped into them, hugely jolly and funny. As it drew to a close, the last gig was a mammoth venue in Amsterdam, run by a typically laid-back, equitable and unflappable Dutch promoter. Forgive me if I write the Dutch dialogue in a possibly stereotypical manner but I'm afraid it is simply how it happened and much funnier for it. Muttley was *particularly* badly behaved in Amsterdam, and everyone on the tour was absolutely convinced they would never play there again, or indeed be safe in the city in perpetuity. Muttley stole, Muttley badgered, Muttley snorted and bellowed. He staggered, fell and generally roistered. His speciality was riot, and he excelled at it. The last night of a tour is always particularly festive and either one of the best times to see an act perform, or the absolute worst, depending on the abilities of the act to handle their cups.

Dastardly's managing a quick fumble with an interested party in the backstage toilets was nothing in comparison to Muttley's behaviour that night. Muttley was a legend. An unkillable terminator. A never-ending liquid prank on legs that rivalled the powers of Quag Allurgie for remaining upright in a storm.

The bill always comes in the morning, however. Leaving at the airport with the promoter, Dastardly immediately started apologising for Muttley's behaviour the night before, as he usually had to, everywhere

CHAPTER 7

they went. The promoter merely laughed in his expansive, generous and liberal Dutch manner.

"Are you kidding Dashtardly!? I got into thish bushiness for thish! I love thish guy! Muttley is *alwaysh* welcome in my city! He'sh a true *Rockshtar*!"

"Thank God!" replied Dastardly. He was convinced it was the usual shambles. "I'm so relieved, well, thank you so much! I, for one, cannot wait to come back!"

The promoter's smile switched off like a light.

"Oh no Dashtardly, you are mishtaken. For you there ish no nexsht time."

Turned out his fumble in the bogs was with the promoter's spouse.

* * *

On the morning of Love Parade UK, I was back in our bus when I heard the chanting start. The simple refrain was crystal clear.

"MU-SIC! MU-SIC! MU-SIC!"

The boss knocked on the bus door again, this time looking a bit stressed.

"I don't suppose you fancy starting now do you? Only the police are a bit worried about crowd control. Can you manage four hours?"

Pfft. I used to play eight hours straight in my residency at the time every week. Piece of piss. When I got up the stairs to the stage I could see the problem. In less than an hour what I seen had doubled in size. There were approximately 20,000 faces, all looking at an empty stage and chanting for music. I will never forget this moment as long as I live. It felt to me, perhaps, like lighting the Olympic Flame.

I walked out onto the stage to a huge roar. I didn't think about it for a second. I reached into the box, and I didn't even have to play it. I just held the record in the air. The roar was, as any sports fan knows, unlike any other sound or feeling. I just stood there like an idiot holding a bit of vinyl in the air and they went batshit.

Which was nothing compared to what happened when the needle went down.

It was 'Jump Up In The Air' by The Raid. Todd Terry, basically. It was a good way to start. If you listen to the tune, you will see why the first drum fill would make 30,000 people go utterly ape. Try to picture the scene. A sea of people as far as the horizon leaping up and down in waves like a vast, choppy ocean. Never known anything like it, before or since. Quite the sensation. And literally the first minute of what was going to be a very long 48+ hours of continuous raving.

After exiting the stage on an incredible high (and funnily enough, handing over to our friend DJ Dastardly) I drifted on a cloud back down to the bus. Usually, these big things leave me cold but this was so HUGE and deeply vibey. Also, very much about our scene. Kids had travelled from all over to be there. I don't think anyone had any idea just how vast it was going to be, least of all the organisers. Next, I had to jump on a truck and play at several locations in the parade of floats. I was used to this version of things, having done it a couple of times at Notting Hill. I was on Quag's float at one point. He was most amused at seeing my head blown-up to the size of King Kong's on the giant screens. More floats, buses and trucks were visited and played upon. Then back to the tour bus to prepare for the live show.

Mighty Kwowser was with us. At the time, I shared a flat with him in Soho. He'd made an extremely rare foray outside of the square mile and what's more shocking, into the deep country. As we played, Kwowser found that if he ran to the front of the stage and threw his hands in the air, 50,000 people would do it back to him (the numbers were growing hugely by the minute). I couldn't count by now, my tiny superpower was overwhelmed. There were people not only to the horizon in front of the stage, they were in all directions around it too. Completely surrounded on all sides. The small area of trucks and stage area that seemed so large at the start was rapidly dwindling in scale, massively outnumbered, a small collection of ships moored around a rig, adrift in a sea of frothing kids.

Kwowser and I don't exactly look like twins, dizygotic maybe, but the front row of the crowd was quite far away, and although huge TV screens beamed the stage details out to the crowd it might not be clear who was who. I played bass and drums when we played live, so to the uninitiated

CHAPTER 7

it might look like Kwowser was in the band, or some sort of maniacal cheerleader. Or, he discovered to his great delight later, me. As I mentioned briefly in the first book, Kwowser was a professional door picker, amongst other things. As well as getting hired, fired and barred for life on a gig I helped get him in Ibiza, he was also famous for being so rude to kids trying to get in the door that he would sometimes make them cry. He was an old school London fashionista. He was called 'Kwowser' because he was obsessed with trousers and especially ones that made him go 'wow'. He once amused me greatly by appearing out of his room with a great flourish and declaring to nobody in particular in his Mick Jagger-esque twang:

"Oooo! I've got 64 jackets!"

...and promptly dove back into his room to count more items of clothing. I loved him dearly for his terrible manners, awful sense of humour and for being singularly the worst drug dealer in the world. He'd literally not sell drugs to people he didn't like. And he didn't like anyone. He was like a one-man 'just say no' campaign. His sense of humour was basically double Y chromosome stuff. Despite being quite camp he was basically alpha male in his head, so jokes were at everyone else's expense and the harsher the better. This manifested itself immediately as we got offstage of the biggest gig we would ever play. Kids immediately surrounded him thinking he was me, having been running to the front of the stage and waving his hands in the air, it may be fair to assume that a DJ in a band is only capable of doing that and not much else. He found this delightful for the next 48 hours and each time he was 'recognised' was a version of this:

"Ooo Secret DJ you were great today on stage! I didn't know you coul..."

"YEAH MY NAME'S SECRET DJ, DON'T FORGET IT! I'M WAAAYY TOO IMPORTANT TO TALK TO YOU, NOW FUCK OFF!

"Pause."

...AND YOUR TROUSERS ARE SHIT!"

The kids would wander off in a daze, mumbling that not only was I much changed since moving to London, even my accent was different. He impersonated an evil, slightly camp version of me at every opportunity and made sure I was roundly vile. Often right in front of me. I thought it was hilarious. Until the internet came along, that is, and every daft joke you ever made suddenly comes home to roost. But that's another topic.

Our Love Parade live band show could not have been better. Once again it was BBC Radio One, who were always good to me, not only providing the stage but putting us live on-air to the entire population of the UK and further. What was new for me was, for the second time ever, one of my family was there. Specifically, my Mum. Who'd no real clue what it was that I did and how it was received. To see my colossal noggin on a vast screen, hundreds of thousands cheering, be the first, middle and last act... it was quite an eye-opener. Even if my parents cannot comprehend the bad language, the drugs, the terrible unchristian activity, the idiotic carry-on, the crushing disappointment in their child... at least moments like this make some sort of sense. They can see it isn't entirely nonsense. OK. Scratch that. Mostly nonsense, granted.

I think it was the best day of my life, maybe. Yeah, quite possibly.

This sort of thing can never happen again, unfortunately, and not merely because the local NIMBYs crushed it. There were 'officially' 300,000 people there but the police put it as many as 400,000. Nearly half a million, possibly. To put that in context, The Beatles at Shea Stadium was only 56,000. I heard there were 12 arrests and none were charged. Can you imagine? That is such a low number our scene is practically in-credit. Half a million souls, and no crime. Yet it was banned from that city, and later, from the nation. You have to wonder if it was the fact that it was free, that there were so few 'barriers to entry', that I got to play to hundreds of thousands and someone trusted Quag with his own float. Maybe that sort of thing was the real problem. We made too much noise. In all senses.

It could be argued this was some sort of fulcrum. A peak that we never bested, nor came back from intact. The most tragic postscript was in Germany, though. Moving the original Parade away from Berlin to Duisburg, and attempting to manage the chaos by holding it in a closed-off area rather than make access free, proved a tragic error. 21 people died of suffocation and 500 were injured in a crush, with the organisers, police and local authorities all blaming each other to this day.

CHAPTER 8
YOU KNOW THE HONEYMOON IS OVER WHEN...

On the other side of the coin, the smallest outdoor gig I ever did was for a friend of mine's wedding, relatively recently in fact. This was only the second wedding I'd ever done, the first being a very grand affair in Ibiza. When I started in the 80s, the idea of a DJ at a wedding was pure mobile disco territory. The opposite of what we were trying to achieve. And again, on-topic perhaps, the whole shebang has gone full circle and now every wedding has to have a fully credible DJ. Especially in Ibiza, where there are several weddings every single day over the season and quite a few off-season.

To say my mates are not part of the scene is not entirely fair. I met the groom cross-eyed and quadra-spazzed as a raver at one of my many after-hours parties. But the Bruce Wayne to his Batman was a highly respectable daytime job. In fact, he is a TV news personality. His bride, one of the heads of a major news network. A soon-to-be-wed current affairs power couple. It was an honour to be asked to DJ. I think one of the reasons no one ever asked me before is 'cos they think I would be too fancy to do it. Not so. I was deeply flattered. Although not the marrying type personally, I see weddings as major life events and extremely important. The bride, however, was somewhat dubious about my being involved. Possibly for good reason.

This lack of confidence in me may have something to do with the fact that the groom and I had spent some time in Ibiza 'making a documentary'. I put that loosely as the end result was resolutely ignored by the BBC on the grounds that it was a roasting hot potato due to Ibiza being basically 'drugs' in their minds, and they'd just been caught with their fingers in the till in a major financial scandal. The timing was poor, to put it mildly. Ironically, there wasn't a single mention or so much of a whiff of drugs in there, it being mostly about Carthaginians, crop rotation, and salt as an industry. This 'shoot' was mostly me winging it, completely ignoring my infinitely wiser and vastly more experienced buddy, spending days in the blistering heat and boiling nights interviewing the local salamanders, those luminaries who simply did not exist until the sun went down, and had their breakfasts at midnight. The daytime is not your friend if you are serious about the disco. It is deeply unsurprising that most night people are, in fact, resolutely night people.

A third musketeer arrived in Ibiza. A grizzled and highly experienced war photographer was to be our film cameraman. Landing straight from an assignment in Afghanistan, he proceeded to complain bitterly about everything but, in keeping with the job proceeded to do a stellar turn as a professional. On night four, after constantly racing around trying to meet the schedules of the various night-lizards and get the right light at sunrise, the right light at sunset... the shutterbug veteran hit a particularly keening note of displeasure at the gig in general. I turned and asked:

"Dude, are you expecting me to believe that a couple of days and nights in Ibiza is harder work than a major conflict zone?"

"You know, believe it or not, we do actually get to *go to bed* in Afghanistan," was his weary reply.

We later ended up doing interviews with the excellent German promoters and stars of 'Cocoon', then residing at Amnesia. A superclub was another new experience for my pals and one they were similarly uncomfortable with. Trying to find a free spot just to be able to tip our elbows to drink was not easy. Even in the VIP overlooking the main DJ booth. The maître d' for the exclusive area whizzed back and forth across our attempts at shouted conversation as we foolishly thought we had found a body-free spot. It was merely the well-beaten track for the staff to hustle back and forth for the millionaires all around. Every couple of seconds, someone hastily pushed past or howled for us to get out of the way. The groom-to-be getting more and more annoyed and redder, redder and redder in an already frankly rosy and slightly sunburned face. As disco fate would have it, we've all found ourselves victims of The Dropout. That moment when we are bellowing at the top of our lungs just as the never-ending thunder of the music decides, for one inexplicable moment only, to drop out completely.

CHAPTER 8

"LOOK HERE!!" came a massive cry in a beautifully trained, cultured and highly strained voice,

"I AM AN *ENGLISHMAN*! AND I DO *NOT* ENJOY BEING JOSTLED ONE BIT!!!"

So roared the newly christened 'Jostler'. Right at the moment of sudden, absolute and dead silence. The music missed only a few seconds before kicking off again. Eight beats were enough. Scarlet turned to purple. Exit imminent.

I love The Jostler. He's an excellent person and spends much of his time risking his life to bring you the news. I mean that quite literally. As well as this tremendous strength of character, he simultaneously manages to be in the photo of the crowd on one of my albums, clinging onto a column as if he were in a storm at sea, completely sideways, fully off his nut. I love people like this. Able to stride two worlds. Not in a furtive way at all. One day they rave. Another, they read the news. Like a normal person. No one quaking in fear at society judgement. One of the biggest hypocrisies we labour under these days is that you somehow cannot exist in normality having sampled extremity. Politicians lie through their teeth that they never did drugs, when everyone knows they did, and some still do. They go to church services while simultaneously ordering death, dealing in open corruption and lying, lying always *lying*. Yet if someone is honest and open about their own past, they lay themselves wide-open for the very same hypocrites to lambast them for living an adventurous life. Bizarrely, in their topsy-turvy world, having *lived* makes you somehow *less* qualified to lead. I'd vote for someone who had an actual past in the real world over a pompous toff who'd done nothing but spend Daddy's money any day. The purpose of this vast hypocrisy is control. Sadly, our system is owned by the same people who practice this vice the most, and change is unlikely. So far.

Don't get me wrong. Jostler was young, free, single and a man of his own destiny when he troubled the dancefloor. Now those days were far behind him and his impending nuptials beckoned. However missing his flights to get back to work, and his fiancee, during our filming in Ibiza somewhat tainted *my* credibility. This was not uncommon amongst my friends however, my being something of a human sicknote when it came to friends visiting the island.

Anyone who comes to visit, and not even necessarily visiting me personally, will use me as an excuse or general fall guy when talking to their spouse. Memorably in the early days of mobile phones, I was with a friend who apparently was here without his wife's knowledge, having told her he was off to some sporting event or other. Like clockwork, and right in front of me, he'd tried to blame the entire fiasco on me. Like I even want people to appear here like a raging holiday monster. Calling me for pick-up from the airport, drugs and free clubs at 5am on a Wednesday. If I did the same to them from Heathrow, they'd literally never speak to me again just for the call, never mind actually get out of bed. But for some reason people say things to me on a Monday like:

"Ooo I bet you are down the front at DC10!"

...and I am forced to tell them the truth. That I've been descaling the shower heads and the most exciting thing I've done that year is to do some brass rubbings in a rustic church. My raging days are long behind me. Mostly. Although 'raging party monster' is entirely relative, me taking it easy on a Sunday afternoon probably looks like Sodom and Gomorrah to my dear old Dad.

I digress, my missing-in-action mate's furious wife was on the other end of the mobile phone from England, and just as she was losing the plot, he turned the speakerphone on.

"I KNOW WHAT YOU ARE UP TO OVER THERE YOU FUCKER. I CAN *HEAR* YOU GURNING. I KNOW YOU ARE THERE WITH THAT SECRET DJ DICKHEAD, PONCING ABOUT IBIZA LIKE HE IS FUCKING MAGNUM OR SUMMAT".

To be fair, I do wear a moustache well and have been known to solve crimes in my spare time. And I have a Higgins. I assured her the Lamborghini is mine, however, and not another loan from Robin.

So, all Ibiza adventures aside, you can see why the future Mrs Jostler was highly dubious about my being anywhere near her wedding. Her only real experience of me being as some sort of phantom kidnapper and resolutely failed documentarian. I was 'An Ibiza DJ'. Equal parts exotic and ridiculous. Made all the more inappropriate by the location of the wedding. Deep in The Shire. One of England's most picturesque and olde worlde locations.

The Jostler also took it upon himself to look at this as an opportunity for nuptial hilarity. Subtly implying that I was a 'top notch Techno' sort and all-round noise merchant. He confided in me one day that he wanted to play a prank on Mrs Jostler-to-be and asked that the first record would be the most horrific banging firework display of unpleasantness I could possibly muster. I said I can go one further than that and used my contacts to rustle up not only a gigantic Funktion One sound system but have it painted white for them. The ratio of pure audio power to venue/people being somewhere around the order of magnitude of 10,000 watts of pure evil to one oppressed pensioner. Let's just say it was touch and go that it could even physically fit in the room, or through the door. The Jostler jiggled with glee at the prospect. I was a little dubious, knowing Bridezillas are not to be trifled with.

As the happy day arrived, I realised my folly. This wasn't like the usual gigs. I'd have to collect the colossal fucker of a sound system and drive it across the country, and worst of all, in and out of London on a bank holiday weekend. It was a *monster*. Being spotlessly white didn't remove any of its beastliness. The excellent audio firm, London legends based in Crystal Palace, helped load it a little. A stark reminder for my bones and sinews that humping flight cases was something I'd not done for 25 years or so. Your mind thinks it is familiar, easy even. Your body starts protesting that assumption immediately. Just putting the things into the truck was more physical labour than I'd done in a decade. Then the drive...

Arriving the morning of the wedding, I discovered an idyll that time forgot. A delightful farm, a quaint medieval-style set of tents overlooked by an ancient castle. Not even a carefully chosen wedding location off the internet, but simply the bride's family home. I heaved a sigh and began the epic set-up. As Mrs-Jostler-to-be came frantically hustling up, hair in bridal rolls, her face said everything, up to and including 'what the fuck is *THAT!?*'.

I'd not forgotten much of my early years of tech work, but I can't say I was particularly au-fait with these new streamline systems that were computer-driven with automatic crossovers and preset EQ. A little like asking a vintage car enthusiast to tune a modern racing car. After the initial shock of seeing her beautiful rustic tent apparently being guarded by two giant sinister fridges that poked the roof slightly out of shape, she charged over to discover me on the floor, crossed legged and cross-eyed trying to made head-or-tail of the pure science in front of me. I just looked up, sweating, exhausted and harassed and told her:

"I've never done this before!"

She simply glared pure murder lasers and stormed off.

The wedding was truly delightful, I have to say. Intimate, and with the cream of UK current affairs and television, all frankly *very* interesting people, all with something to say and for a change I wanted to listen. I had a great time. Which surprised me greatly after the epic quality of the journey and set-up. As the speeches ended my moment loomed. The bride looking more and more apprehensive. The Jostler hugging himself with glee. Dear reader, I couldn't bring myself to hurt her anymore, so suffice to say I only played about 30 seconds of face-melting Techno. Just enough to make the Jostler happy before immediately segueing into some classic wedding hoe-down, cheers erupting after initial unbridled terror. What I had dreaded for months actually became one of the most fun gigs I've ever had. My child, you KNOW you are a DJ when you can play completely unknown House and Techno to a crowd of normal citizens, children and old folks and every man-jack of them pogo up and down merrily. I'm no ego monster, of course I softened them up with disco, pop and classics! I've watched TV, I know what humans get up to enough to do a fair impersonation.

Just as things were really getting going, the Jostler came running up to me excitedly and without a drop of irony said.

"I really need you to make an announcement, it's pretty urgent."

I was stunned, I hoped no one was injured. An announcement in the disco industry is usually an extreme circumstance. I held my breath…

"Can you announce it is time for Pasties and Cheese?"

CHAPTER 8

I'd never got on the mic in my entire career, so I think the look on my face said everything he needed to know. He did it instead. Shortly after, I turned the music back on and someone screamed at the top of their lungs:

"*LETS 'AV IT, TAVIT*"

...in relation to a small crew of youngsters from Tavistock being guests. As 4am approached, there was a kerfuffle. A neighbour arrived to ask to turn the noise down. The Jostler asked if I could turn it down a notch as next door were unhappy. I shouted for the father of the bride's opinion on the matter and he disagreed vociferously, enjoying the Techno and cider immensely, and motioned magnanimously for everyone to continue full speed ahead. I discovered the next day that the neighbour was the next farm, over four miles away. Also one of those enjoying the Techno and cider was the local Chief of Police. I was not in Kansas, Toto. I was a maniac adrift in Tolkien's Shire. It was possibly the smallest gig I'd ever done. But it was way better fun than any one of the biggest of outdoor shows.

INTERLUDE
BRIGHTON ROCKS

We were due to hook up with Bass Terrorist in Brighton. Terrible name, lovely guy, still very much the first true martyr of our scene. For some forgotten reason today, Tour Manager had sublet the driving job to Sticks. Sticks was a drummer from a famous Goth band who was possibly the only person who took more amphetamines than TM and was technically still alive. Sticks famously was the only person who'd been barred for life from Top of the Pops thrice. One time in the 80s he went onstage and casually leant against a prop column, which immediately toppled and created a domino effect that destroyed the whole set. Barred for life. Mainly for his reaction to it, which was complete indifference. Sticks was my generation of working class artist, who might wear tons of hairspray but would knock you out with one punch if you deserved it. Since his heyday, he'd settled into a life of powerful stimulants and long-distance lorry driving.

Oh yeah, the second ban from the UK's only mainstream music TV show was arriving there a second time in a gas mask for a disguise, and ripped off his tits on pink champagne. Then on live TV, he head-butted the cymbals of his drum kit enough that blood spurted and sprayed in many directions. I was absolutely possessed with an obsession to get him on a third time. And I did. Got him to play a MIDI drum kit and drive me to one of my band's appearances. True to form he was out of his mind and started lunging and lashing-out and swearing at a roving cameraman as he played, once again live in front of millions. Barred once again, something like 20 years after the second time. A great day for all agents of chaos, everywhere. Something I watch repeatedly for laughs. Well, also watch advisedly.

As usual Tour Manager had one job with that TV appearance, which was to 'tape it'. Simply make a VHS recording on the night of live broadcast. One of his many bizarre hobbies that he engaged in with ridiculous intensity was home-made porn. As I excitedly watched the debut of this band with my family after coming home from the studios the next day, we crowded around to watch my triumph. The second it ended, there was a bit of snow, white noise, and a cut to a very familiar-looking room, apparently in negative. It was Tour Manager's bedroom on night vision. You have never seen me move so fast.

My Grandma said:

"Oo, what was that? Was it 'Badgerwatch'? I like that…"

I've no idea what is on the rest of that tape, God help me if I ever learn.

A weekend with both Tour Manager and Sticks was going to be rather large. Sometimes travel with drug loons is like being in a spaceship or TARDIS. You can close your eyes for a moment, open them again in a different galaxy entirely. Especially with Sticks driving. He considered himself a professional driver, which mainly meant driving for ridiculously long distances on massive amounts of whizz, grinding his teeth and ignoring any and all advice. Advice like road signs or directions.

Now I may not have mentioned that Tour Manager had a ridiculous car. And if you have an awesome car, you will drive everywhere in it. We did. At the time it was one of the fastest production cars on the planet. Frequently faked. We rolled up at the seaside city and pulled into the hotel car park, at stuntman speed of course if Sticks was at the wheel, and parked, or skidded to a dangerous halt more like. T-Man had been unconscious for the journey and was his usual woozy and horrific self when unrefreshed. He staggered out of the car and screamed,

"FUCK OFF! FAKE!" pointing wildly at the car next to us. We'd managed to pull up to a car very similar, but to the expert eye had clearly had extra badges and trim added to 'upgrade' it. This delighted Tour Manager usually. He was ever-so-proud of his car. As the usual staggering mess of hotel reception and check-in began it became apparent that none of us had any money. I was annoyed. Mostly at myself. We did have lots of drugs though. Which sort of made up for it. After much bumbling, a room was found and an introduction to Bass Terrorist was made. A knock on the door came, and a very tall man entered.

"Fuck me! Beanstalk Cunt!"

Tour Manager had that very British skill of saying the obvious extremely loudly and very rudely. It was like a tick. Possibly was actually a form of Tourette's, you couldn't tell with him where the drugs ended and the genuinely clinical began. He and Sticks together were almost like an explosive epoxy. Two liquids that were relatively harmless but highly toxic when mixed. They also performed what we called 'The Loop'. Vast amounts of stimulants often made you repeat things, sometimes within minutes or even seconds of saying it. Sticks piped up with:

"Jesus, long as fuck."

"Beanstalk cunt!" repeated T.M.

This often happened, this drastically and uncomfortably, upon meeting a perfect stranger. This tends to happen with gangsters too, I've found, but it's more of a test. A challenge. These two actually, underneath it all, have hearts of gold. They just have no idea what lunacy comes out of their mouths half the time. I worry that some readers may be completely missing the point of these tales. That I am trying to depict a swan-song. An era that has passed and will not return. A time of rock 'n' rollers, extreme privilege and terrible behaviour. As a warning, not a manual. But for now, try and grow a sense of humour. It will ease the passing of time.

As a form of test, the tall newcomer had two options: take huge and immediate offence or get on the train. He passed with flying colours by immediately demanding some of TM's drugs. Beanstalk was Bass Terrorist's new manager. The conversation moved to how we got there. Ending with, a now fully recharged Tour Manager, delightedly recounting parking next to 'the shit fake-mobile', gleefully pointing it out through the window:

"You can't miss it, it's the shit fake one next to the real one."

"Ah yes, my car, you mean?" said Beanstalk.

Now for a normal human, this would have been a moment of high, of not mortal embarrassment. For Freaks, it is merely open season. So overjoyed was TM at this revelation it became part of The Loop for all time. Almost no moment passed for the next 48 hours where TM didn't relive his joy at outing the faker. Beanstalk wreaked his revenge immediately by doing all TM's gear in. Later, in the club, TM was incensed to learn not only was he now dry of substances, the Beanstalk had the nerve to call and ask for more.

Brighton has most excellent clubs. The city on the sea serves very much as a retreat for Londoners who have made their fortune and had enough of the capital. On top of this layer of bohemia is another crust, based upon what I term 'the coffee filter' theory of geography. I've seen much of the world and noticed wherever there is a geographic southern point, especially near a conurbation, a lot of lunatics collect. This was writ large around Brighton in the mid 90s when the Conservatives, in their mania for dismantling, closed some of the biggest asylums in Europe, simply letting many of the mentally ill loose. Some died, some went to prison fairly quickly, many simply gravitated to the streets of the coastal area to survive as best they could. Some even became citizens after time. Brighton was a special place. Still is, if not gentrified heavily these days. The best clubs are in glorious Victorian arches that face the sea, under the promenade. For a while, one of the best places to rave in the world.

Possibly fuelled by the derision for his mock wheels, Beanstalk arrived at the venue and proceeded to be absolutely awful at every turn. Proof if ever was needed that the addition of large amounts of drugs to someone generally takes-away in equal measure. Sticks decided that he'd had enough and with the slow deliberation of a master craftsman, pulled over a stool, methodically climbed up it carefully carrying a full pint, and poured it with detailed slowness over Tall Man's head. Credit to the big feller, he stood and took every fluid ounce.

Not waiting to be ejected, and the next day already over the horizon, our party made an escape and found, all too frequently, ourselves wandering around a strange town at a desolate hour of the morning. Seaside towns are like the stage sets of westerns. All front. Once you go back from the sea inland, they get weirder and weirder. Nothing in Brighton is weirder than The Pavilion. The vanity project of the profligate buffoon Prince Regent. A grotesque and inappropriate palace dedicated to untrammelled ego. Naturally, it was a magnet for us.

Upon rolling up to its ridiculous facade, we discovered it was just opening up. A small gaggle of American tourists were up with the lark, keen as mustard to do some hardcore gawping. Tour Manager immediately went into Toff Mode. As if the very bricks and mortar brought out his inner demented aristocrat. He launched himself past the tourists and bounded up the stairs, extemporising on the glory of the architecture to no one in particular. Closely followed by security, as he'd forgotten to pay. He had lots of money, just never on him. It wasn't a trick, he was almost psychotically generous, he just frequently forgot about money. Often having to call the ever-oppressed accountant, Neil. Poor old Neil would get the maddest requests at all hours of the day from all corners of the globe to resolve a fairly trifling matter. Yes, you are correct, Tour Managers are also supposed to handle the money. He began gesturing at me incomprehensibly. Clearly trying to instruct me upon something arcane.

T-Man was some way ahead of the posse of security, leading them in his wake less than being escorted. He mouthed something to me as he approached across an obscenely garnished hall, holding his hand to his ear in the universal sign language for 'telephone'. As he approached across the marble and tapestries, wild hair and beard flowing, a 'V' formation of heavies behind him, he lost patience with my obvious inabilities with telepathy and started roaring at me over the heads of the tourists in front of me:

"Neil! Neil!"

…the immediate effect of this was, for those tourists still young enough to do so, a most hurried attempt at genuflection.

CHAPTER 9
THE CRACK OF DOOM

Nowadays, Russia has a thriving and highly legitimate electronic music scene. The first time I played Moscow? Not so much. In fact, I was surprised to be there at all, really.

"I am Anatoly! Here you are today Mister Secret Man. Welcome here!"

I thanked him and asked how long we had until the gig.

"Oh many time. Plus to meet several beautiful ladies."

I wasn't particularly in the right state for several beautiful ladies. I wanted to sleep if it was feasible. Do the gig. Then go home. Sadly nearly every time you arrived anywhere at this point in the history of our scene, your hosts were party people and fully expected you to party too. At all times. This happens still on occasion, but much less so.

As we stumbled out of the airport, quite a sight met me. Contrary to what you might think, we almost never get limousines. Limos are silly. For hen parties and people brainwashed by TV who wish they'd had a Prom like in American movies. This was not just a limousine, but something more akin to a military staff car. Also, suspiciously, *very* low on its axles.

"Is that what I think it is?"

"I do not know what you are thinking Mister Secret Man."

"Is it an armoured car?"

"Oh yes. Very armoured car."

"Wow. OK."

He opened the door and the back already had two occupants. Again, not unusual, sometimes a few DJs got picked up, or promoters brought friends to gawk at the DJ. These didn't look like either.

"Anatoly, are these guys security? They look a lot like security."

"Oh yes. Very excellent security."

"Friends of yours?"

Sometimes friends of the promoter were security. I've got friends who work the doors all over the world. They are people too.

"Oh no."

I said hello, neither of the heavies replied.

The limousine/tank, which must have weighed well over three tons fully laden, very slowly crept out. After a while of oppressive silence, one huge guy next to me, the other opposite. I knocked on the separating screen, as Anatoly elected to sit up with the driver.

"Anatoly, are these big fellas military? I'm getting a sense they are."

"Oh no, no military. How you say it? 'Off duty', yes?"

"So they are mercenaries?"

"Oh yes!"

"Is that good or bad?"

"Oh, very good! The best! Best Russian men."

"Anatoly. Are they Spetsnaz?"

"Hey, very good! You know Russian!"

"Not much. I heard they teach them cannibalism, and they are pretty handy."

"Oh yes!"

"Anatoly. WHY are there moonlighting Russian special forces in a large armoured car? And why I am in it with them?"

"Ha, ha. You are funny Mister Secret Man. Tonight will be much better than last week. Is good to laugh!"

We decided to miss the hotel and several beautiful ladies, much to the chagrin of Anatoly. The club also had a restaurant so we were to eat there. It was not the sort of place I was used to. Clearly everyone in there was very rich. Dancing was pretty desultory and the sound system not particularly loud, or sounding good. I'm a stickler for sound systems, being something of an obsession of mine. Sometimes you arrived and it was pretty clear that your hosts just kind of flew you in as a status symbol, rather than as a DJ who might fit into an existing scene and music policy. In the past it happened a lot in the Emirates, Russia and more recently, China. Wherever there was new money, the new money wanted DJs. Sometimes any DJ would do, the more expensive the better. Sometimes the hosts were highly legit fans and really wanted to start something real in their home towns. Sometimes, like this, you were just a thing to be paraded around. Like a novelty animal in a fancy cage. I always do my best, however.

CHAPTER 9

The gig was fairly creaky. As was I. Brighton had knocked me sideways. The system a little strained, the dancefloor a little dry, most of the crowd electing to sit at tables on a level overlooking the floor. Anatoly came over with some drinks, put the tray down, took a chromed pistol out of the back of his trousers, plonked it down next to the drinks, gave me a wink and left it there as he exited. The two sides of beef that came in the car stood behind the booth all night.

By the end of the rather dull festivities, I did what I nearly always did and tried all I could to avoid any adventures (I failed may times over the years) and asked if, rather than the hotel, they just take me straight back to the airport. I'd kill the hours there. For me, there is nothing worse than being THIS close to a comfortable shower and bed but only having to get out of it as soon as you get in. In those days I'd happily stay awake for four days and nights if it meant a couple of days solid rest after. Compared to today, I even found it relatively easy. Just one weekend's itinerary from those days would kill me now. I'm not kidding. I'd die.

Anatoly was as jolly as ever but he was genuinely crushed that I had no interest in several beautiful ladies or was willing to miss my return flight in order to drink my own weight in vodka. I felt bad, and I said as much. I was sorry to ruin his fun.

"Oh no! No thing is ruin Mister Secret Man! This was BIG success for me." For some reason in Eastern Europe they always address you with your full name.

"Do you want your gun back? I don't think customs will allow it."

"Ah, you are funny! Also, you play many good record. Which was big relief for me."

"Why Anatoly? Why the cannibals and the pistols and the journey in a tank?"

"Oh yes. You should ask before. Last week DJ is very bad music. So he is killed in the face."

Good to know. Sometimes in these situations there is a large clumsy waltz whereby a few quid is attempted to be shaved off in currency exchanges, despite all being arranged up front. Or, in one instance, being taken to a remote disused Romanian ski resort for three days while they 'try to arrange for the money' and try to pay you in 'good times', which technically is a sort of festive kidnapping. Or once in Switzerland someone offering to take the money to you, and simply walking out of the venue with it instead. Getting paid was a lottery sometimes and thank God it all happens electronically and in-advance now. I was lucky this wasn't one of those times, but frankly, had Anatoly paused for just a moment with the wages I would have told him to keep it and ran into the street shouting for taxis or for the police, possibly pocketing the shooter on the way out the door just in case. I've since had some delightful visits to that great country, but never again quite so steeped in potential danger.

It was now Sunday and I was lumbering along in the fancy tank to the airport. I'd managed to convince my hosts I didn't need the escort as I was unlikely to be murdered inside the car having already made an escape. Yes, usually a tour manager takes care of these sorts of things, stuff like getting paid, security, and local transport. It must be great to have one. I must try it one day. Sundays, though. Bane of my life.

Sundays have frequently found me in all the worst kinds of pickle. I pressed my face against the cool glass, trying to dredge up a vague number of how many Sundays. I lost count. I'd spend possibly the most of all my many many lost hours on Sundays. Decades of not going home when you really should. Missing flights. Sometimes even deliberately. Spending everything you just earned on extra nights in hotels the promoter has a cheap corporate deal with, and you do not. Waking up to find just a few hours past checkout has cost you half of everything you earned the night before. If I could have every bit of wasted time and frittered cash back by reclaiming every lost Sunday, I'd be a very rich 22-year-old.

Sunday though. It is the 'day of worship', but exactly what you worship is open to interpretation. I myself had a franchise of afterparties in a few cities than ran only on Sundays. I'd do my Friday and Saturday nights and then spend the Sabbath roaring around various cities. I think it is one of the biggest factors in really doing me in. At one point I had an infamous residency in Ibiza on Sunday that started at 10pm and finished at 7am Monday morning. Then my own event would be Monday night. For about three years solid I started travel on a Friday and was still awake and working on a Tuesday. Before you envy any DJ, bear in mind that some of us haven't had a weekend to ourselves in a very long time. If you have any degree of success you have no days at all to yourself. Think about it. You literally never stop working. For years. You think playing records for a living is easy, try doing it without sleep, or days off, in three different time zones, and all done solo. Every single day. For decades.

Some countries are ALL about Sundays. Spain and France love a party on a Sunday, and LGBTQ+ folks consider it their day all over the world. The most memorable for me was Indonesia. Like a lot of overtly religious countries it operates a very efficient and completely liberal counter-culture that is almost invisible unless you are shown it. The most Muslims in the world are in Indonesia. And the biggest afterparty. You think Berlin is cool? You should have gone to 'Stadium' in Jakarta before it was closed down.

If a culture is very repressive, people want to party even harder. People are people. Whatever the 'rules', people used to them know how to break them. Arriving at Stadium on a Friday and leaving on a Monday was a regular, weekly event for its hardcore clientele. You'd arrive at a vast mock-art deco facade. As you move in you see a vast atrium, four floors with a huge well in the centre, almost like a dark shopping mall. At the top of the well is a huge sculpture of a dragon in-flight. Inside people were openly out of their gourds everywhere you looked. There were restaurants, karaoke rooms, hotel rooms, brothels, shops, and all kinds of esoterica in every dark corner. You could literally come here and never leave.

It could take hours to walk around it and maybe a whole day and night to see every corner. I was told proudly by my host that they were one of the only places in the world that accepted credit cards for *everything*, stressing the word with a stage-wink. I got the feeling you could arrive in here and leave bankrupt. It was always at fever-pitch. The music was great, very of-the-moment and frequently played by international guests. It was, perhaps, the Frankenstein's monster of clubs. A beast patched together of everything one mad genius thought was 'good'. Crammed into one tormented body. Massive, impressive and frightening... but somehow terribly wrong.

Though perhaps my perception was skewed by the return journey. It was an impressive place no doubt, and some of the best 'street food' I ever had, back when that meant rare food you ate from a cart in a street that you could never get in a restaurant without paying quadruple, not an overpriced hipster burger in Hackney. However, tasty as it was, I got the shits pretty bad in the airport. It happens. My guts are pretty robust after being exposed to pretty much every bacterium the planet has to offer, but now and then I am reminded I am nearly human. There was a writhing, panicked and quite sweaty attempt in an airport toilet to sort out this trouser problem. Which mainly involved getting rid of the pants in as unobtrusive a manner as possible and then trying really, *really* hard not to do it again. Lucky for me I'm the sort who carries spare everything. You have to with no tour manager.

I figured it might be the heat, but I seemed to develop some sort of rash immediately. As I got on the plane, I parked in the seat almost as flat as a plank of wood, or a cello in its case, barely bending in the middle. It started to get quite painful. I've had some bad, even terrible flights. This was top five. The rash was like a stabbing pain eventually. I was a bit alarmed. It seemed to escalate faster than an argument with an online drunk. By the time the blessed announcement of landing came I was almost gritting my teeth. The pain was shocking. Not helped by my constantly and sneakily trying to cop a scratch. The train journey after landing, back into Central London, was equally hellish. I'm a pretty rational person so I was wondering over and over how a simple mishap with liquid guts could lead to such a painful rash so quickly. I was, forgive me, mentally trying to get to the bottom of it. I was lost. What do I know? I'm a DJ, not a dermatologist.

* * *

I was exhausted when I got back in. First thing I did was get myself a triple tequila and a handful of painkillers. I didn't do anything further but launch myself into bed fully dressed and hope that lying face-down along with the booze and pills would make it go away. And it kind of did.

I woke almost screaming. The stabbing pain was colossal. It was the middle of the night. I felt a sharpness like a splinter, and as I was lying down finally, managed to get a good rummage and felt I found something down there and switched on the bedside lamp.

CHAPTER 9

I opened my hand and there was a spider sat there as big as my fist. I literally leapt into the air. Then I landed. Then screamed to myself: "WHY AM I STILL HOLDING IT!!?"

...and then hoofed it across the room like it was a live grenade. It lay there, stunned. Then I had a moment of clarity. This new species of crevice jockey must have been the pain all the way from another continent. A stowaway. I had no idea if it was toxic. I chucked the water out of the bedside glass and leapt over to it and placed the glass over it. It barely fitted. The thing was massive.

I felt odd. I was engaged in an international trouser crisis. Maybe it was poisonous. It was so big it might tip over the glass. The glass I had the tequila in was larger and heavier, and in my delirium I figured it 'contained alcohol fumes' that might stun or kill it. So I swiftly changed the glasses over his prison. Somewhat reminiscent of when Indiana Jones replaces the weight of the golden idol with a bag of sand. Nervously. Quickly. It didn't seem to notice. I then started ringing zoos. Seriously. In the middle of the night. Then the tropical disease hospital. I got through to a nurse who patiently explained that they had few specialists in insect bites working at 3am, and didn't have a lot to offer at the best of times. She hazarded a guess that if I had been bitten repeatedly for the last 20 hours I'd probably know by now if it was deadly. And no, she did not personally know of any species of 'Arse Spider' in existence. No, that was a funnel-web, and Australian. No, there's no such thing as a 'bummel-web', dear, go to bed.

Who can sleep with that arse-bother going on?

I went into the bathroom and, via a hastily-constructed Rube/Goldberg device of silly proportions, managed to get two mirrors to inspect my crevice. A brief patent idea flashed before me, using the mirrors on sticks that check for bombs under cars, re-purposed for the bum-squad. Bum disposal expert that I now was, I got a view of the injured party, i.e. my poor undercarriage. My new friend had had a field day in there. My arse was covered in bites that produced massive welts. I looked like a disappointed Space Hopper. I couldn't sit down for weeks. I advise caution on the road, hitchhikers can be dangerous.

INTERLUDE
FUDD 'N' BUGS

On the journey back from Brighton, possibly as part of a lack of, or possibly over-refreshment (it's hard to tell the difference really) T-Man started getting paranoid. It manifested as demanding to drive and then worrying about the load and its effects on the tyre pressures. The implication being that Sticks and I were fat, of course. One of his favourite topics. To be fair, it was his car. Unfortunately for us this meant lots and lots of pointless stops for his constant diet of sugar and cigarettes, and to fanny about and twiddle with things that were perfectly fine.

We pulled into a service station. Things were getting even weirder, as usual. As we decanted all over the place like a manky, gawky spillage. Sticks was extremely concerned at that moment about the game 'paper, scissors, stone'. He didn't get it, he'd never understood it and claimed he didn't even know how to do it. I was flabbergasted. He wasn't kidding. I called Tour Manager over.

"Listen, he doesn't know what 'paper, scissors, stone' is. Show him with me..."

"Neither do I!" replied the vagrant Duke.

"What!? Don't be ridiculous. Don't be stupid... show him!"

As usual, a small crowd was gathering to watch the idiots. I make a fist and pumped it up and down thrice and made a scissors with my fingers. Tour Manager looked at me blankly. I was getting annoyed again. I cried out,

"It's easy! Come on man for God's sake! PAPER... SCISSORS..."

"...HITLER!" shouted Tour Manager.

Possibly alluding to me, or in his own world, playing the game. Who knows? The people around us looked appalled. I started laughing hysterically.

Tour Manager bustled off frantically to carry on with his pointless task. Everyone around started clutching their pearls, gathering children and generally huffing and puffing. I'd gone through the envelope again and stopped caring. I paid for the petrol dismally, failing at every stage. Pockets too difficult to navigate. Money too weird to handle, mathematics impossible. Which was our pump? Where is a toilet? Who am I? Why am I always in a petrol station?

I stumbled over, the car had gone, of course. Why would it stay in one place? That would be way too easy.

"Excuse me…"

I began, but the person I was asking had hurried away, as they frequently do with me. I started looking around, not very efficiently. Eventually, I found them. Sticks suddenly unconscious in the back seat, for when a Freak crashes, they crash without preamble. Conscious and noisy one second, the next under a table, comatose. Tour Manager was looking even more perplexed than usual, holding a dripping tube and scratching his huge beard like a cartoon. Under the car, and stretching a considerable distance in all directions, was a very large puddle.

"Car trouble?" I investigated casually.

"STUPID machine won't inflate the tyres. Every time I try water comes shooting out. It's clearly malfunctioning in a serious manner. I've caused a biblical flood."

"T-Man. That is the water hose. For the application of water. The air hose is next to it. You've just tried to put water in your tyres."

I inspected more closely.

"And what's more, completely confounding physics, you seems to have managed to get some in!"

"Well, obviously, these tyres are faulty," was his inevitable reply. As if they had somehow filled themselves with H20 instead of merely 02.

We squelched along at a very sedate pace until we could find the next station, suitably far from the epicentre of our previous automotive embarrassment.

Tour Manager operated solely on Clarkson Logic. This is a mindset I have observed in certain males and made most prominent by the former presenter of the petroleum-obsessed TV show 'Top Gear'. Clarkson Logic is a set of principles based on the empirical evidence that whatever contradicts you, impedes you or generally obstructs is clearly a conspiracy and nothing whatsoever to do with yourself. For example, if a car does not perform to your liking it is a dongle, manifold, funny looking thingy, design flaw or national stereotype that is clearly the problem, never once do you consider that you might be shit at driving. Not ever. 'Operator error' was the closest Tour Manager ever got to describing his own fuck-ups.

Sticks started to revive, which was bad news. The two of them on a comedown together was like matter and anti-matter colliding. A catastrophic Waldorf and Stadler of cosmic proportions. Two gigantic egos utterly incapable of compromise simply clanging against each other like Scylla and Charybdis. Being caught in the cross-grump was no joke. This was going to be a long return journey as we sloshed up the motorway.

Don't get me wrong. They loved each other in a very tender way. They were just incapable of showing it in any way other than various forms of ascending abuse. The more horrific they were to you, the more they liked you. Savagery was a gift, bestowed-upon to the respected. However, when they loved, it was truly epic. Like two bison taking huge run-ups and butting each other. This didn't just mean the constant swearing, curses, brutal nicknames and shouting matches. It also meant a series of practical gags and one-upmanship. This is the eternal vortex of the straight white male. Especially those from the monochrome, distant past. Forever condemned to express emotion in only the most basic and highly competitive manner.

The love war between Sticks and the Tour Manager peaked in the form of a feud that took place over a few weeks back at headquarters. At the time all three of us lived on the huge upper floor of Tour Manager's palatial manse. The ground floor had been converted into a massive pub and club, formerly a large hotel, before that, his ancestral home. No, not 'Spunky's Muff' in the middle of the city. Above us on the third floor was T-Man's utterly delightful old Mum, who floated about in a kaftan constantly making everyone lunch and dinner (a reflex from the hotel days, and her way of communicating) and being acutely accurate whenever observing any of the Freaks that paraded through. The double act between T-Man and T-Mum was almost as hilarious as our own. I'd be constantly shocked as he'd use foul language at her casually and completely without malice, while she'd take it all majestically in her stride, as only the truly well-bred can. There's a huge similarity between the very bottom and very top of the class system in the UK. The very posh are frequently not particularly rich, sometimes even heavily burdened financially, effortlessly rude and utterly disdainful of conventions. It's the middle and upper-middle classes that are prudish, grasping and superior.

T-Mum was lovely. I thought she was fantastic. Not least of which when finally introduced to Quag Allurgie, who as we have learned, is supernaturally charming, she simply went "Pffft" when I asked her what she thought of him. Her judgement on something was always absolutely spot-on and laser-precise. I will take to my grave her commentary on me to Tour Manager:

"I like that Secret DJ, he does what he says."

Words to live by right there.

Largely she went unmolested in her sprawling attic complex, and we had the run of the middle floor. Huge rooms that had variously been ballrooms, media hubs, bedrooms, recording studios, offices… you name it. She was blissfully unaware of most of the nonsense on the two floors below, but by no means ignorant of the idiots and their foolishness. Sticks and Tour Manager's feud was so loud however, that it could not possibly go unnoticed by anyone within a square mile.

The grand feud started fairly innocently with Tour Manager going through a period of rest. Which for him meant being awake for three days and nights solid and then passing out in strange places. He's the only person I know who has actually passed out in their plate like a cartoon. Once found in the conservatory, at peak lunchtime, snoring into a lasagna surrounded by customers.

This time he'd passed out like a tiger-skin rug in his front room upstairs. I remember it vividly. Sticks brought some people into the living room… complete strangers. Tour Manager was lying on the floor absolutely spangled, unaware of pretty much anything until a group of people loudly entered. It was the brewery area manager and a couple of minions. Sticks casually remarked:

"Ah, here's the embarrassing shitty mess who allegedly runs the place," and took the tour somewhere else. T-Man clocked-it, but was too out of it to reply.

War was declared immediately. Tour Manager's new frenetic and pointless hobby from that point onwards was labelling anything he could find with 'Fuck Off Sticks'. Ideally, it needed a complex preamble. I first saw it when T-Man asked Sticks to put in a video tape when we were watching TV. Sticks lumbered over, pressed eject and the tape already in there had 'Fuck Off Sticks' in large cheerful letters across the spine. A couple of days later came the reply from Sticks.

Now Tour Manager loved gadgets. Any gadget ideally, but he was particularly fond of having the largest and latest car, computer and phone. His flip-top phone was the hottest and most expensive thing at the time. It rang. He, James Bond-like, flipped it open ostentatiously and discovered a small calling card within that simply read 'WANKER'.

"D'oh!" cursed T-Man, answering the call while looking at the card.

"WANKER!" shouted Sticks into the receiver, calling from across the building into the telephone he'd called from.

Tour Manager then went on a reprogramming mission. Anything in the venue that could carry text was to be re-purposed. Didn't matter if it was essential to the running of the place, it had to chime 'Fuck Off Sticks' when pressed. TV monitors in the bar areas had to read it, even during the day and roundly-acknowledged 'family time'.

T-Man would go to the freezer where he kept his poisons and get out his wares and 'WANKER' would be spelled out in ice. In-turn, T-Man would spend hours creating fake labels with his computer and printer for all the cans and bottles in the fridge to subtly say 'Fuck Off Sticks' on them. Some not-so-subtle. Sticks might be holding a bottle with it written on, unawares, for some time with T-Man giggling and shaking with joy nearby, and if no one noticed, he'd drop a hint.

Sticks then upped the ante by programming all the computers to say, in the slight weird woman's voice they can be elected to use, "Tour Manager is a cunt" every few seconds for the entire duration they were on, and for weeks no one knew how to stop it. Both of these beasts on colossal amounts of stimulants could lead them to spend days in research and development for their japes.

T-Man responded by writing in childlike scrawl on his own shirt 'Fuck Off Sticks' while still wearing it, so it was disproportionately crammed to one side. He promptly forgot he was wearing it and went upstairs to visit his Mum and her three sisters. Her Ladyship peered over her half-moon glasses on a chain and remarked:

"Sticks... off... Oh dear! What on EARTH is that?"

T-Man took one look at her, grabbed the shirt to inspect it as if he'd never seen it in his life, and with the amounts he was taking, could easily be the first time he'd seen it since he wrote it, promptly exclaimed:

"STICKS DID IT!" and ran off like an eight-year-old.

"Why would he pen an insult about himself?" one of the aunties pondered aloud.

"BECAUSE HE'S A WANKER!" came a shout from below.

The war of attrition came to an end when, at some expense, Sticks had made a vast vinyl banner. Something like 30 feet long and 10 high and attached it to the facade of the manor via ropes out of the middle floor windows, which was visible for a mile saying:

'T-MAN IS A WANKER' in huge letters.

Tour Manager was 50 at the time. Sticks was 48.

At one point I was sat in a corner as the two of them went at it. I was feeling rum and uncanny. Slowly their bickering made them morph in front of my eyes. They had on huge powered wigs and make-up. They were surrounded by opulence and ladies with fans in huge dresses. A sinister cardinal in the corner cast a dark eye at Tour Manager and exclaimed:

"I do believe the Duke here is pregnant... with a witticism!" he chortled triumphantly.

"The Cardinal can FUCK OFF!" was the riposte.

"Wanker," agreed Sticks-in-a-wig, nodding sagely.

It's at times like these I look at the camera with my best Oliver Hardy face and wonder why I am here and what I did to deserve it.

They tried to rope me into their lunacy, only once. I'd been out working. One of us had to. As I returned I bounded up to the huge living room, in the days when bounding was still in my repertoire, which had its own small set of steps in turn, and froze in my tracks.

Something was not right. Both of them were sat in the room quietly. This, in itself, was deeply unusual. I have an eye for the unusual. For example, I once warned T-Man that Quag was going to do something devious very soon because I came across him in a hallway of T-Man's club and he stopped talking to the person opposite. Quag would never stop doing anything for anyone unless he didn't want you to know about it. Right on time, two weeks later, he pulled his event out of the club for a better offer and promptly ruined the venue. No one believed me at the time when the warning was given, of course.

So these two sat all-too primly 'watching TV' in the pose of someone trying a bit too hard to look like someone watching TV rang ten bells in my head. I stopped at the threshold.

"What are you two dingbats up to?" I asked.

"Just watching TV, totally normally. Love TV. It's good. You should watch TV too."

"You both are extremely weird. Way weirder than usual."

"I am not weird. This television is SOOO good. The various programmes are particularly engaging today."

The penny dropped, and lucky it was just a penny. I looked up and balanced on the door was a large bucket of water.

"Christ you two amateurs might be perfectly matched, but you'll have to get up earlier to fox me. Ideally before the crack of 4pm."

"DAMMIT!" cursed a thwarted T-Man.

A few minutes later, I heard a great commotion. The two of them promptly forgot it was there, and it crashed down on his 75-year-old Mum coming in with his dinner on a tray. Scenes ensued.

CHAPTER 10
RESIDENT EVILS

It could be said that my two specialities, over the years, were back-to-back DJ sessions and being a resident DJ. They are the things I have done the most often, sometimes simultaneously. I'd say a solid 75% of my gigs over the last four decades were as a resident. I think perhaps it's the most important DJ role in our business. The decline of residents in-favour of huge names is another large contributing factor to our journey from the light to the dark.

Because while the music isn't always demonstrably from the USA for me, the set-up of nightclubs definitely is. Like it or not, every major club in the world is modelled on venues from 70s/80s New York or Chicago. Not always in layout precisely, but in the trilogy of dancefloor, sound system, DJ. In the early, cocksure, gay and heady days *all* DJs were residents, and the resident ruled the party. It was the norm to only be able to see David Mancuso exclusively in his Loft, Levan and Knuckles at the Continental Baths or Siano at the Gallery. The captain of the ship, piloting to the journey 'til dawn, the personality of the resident DJ defined the entire club. But for a quirk of etymology, House music itself, named after the music that Frankie Knuckles played at The Warehouse, might just as easily have been called 'Knuckle music'.

At the birth of the scene in the UK it was the same. Each club had its DJ, and only later did they slowly start to cross-pollinate. This continued through the 90s and early noughties: the genesis of Sasha's legend is inseparable from his regular spot at Shelley's in Stoke, Junior Vasquez *was* Sound Factory and Twilo in NYC, Body and Soul needed no other input other than the holy trinity of Kevorkian, Krivit and Claussell. Paul Oakenfold became so synonymous with Cream at Nation in Liverpool that when he left to 'go global' and was replaced by Seb Fontaine, it was the biggest news in clubland since the invention of the glow stick. It's only today that many bad clubs have relegated the resident to being the human equivalent of having a CD on. Background music, killing time. Witness the shitness as people file in, check their coats, get legless and kill time until the overpriced guest.

So why did the guest come to dominate and the resident be consigned to the shadows? Could be that it's just a question of glamour, that the weekly toil under another's shadow is not as 'fun'. It's way faster now to suddenly emerge from nowhere as a 'producer' and be asked to start doing gigs straight out of solitary years in the spare room. The dumbing down of our young crowds into thinking only new big names in lights is of any worth may be a large factor. Perhaps it's just all about money as usual. As a DJ you just make far more as a travelling attraction – while there's far less responsibility involved in simply turning up, making small talk with the promoter over a meal, playing a two hour set then hitting the hotel only to fail in getting a bit of shuteye before yet another flight. Ultimately, perhaps leading with your ressies is a luxury that died in the 90s along with other extravagances. Likely it's all the above and more.

The clue is in the name. Resident: your disco-insurance that there is a base level of quality for two-thirds of the night that *resides* in the place without fail. The attitude of the club and its promoter is the setting for the jewel in the crown, however. It's not enough just to be good at playing records; it's a team effort. To understand that the common denominator between every single (no exception) great club is that they honour and understand their residents is to understand all you need to know about what this club thing we do is all about. Many venues and promoters are rainmakers who claim to be the architects of the special bond that happens, but many are mere custodians at best, caretakers of the 'thing' between ressie and regular. And the resident cares. Far more than the promoter, they are the ones with their bits on the line if things look or sound bad. "From the shiny-ness of the mirror ball to the frequency range of the bass bins", as Jon Da Silva said about his residency at the Hacienda.

The crux of the matter, is, of course, The Crowd. Ultimately, they make it happen. The essence of a proper club and perhaps its core definition is a double act, a waltz to the music of mutual rapport between its regulars and the resident. It's usually done organically over years, usually far away from the artificial photosynthesis of hype and attention. It even boils down to knowing who occupies which space in the club. The Hacienda famously having different areas representing different local types. How can a nomadic DJ superstar, not-so-fresh from the airport pluckily clutching a fist-full of USB sticks and a hotel keycard hope to possibly build that kind of rapport? Let's be plain. All this is not consigned to some 'golden era'. Today, all over the world, the absolute and unquestionable common denominator in every highly respected club is that they understand the importance of the resident above all else. Giants such as DC-10 and Fabric are built on it.

I absolutely believe in the resident DJ. I think that is clear. Even without a residency, I think like a resident. If I'm a guest, I often ask to play back to back with one of the club's own. I believe it's the making of a good guest to be or have been a ressie. In my imaginary undersea kingdom, it would be compulsory to have served as one. There are many counter-arguments, however; where is the new blood? Who wants to see the same face every week? How can someone progress in that situation? When I try to answer and drum up some examples of great clubs that don't utilise the residency, I come up dry. Parched. Or rather I come up with a list of shit clubs. Try it. I may do a graph that shows the quality of resident is directly proportional to the success of the club.

Some of the biggest names started as, and still are, residents... and by big I mean legendary-over-decades-big not woke-up-this-morning-EDM-big. It doesn't take a genius to work out being a resident had everything to do with the making of our outstanding best. Another argument is that it's fair enough for promoters to say 'it's a question of economics'. The big names bring the big amounts of people. Fine. Then it's also fair to say you're all welcome to each other.

The well-loved resident also removes all shadow of a doubt. You KNOW it's going to be good even if the guest is a giant plonking megabollock. Clubs with revered ressies are always buzzing. They are a cut above frankly. Good residents without question challenge the guest to step up. This isn't opinion, I've seen it so often it's almost funny. Guests you wouldn't just write off by rep but you'd seen several times go through the motions for the money suddenly find themselves sandwiched between two legendary ressies and a hyper crowd and suddenly they remember how they got there and what it took and they reach inside themselves and find it. You deliver or die when the stakes are high.

You see, *House is a feeling*, and if all you get are big names jetting in, there is no connection and consequently no feeling. Emotion is entirely about contact with something. The connect of the crowd and resident is totally about that, and when it's right, the guest just has to fit into it just to keep up... and the good ones do. Before you know it, you are one of the handful of world-beating clubs that bases what it does on its residents. Yeah, it really is that simple.

Not simple enough? All the world's best clubs are all about the residents, to the point where the guest barely makes a dent. Ibiza is almost entirely residencies by the biggest and sometimes best. This is not a coincidence.

* * *

My residency at this brand new superclub wasn't my first, but at the time it was certainly the most prestigious. It was the big league. Not merely in looks and wage, but playing the whole night in the second room. From open 'til close. Every single week. Sometimes twice a week. Suffice to say I was buzzed about this new gig. It was a *proper* residency.

However, in hindsight, like so much of my disastrous career, I was blind for most of it. Too high, too happy, and *way* too engulfed in the music to see what was going on elsewhere. Alarm bells should have rung day one when in fact I was too busy ringing my Mum to tell her I was in a hotel opposite on the balcony and the promo video I'd directed for our band was on the big screen opposite, off my tits with pride and joy. Highly insufferable too, more than likely. Too buzzing to notice the guest list at the opening was all shades of very wrong. Celebrities favoured over dance music press. Actual paparazzi outside. Lasers and shit. I was very much at the peak running-around-like-a-man-on-fire stage of my career and highly managed by Chib and one of the biggest agencies in the world. Point is, I wasn't very involved in any of the decisions. I was on the road, pushing people into pools, talking gibberish at afterparties and licking my own eyebrows. Not saying I would have done better either, decision-wise.

Don't get me wrong, it had all the right stuff. On paper. Those in charge had a strong pedigree and loads of experience with a clear vision. They were from out of town, however. I may have mentioned how the team sport mentality is a cancer in our biz. There are regional rivalries that are frankly embarrassing, a species of regionalism that is 'banter' when they want it to be and often pure hate in reality. A big part of that 'you're not one of us' disease that is the opposite of Acid House. Although many of the dancers would travel the world to party, the owners of the venues were frequently deeply opposed to their competitors. In this instance, our superclub was trying its hand in a new town. Millions were put into this new venue. What many of us there didn't realise was that there was a 'home-grown' venture also due to open. Local, savvier of the environment and very much more about being alternative. So much so, in fact, that they delayed their opening, at huge cost to themselves, in order to present themselves as the 'alternative' to the new, shinier and 'foreign' venture. It was *extremely* shrewd.

Sometimes, in terms of marketing, all you have to do is point at something and say "You see that? We're not that." Really. It's that simple sometimes. I'm going to call the home team in the city 'Basement' and the away team 'Tower', or as I referred to it for years after 'The Towering Inferno'. The Tower Club concept was actually all about the working class and its aspirations. There was an element to clubbing that ordinary folks, who let's face it, were behind the whole shooting match in the first place, were keen on things being quite posh at this time. They wanted a large night out. A night to remember. At this time too it was common for people to travel a thousand miles to go to the club they liked with the DJ they wanted. There being a lot less of both venues and acts at this time. People would spend months planning for their big night out and a lot of their hard-earned on it. Team Basement was for a far more middle class, urbane crowd, who liked it moody. Who were highly cosmopolitan and as such, had more money but pretended they didn't, and very much dressed-down instead of up. Personally, I liked both places, had a lot of friends working in both venues. Yin and Yang. Both had superb sound systems and DJs. Many people went to both.

Then the sneering started in earnest. Club Tower was 'shit'. These foreigners didn't understand 'our' town. Tower was rubbish. It wasn't actually. I was there every week. There were some *blinding* nights. What it did have however was a horrific right-wing local council who hammered it every week. What Club Basement had that Tower did not was drugs. By no means involved in them! No Sir! Just had nothing like the same restrictions. Club Tower had a door policy like a current airport. Metal detectors. Even dogs at one point. Massive amounts of security staff. Searches of a most annoying and thorough nature. It had to or it would be shut down. Comparatively at the time at Club Basement you just got a cheery hello on the way in. Club Tower seemed less of a good time because it was dry as a bone. Drugless Douglas. You got the lot taken off you if you had any on the way in, possibly you were handed over to the police, and could not find any if your life depended on it once inside.

Tower opened initially with a 2am license. Archaic? Absolutely. Unworkable? Without a doubt. That's ok, said Darth Council, we'll review it after you open.

"Yes, you'd better, because most of our clientele come from out-of-town, and if they get turfed-out at 2am they will have to wait something like five hours for public transport to get started properly. Particularly on a Sunday, when transport is at its worst."

"Ah! It'll be fine! Don't worry. We *want* you to succeed! Let's look at it again next week. Meanwhile, good news! You can go on 'til 3!"

Years passed. Not only were customers stranded after 3am, forced to get outrageously expensive licensed cabs for huge distances homewards, all the business projections were for a place that earned money from 11pm 'til 6am. The council were effectively *halving* the income of a vast machine that employed hundreds. Over at Club Basement everyone was having a whale of a time and earning quite nicely comparatively. Indeed after Tower closed for the evening, all the staff and many dancers would pile over to see our mates at Basement. I was one of the few DJs who has played at both. Spent a *ridiculous* amount of off-duty time and money at both too.

I personally spent HUGE sums inside Basement, after finishing up at Tower. Huge for me anyway, nearly everything I earned that week. Had some killer morning sessions. We also had some awesome nights in Tower, but the people having an awesome time were working class kids from out of town. Not super-cool locals. Guess which way the hype was going? Of course. Tower was shit, Basement was ace. All the people who worked backstage in our industry soon stopped going to Tower, it was grotesque for them to have to mingle with people with accents! Good lord, some of them were from the *provinces!*

Club Basement could do no wrong. Not only because it was genuinely great, but because it wasn't Tower. By now a full 'us against them' narrative was in-place, imposed from the outside entirely, as in reality, we all got on famously. The industry finally fully rejected Tower and only went to Basement. Then things *really* started to go bad.

Evil Council declared out of the blue that Tower had a, wait for it, *drug problem*. Ta daaaah! To be fair, this was absolutely true. It had a massive drug problem, it didn't have any. Anywhere. To those of us working there it was bordering on the hilarious. Not only was it the driest place in town with the harshest door policy, it was now being told to be even harder on people. Conspiracy theories started to appear that other clubs had influence at the council, all sorts of rumours. But the bottom line was, since the day it opened, the council would just not let it breathe. Eventually and completely unsurprisingly, it folded for good. The license revoked. Millions and millions poured down the drain. About 300 people unemployed and due to the nature of the closure, a large chunk of the door staff lost their licenses, and could never work again. All on a whim and a lie. Did the venue help regenerate the area? Oh *definitely*, this was part of gaining the license. Did the council shut it down intentionally once it got what it wanted? Well, luckily I'm not a cynic and can't say for sure.

The fact that years later exactly the same move was used on Club Basement by its own council to try to get rid of it, and take over the area the club had cleaned-up for them, and the whole industry totally lost its shit over it this time... well, let us just say the irony was not lost on me.

So do you see what this is telling us? The problem isn't always poor lineups or what clothes people are wearing or what records are played... it is about politics, business and an industry that is more concerned with how it looks, than how much it supports its members, protects interests, or lobbies to influence policy.

Most of this was lost on me at the time. I didn't find out about much of it until years after. I didn't lose out in any way. Much worse things happened before and after, as you will know if you read my first book. Around that time I'd never been busier. I wasn't particularly concerned with anything that didn't involve getting the flight on-time and getting mangled for the rest. Which is one of the reasons I was at the wrong club in the first place. I was letting the biz control me. The industry was not only profiting greatly from me, it was telling me what to do, fucking up what I was then doing on their say-so, and then profiting again from the clean-up and 'fixing it'. Sound familiar? Sound like capitalism? Perhaps indeed, that is what we were. 'The Future Sound of Capitalism' with our latest hit, 'Higher State of Awkwardness'.

The rise and fall of the Towering Inferno would become, rather unfairly, a byword for the hubris of a generation of working class Icaruses, whose ambition, fuelled by the Acid House revolution (and, let's be accurate, a LOT of drugs), had outstripped their competence. It synchronised perfectly with the debacle of the millennium NYE celebrations, when a collective brain fart on the part of many of the UK's biggest promoters saw them losing millions on huge follies that no one went to. Looking back, it was the beginning of the end of the age of the enthusiast. Clearly, there was money to be made, but could people like myself, Quag, and the Tour Manager really be trusted with the responsibility? When clubland rose again, it was as if someone had decided that this time things would be very different.

CHAPTER 11
THERE'S ACTUALLY LOADS OF BUSINESSES LIKE SHOWBUSINESS...

Ask anyone in the biz and I can guarantee that if you talk about the industry for more than five minutes, a visceral hatred of DJ booking agents, the people who agree the gigs and the fees (for a healthy cut), will pop up pretty sharpish. Agents, for many in the game, are about as welcome as a massive spider in your arse. Personally, I've had good and bad. They aren't institutionally evil, but clearly most venues, promoters and a lot of DJs are going to have objections because the agents are the money. Also, because our business is essentially a bunch of soon-to-be released kleptomaniac monkeys wanking in a sack, you do need a representative to stop you getting ripped-off before you even get on the plane. It is absolutely possible lately, via the internet, to have a nice wee 'artisanal' career where you do it all yourself. No doubt. Lovely. But if you blow up, you literally cannot handle the amount of interest. If you are managed then that manager is going to want to make as much money for you both as possible. This is capitalism. Then the escalations start. Because capitalism must always drive cash value upwards. At least it seems that way to us lowly mortals. Ironically, Libertarian billionaires now drive cash value *down* in order to control a market, using short selling, negative equity and apparently contradictory techniques to get even more obscenely wealthy.

But the drive of agents pushing up DJ wages is arguably the biggest factor in turning our beloved disco into a casino's counting house. I saw it myself very early on. Some of the earlier big gigs I worked at in the late 80s saw a shift in prices from DJs costing about £300, perhaps £500 at a push for the biggest to suddenly doubling and tripling, almost overnight. At this point, if I was on the internet now, some smug fuck would, as inevitable as the tide, throw in the phrase 'supply and demand'. It's always used, mainly by people who have no argument, and simply want the world to stay the same. I think perhaps that is the very definition of a conservative right there. That someone who is doing obscenely well deserves it at best, is very lucky at worst. Folks wish it was them. The exceptions are the super cool promoters and large venues who still only pay DJs £300, decades later, because it is the 'right thing to do', when in fact it is entirely about them making their massive margins even more colossal. Once again, driving value down is a method of control. You are to be glad and deeply honoured to be playing at super cool spots. For this you are paid less and they make more. Their public reasoning is that it is 'wrong' to overpay DJs. Then they themselves pocket vast amounts. It is correct to redress the over-inflation of talent bills, but you lose the moral high ground when the money saved by your stance does not find its way back to the dancefloor, but flies off to the tax haven.

Look back, the first time this inflation happened was as the 80s handed over to the 90s. The talent bill for the night suddenly skyrocketed due to the DJs being more in-demand. Immediately the profit margins of the raves went down, down and down. So the amount and price of tickets had to go uppity-up. Something that was previously manageable, fun and even intimate quickly became bloated, ungainly and desperate. When things get big, profitable and complex, gangsters move in to roundly exploit the scenario. They might wear an M1 flight jacket or they might wear an extremely expensive suit, but the mindset is almost identical.

A layer of middlemen always arises when things start to get profitable. You could argue that they are completely surplus. You could argue they are essential. It tends to be proportional to how much money is at stake. In a sense, as a safety device, agents are invaluable when it comes to ensuring and insuring large events and big names with big draws and even bigger drawers. Big pockets on big pants mean big business requiring big players.

A good agent thinks strategically, looking beyond their commission, maintaining relationships with bookers, treating all of their clients with equal respect instead of playing them off against each other and essentially putting their 'main' client first. Unfortunately, these Jerry McGuire types are so rare in every industry they had to invent one from scratch for the movie. Many of the Patrick Batemans at bigger firms with a monopoly on talent are short-termists to whom their own status and the next fee are primary priorities, with everything else very far behind. With a revolving door of DJs willing to step up and take the place of the latest burnout (often thinking that acceptance onto an agency's books means they've somehow 'made it'), there's no real incentive to look after the clients they've got. And with the leverage that comes with having a slate of confirmed ticket-selling DJs on the roster, there's no incentive not to gouge promoters for as much as possible, force inappropriate DJs on them to everyone's detriment and swan about like a really big swan. Possibly made of jewels.

One of the defining moments for me was when I was trying to book a very major artist to headline a large event, whom I'd booked the year previously. When I got in touch, I was flummoxed to learn the price had almost doubled in less than 12 months. I assure you nothing earth-shattering had been done by the act in the intervening time. I had to ask, *why*? No answer was forthcoming. It put me in mind of another agent who was famous for one-word replies. "No" being the usual one. This was long before completely ignoring someone was normalised. You know, when it was unbelievably rude beyond measure. What's that Little Baby Jesus? It still is, only we are all despicable now? Right. Got to agree.

Anyway, I had a little think and suddenly I had an epiphany and this time called the agent. After a bit of preamble, I said:

"Hey listen, don't take this the wrong way but I've not seen much of your boys in the last year, tell me, just between us... are you doubling their fee because they are playing half as often?"

There was a long pause and then a simple:

"Yah".

And, of course, I did not book them. And yes, where are they now? Probably wondering what the fuck happened to their career no doubt. I would be.

In the 90s a thing started where once we looked on in a kind of slightly disgusted awe at the excesses and demands of our cousins across the pond visiting here, and suddenly started doing it ourselves. Suddenly 'value' didn't just mean money, it was attached to everything. How difficult you were was attributed to how important you are. Naturally, this meant artificially inflating the common skill of being a complete intransigent arsehole. I'd heard the word 'diva' being bandied about for years and just assumed, having had to deal with it once or twice, that it was simply French for dickhead. And once again, notice how currently this has filtered-down to nearly everyone? It is perfectly acceptable to be a pain in the arse now in an everyday sense. "If you can't love me at my worst, you don't deserve me at my best" being the honking fanfare of the nightmarish entitled wanker. WOOP! WOOP! AVOID! AVOID!

What is even weirder is we have been conditioned to *want* it overpriced. No one wants 'cheap'. I saw this first hand when I focussed on afterparties. I thought I was a shiny hero in marvellous boofy, blousy shirts when I'd let people in free or charge a fiver. Again, the problem was value. No one valued it unless it was slightly punitive to their pocket. If something is £30, they will definitely show up to get their value for money. If they paid £10, they are pretty OK with forgetting about it and doing something else. And get this, a couple of people came to my door once convinced the party was a scam because it was free. Asking what the catch was. Don't get me started on fundraisers for charity. Standing on the door with a bucket for the Red Cross and people saying "I don't believe in charity" by the dozen would be met by my promptly not believing in them getting into my club. It truly is shocking how much agile mental gymnastics happen when people don't want to do something good. The attitudes of the 'peace and love' generation constantly cease to amaze.

My latest wheeze/colossally doomed vanity project was fairly recent. It was a very simple jape. Cut out the middleman and connect artists directly with the people who want to book them. It started with getting begging letters for 'flight shares' from agents. You may or may not know that frequently they mass email promoters saying: "Oo, please help! Poor millionaire DJs Stodge 'n' Plinth need another overpaid gig on a stopover between X and Y on Z date, please help!". I figured, why not put those dead dates into an online diary that people can check out and even bid for? Then it grew into a machine for booking DJs. Not only could DJs with no agents use it (AKA most DJs), fans could club together to do

'VIP gigs' and crowd-promote gigs with their fave DJs, especially on the midweek dates that are always free for artists. Yes, big DJs and big agents could use it too. There'll be little change in circumstances for the big dogs other than things would be easier and more open.

Every agent: "Oh wait... *more* open you say? Yes. *Less* of a monopoly is it? I see. Mmmmm. How interesting."

You'd be able to book flights, hotels, cars and restaurants through the system. I even built a prototype and like all good ideas (cheers, yes it's not bad thanks) absolutely no-one with any money would commit to it until someone else did. They all *wanted* to, just let us know when someone else does. *Great* idea by the way! Cheerio!

Let's just say it was *not* popular amongst some very powerful and influential agencies. No Sir. 'Nuff said there. And as I said to all concerned at the time, you may as well come on board with us now, 'cos it's not a case of 'if' this *will* happen, it's just a case of 'when'. Which I can also answer with 'very soon'. I stand by that. In the time since there have been a couple of other failed stabs at it. Yes, I will be waiting with my lawyers when the money comes in. Just kidding. No wait, I'm not.

Middlemen are the soul eaters. And record labels are the ultimate middlemen. I have to say that, with only a little exaggeration, almost everything that came to pass with major record companies, for me, involved middlemen having almost no clue, dismissing everything I said, and then their own choices proving to be utterly, dismally wrong. Once again, you are faced with an industry that perceives its workers and artists as completely dispensable commodities. Deeply stupid and rather annoying ones at that. Something that makes noise in the corner while you are trying to work, like bringing a demented toddler to the office.

Early on I was signed to an 'indie' label that trumpeted its cool credentials to the heavens but I later discovered was owned by the Murdoch family. You don't even have to look very hard these days thanks to the internet, but back then it was much harder to see up the chain. Scratch the surface of any media company and you can often trace them to some deeply unpleasant connections, including in some cases Big Pharma and arms dealing.

As a disc-jockey, I'm always deeply wary of desk-jockeys. Naturally, some are very good people but the upper tier simply did not get to sit down all day and get paid loads if they weren't highly ruthless; indeed anyone with an overabundance of ruth need not apply. All these things start with boatloads of promises. A veritable armada of bullshit sails into view that will just never happen. Usually, somewhere there is a discussion about 'artistic freedom' and how liberal everything is, which immediately goes to pot the minute an actual discussion raises its head. They sign you based on knowing very little. Back then, no idea at all about dance music. Not a sausage. I mean, we were the only electronic disco nitwits they had on their books.

It starts slowly with 'suggestions'. Bear in mind, I've had decades dealing with egotistical knaves who don't know our music, but they do know how to *deal*. It 'might be nice' if you did this. 'Perhaps this might work?'. 'Have you thought about X?' I get it, Reader, you think I'm just cranky. Again, at the time, I was very affable and did whatever they wanted. Which was a terrible, *terrible* mistake. I knew my scene. I'd been part of it since before it was born. I knew that back then, mystery was important. I knew that credibility was everything. I was absolutely certain of how much faster things were moving now. I knew that we were taking the piss a bit, engaging modern irony, so that needed presenting properly. I knew the tunes would need to be able to be mixed by DJs in their sets. I knew what the mastering needed to sound like if it was going to kick in a club, whose sound systems were nearly always in mono. I knew we didn't always need vocals. I knew stuff. They would nod and smile and say how *interesting* it all was, and gosh what a brave new world. Then completely and utterly ignore all of it. You cannot possibly know what you are talking about. Used to run a radio station? What has that got to do with anything? Already been in the biz for a decade? Well, come back to us in another. There is only one role for you in the machine and that is as a silent sausage. Thick as mince and twice as pliable. PLEASE take my advice. Fuck them all. Fight everything. Go at their faces like a spider monkey. They rely on you going with the flow. Being affable and a total pushover is exactly what they need just before they shoot a bolt in your forehead with compressed air after a kindly bit of gentle manoeuvring into the paddock.

Here's an example. CD sales were once huge. Stamping all over the market like streaming is now. It was all about the CDs. So we had a design meeting. What was the packaging going to be like? Well, we were one of their premium acts, so they wanted it to be impressive. OK I said, it's going to be transparent. The CD will be see-through, as will the inlay and the case. New technologies in packing were coming through. We wanted it to look like the future. "GREAT" everyone enthused. Enthusiasm was what they did. Everything was brilliant and amazing and awesome. Long story short? None of that happened. They did the cheapest version they possibly could and it looked like shit. Crucially, without us knowing. Months of detailed to-and-fro was simply theatre.

Compared to the biggest issue, this was just cosmetic. The trouble with future music is that you'd damn well better not be late with it. Clue is in the name. When we worked on our album no one had heard of, for example, Daft Punk or Basement Jaxx. They didn't exist in the wider public sphere. After much wrangling, meetings, faxes, tour schedules, remix deals, phone calls, masterings, photo sessions, artworks, retail discussions, changed schedules, re-scheduled schedules and general fuckery, suddenly it was two years later. *Two entire years* to go through the colon of a big label. By the time we actually hit the shelves, we sounded *old*. Instead of one of the pioneers of a new vibe, we sounded like a pale imitation.

Another example. Public Relations. I had a bit of experience of this, in another life, and I had a very clear idea of who we were and what we were doing. We'd already worked with a larger, more successful band. This whole project was a spin-off of that. It was to be a sort of piss-take vibe with a large nod to the KLF. We had been big fans of the Situationist International for some years. Had already 'pranked' the industry once or twice. There was punk in dance music, always was. The element of how this was perceived was *everything*. I won't bore you too much with just how impossible it was to get this across to them, so let us use the example of the photoshoot.

"Well," says I, "we're in luck because photos will be easy, there won't be any!"

"We can't possibly market anything without photos of the act."

"Yes, but I said very clearly when we started you will never see our faces."

"We cannot possibly do that, it's unheard-of."

"Really, what about The Residents? What about GWAR?"

"Who?"

"DJs and producers don't use their faces, they use their hands. We want to make a commentary on the beauty myth. If we have to compromise, let's use our hands. Making a 'V' sign to fuck off the concept of 'pretty'."

"That is a ridiculous idea. We will drop you if you don't do photos."

End of conversation.

Literally the month after I sent them photos of our hands making 'V' gestures, and was told it was stupid, American rapper 'Kid Rock' did an entire global marketing campaign with just his hand 'giving the finger'. It was hugely successful.

Then we did the photoshoot they wanted, with a very respected and excellent rock 'n' roll photographer. We had to. It was extremely expensive. I sat down with the PR person.

"The dichotomy here is that we are being playful and ironic with the music, so to counter that the image has to be extremely serious. Very deadpan and grave."

"I understand, that makes a lot of sense."

Couple of weeks later I opened a major magazine, buzzing my tits off that we were actually *in* a magazine. Centrefold. Main feature. My guts churned and my smile fell right off my face and into my soup.

She'd used the out-take pics from the session of us clowning around. The ones I said must be burned with fire.

"It's fun! Makes you stand out!"

"AARRRRRRRGGGGG," I replied. We wanted to look like Kraftwerk, ended up looking like Madness.

Once again, all completely under the counter. They said one thing, did the opposite behind your back. This was a theme. Something that persisted for many years, not just with me but with friends in the biz. And don't forget, most of my ideas were about saving money. This wasn't my first rodeo. I knew that it was *our* money they were spending. Understand this, they have budgets they HAVE to spend. If a department doesn't spend and even overspend by the tax year turnaround they don't get given as much the following year. Savvy? They have to spend your money to survive. No wonder they ignored my thrift. No wonder they tried everything they could to 'normalise' this weird new thing. Defang it. Geld us.

Many years later, once again, sat in a design meeting. I went in with something like:

"Everything we have done so far is monochrome. We started as a free party in Ibiza and literally printed all our things on a cheap and elderly photocopier. It is our style. Our 'brand' if you are going to force me to use that word. It is who we are."

"Perhaps it needs just a splash of colour?"

"OK, well. More importantly, no one else is doing it."

"Perhaps, however, it needs just a splash of colour?"

"Literally, no one in the racks at HMV, Tower or Virgin is in black and white."

"Perhaps just a splash of colour, for impact?"

"Impact? We will *shine*. Stick out like an accountant at a carnival. The only vicar at the vogue ball."

"Is there nothing to be said for a splash of colour?"

After a while, you start to realise. If you arrive with all the answers it is the opposite of what they want. You don't need them. Their slightly preposterous middleman job is thrown into sharp relief. They HAVE to make a daft contribution to justify their existence. If they don't stamp their face on it somehow, what is the point of them being there? It's like the executive who thinks everything needs a happy ending, then the version of the thing where everybody dies is a colossal global success.

I've hinted at how mad the economics are in the first book, so no need perhaps to be confused at how you are number one in eight countries but somehow owe the record company money. Like I say, they have to spend your money to justify their fat salary. They have to run you ragged across the globe to make sure they can sit in an ergonomic chair all day.

Do you see it yet? Office politics, the myth of money, lies, lies and more lies and being roundly manipulated at all times are simply how it all *works*. And there is just a much larger version of all that is making the world go round. This is the machine.

Yes, correct, the entire shitshow is a fucktangular rhomboid of kack.

CHAPTER 12
UNINVITED GUESTS

While the nightlife industry that grew out of Acid House thrust many of us into positions that we'd never otherwise have found ourselves, as it matured it became clear that our new utopia had also attracted its fair share of utterly ruthless and shameless opportunists, as well as money and investment from some extremely dubious sources.

In the late 1990s, Gatecrasher was one of the three biggest UK superclub brands; but while Ministry of Sound and Cream went on to become global powerhouses, Gatecrasher ventures suffered a variety of calamities: fires, floods, and at one festival, a death. For a while Gatecrasher even teetered on the edge of cultural phenomenon status, as the late 90s style press, ever thirsty for a Shibuya-style youth subculture in the UK, feted briefly the 'Crasher Kids', a group of club regulars who sought to outdo each other every week with their daft-yet-somehow-lovable UV outfits, 'TUNE' and Mitsubishi themed accessories, and props ranging from kids' ray guns to pacifiers. Perhaps the best thing was the way the appalling outfits irked those DJs who despite playing infant-friendly progressive trance, imagined they deserved a classier crowd than gurning high steppers with furry boots and Lego in their hair.

Eventually, over the years, their enterprises all appeared to closedown. Numerous companies that made up the Gatecrasher empire have gone under in the past three decades, leaving hundreds of known creditors out of pocket - yet the Teflon brand and its sole owner and director, Simon Raine, keep rolling on.

The final nail appeared to be when the huge Birmingham Gatecrasher nightclub closed in 2015 after the city took away its license following a knife attack and an alleged fight involving security staff. It was already on a final warning after police ordered a temporary closure when a customer was left badly injured in another security incident. This followed news stories all over the UK of poor practice, non-payment and even ethanol being served to youngsters rather than vodka.

Prior to that the company had already flopped abroad in 2014. Gatecrasher arrived in Ibiza directly off the back of a huge pre-pack administration deal (a UK deal with the Government whereby an insolvency procedure takes place. A company arranges a deal to sell its assets to a buyer before appointing administrators to facilitate the sale. It's a powerful, legal way of selling the business on to a trade buyer or third party. Often back to the original owners under a different name, leaving those owed money with nothing). It shut down several flagging venues in major Northern and Midlands cities and left 233 official creditors out of pocket. Under this sweet deal, two of Raine's companies, TipTopTap, and Late Night Watford, went into administration. A £4,000,000 debt owed to working people was entirely discarded but the business - including the flagship Birmingham HQ - was bought out by Raine's other firms, leaving some of those left out-of-pocket to watch as Raine, who owed them so much, cheerfully started up again in Ibiza.

Alas, within merely eight weeks in the Balearics, Gatecrasher was in trouble once again. By the end of the season, it was practically empty and open only one night out of seven, compared to every night at the start of the summer. The venue's Dutch owners issued a distancing statement and the Raine in Spain left quickly on a plane, returning to the UK leaving staff and suppliers unpaid. One ex-employee described "an attitude of non-payment from the top down". Young street promotion teams were owed, and left to protest outside the shuttered club doors. To add insult to injury, Raine photographed the protest and then took to social media to claim the club was so popular, people were queuing in the daytime. You almost have to admire the brass nerve.

The 'Raine of terror' did not end when everything closed. Time passed and once again they popped up in Sheffield, openly holding Gatecrasher events once more and were also quietly behind another venue. Once again, like clockwork, everything began to run into trouble. My own favourite story of Raine's activities was learning that as well as so many of his clubs so unfortunately burning down, he was a partner in the Sheffield Ski Village, which also burned to the ground. Snow being a most notoriously flammable material.

Not paying anyone is a common theme in the game. The sharks know this. They understand that the happy wee otters are petrified of grown-up stuff like lawyer's letters and wring their little hands when the documents arrive. The letter might be laughable and not worth the paper it is written on, but for one simply to appear on their little aquatic doormat is enough for some to totally lose their shit. One of Gatecrasher's favourite legal tricks is to barge into a town and then copyright the name of each competitor who'd been there for years. Then send a 'cease-and-desist' letter saying they have to stop trading under their own brand. I've personally got friends who obediently stopped working immediately, rather than fight this horrific amoral manoeuvre. These tactics are the world of big business. Capitalism. Very *very* wrong indeed.

It's not new either. Raine has been operating with impunity for over 30 years, but there's an even longer, ongoing story from the pioneer years: Trax Records in the USA not paying its artists, the very progenitors of American House music itself. Adonis didn't get any royalties from Trax for 35 years. Larry Heard and Robert Owens too. Other legends are also disputing decades of wrong. Let's not mince words here, the label owner was white, and all these artists were not. Not paying artists is as old as time in the music biz. Particularly black artists. The capitalists adding their names to music they had no hand whatsoever in writing, or being a 'producer' without ever going into a studio, or knowing nothing at all concerning the artistic process, but claiming credit regardless. It goes back to day dot. The music business is built entirely on foundations of rich white men exploiting minorities and women. Stealing the music, the credit and the money. It's not just barefaced highway robbery, we've spoken before about Gatekeepers. They aren't just assuming stewardship of everything, they are also white people managing access for black people to their own culture. White Gatekeepers aren't just holding on to the power in terms of money, they set themselves up as experts, industry figures, journalists and even as philanthropists. 'Allowing' and 'gifting' access to people of colour who shouldn't need permission from anybody to be involved in a culture they were instrumental in creating.

While our thing started in many places at once, there is no doubt whatsoever that Black, Latinx and LGBTQ+ communities took the thing and ran with it. Made it whole. Made it theirs. House and Techno most of all. It is almost obscene how Techno has been whitewashed into an almost cartoon and highly beige EDM parody. It doesn't stop there. Rich white musicians are wearing African clothes and giving their 'work' African names to legitimise their appropriations. The gentrification of what we do is not merely about money, the cultural assimilation is also highly racial. Gentrification and globalisation are utterly *white*. Bleaching the planet the shade of dry bones. Why be coy about it?

And now we start to see the new breed. The ultra-rich Tech-Bro and EDM Bro, to-ing and bro-ing together to such a degree they have merged into one beast: actual billionaire Tech-Bro DJs. The white faces behind global gentrification actually have the sheer nerve and entitlement to announce themselves as artists. With the funds, influence and self-confidence so vast it borders on stupidity, it all aligns to find them paying for their own gigs and starring at them.

Some might argue, 'fine, leave them to it' but that is way too naive. This is the ultimate, boss level of the commodification of culture. Proximity to power is all that matters. Not content with owning everything, they need a live crowd to salute their beige magnificence. The volume, the relentless banality, the huge crowds, the obscene costs and even more horrific wages. Power. Not art. Fascism, not community.

This right here is how the language and narrative have been hijacked. To talk about these things isn't quite verboten, it's more insidious. It's 'boring'. It's obvious. It's something you think you've heard before, as if that is a reason to shut up about it. Nothing is changing. Social mobility/class distinctions, use what buzzword you will, the dialogue almost never reaches action. Their assault on us begins with language, murdering journalism both figuratively and sometimes quite literally. Making correct thinking and goodness weak or dull at best, an extremist voice at worst. Gentrification and globalisation have an all-encompassing effect, to turn workers into zero-hours 'working poor' and entirely a strata of service industry to the middle classes and super-rich. The working class has essentially been outsourced overseas. Almost nothing is left in terms of industry and labour. Those remnants left of this once-proud, powerful and stand-alone society have been told so often that the reason they are emasculated and unemployed is due to immigrants, they've even started to believe it. It wasn't hard, the rich have been openly stoking racism via the press they own for our whole lives. We are being told completely innocent arrivals are to blame by the very same people who sent all the work overseas in the first place.

One of the other impacts of the new economic normal is that the low wages and long hours mean it is so much harder to be an artist. If you are one, you have to do it faster and cheaper, which makes fast, cheap art. Gentrification is sterilising culture, pricing poor people out, and allowing the mega-rich to hoover-up our beloved movement. It doesn't stop with us either. We're being forced out of our homes and businesses, sometimes by the very same people trying to tell us they are DJs and one of us.

Here we get to my favourites. 'Housekeeping'. A phenomenally mediocre EDM quartet and promoter team based in London. Who could be a better avatar for everything we are talking about here than a DJ 'collective' made of disgustingly rich, white EDM Bros? One of whom at least is a developer very much responsible for some of the physical gentrification of the locations we live in.

Three of them remove references to their surnames, though it would be conjecture to assume anyone is hiding, pseudonyms are normal in showbiz. 'Jacobi' is a regular on the society pages under his spectacular surname of Anstruther-Gough-Calthorpe. Sebastian Macdonald-Hall has a family with a combined wealth of £842m, with them at 168th in the 2020 Rich List. He is part of a huge property empire. Carl Waxberg was director at Citibank for 13 years before launching his own investment fund. Socialite party planner and property developer Taylor HK, or Taylor McWilliams, is the most infamous member. His development company Hondo Enterprises faced protests after installing segregated 'poor doors' in their luxury Aldgate apartment building in 2014. He's been personally working on Brixton. Hard. I don't hate them, I don't even know them. I don't even care if their music is truly awful. There's a lot of that about. What matters is what the rich do to communities and then have the nerve to appropriate what those communities are famous for and pass it off as their own. Sure, eviscerate our district for profit if you must, but do you have to mock us while you go about it?

Astoundingly, vast, giggling money octopus Goldman Sachs has a CEO who fancies himself a DJ, David Solomon AKA 'DJ Sol'. Recently he and beige EDM Bros 'Chainsmokers', courted controversy in New York's fancy Hamptons by doing a huge gig during the COVID pandemic that the local authorities roundly condemned, and the Governor himself called 'egregious' in terms of violations of the health measures required for people's safety. The swanky locality was fully culpable too with 'town supervisor' Jay Schneiderman putting himself on the bill as a DJ too. Yes, of course, the individuals will not take responsibility and 'the organisers' and 'the people' are at fault; traditional politician's responses from Pontius Pilates all over the globe. For me the issue is not so much the line-up, awful as it is, it's the idea that these events happen at all. Tickets were reported at the upper-end to be a staggering $25,000. The entitlement required for anyone to even countenance events during such a time is truly unbelievable.

Rich people aren't evil. I know some. I even like them. They can be just as daft, self-interested, prejudiced and able to rationalise their worst aspects away like we all can. The problem with inequality and gentrification isn't 'evil', it's the disproportionate effect their everyday ills have on the environment around them. We do badness too, it's just that when we are horrible selfish dicks we tend not to dissect communities, destroy the air we breathe, and hammer the weakest by the hundreds, if not thousands. They *are* us. As brilliant and hideous as you or me. Just obscenely more wealthy.

If you have trouble understanding why it is bad that the rich are moving into an area, tripling all the rents and driving out poorer families who've lived there for generations, or you don't understand why it would be horrific that a total stranger arrives out of nowhere next-door to a pub that has been there 200 years and starts to campaign for it to shut because it annoys them... try this:

Urban gentrification is like putting up wallpaper. An air bubble pops up and when you smooth it down it just appears elsewhere. In the big picture it is simply physics. The first law of thermodynamics. Energy cannot be destroyed, only moved around and change form. When actions are taken, there is a knock-on effect. And someone, somewhere will suffer. As long as it is not you right? That's all that matters, yeah? That doesn't work anymore. The world is too small now to fuck your neighbour over and hope no one sees it.

Maybe it all started for me when I was a junior DJ supplementing the non-paying music with paying backstage theatre gigs. Years of pushing wood. Being the lowest in the food chain. Sweeping our filth off the stage constantly so divas didn't cough. Literally catching the fat lady in Tosca when she jumped. Being overlooked and treated like shit by upper middle class performers who thought having an accent was a temporary job, not a lifelong condition. When you spend years standing in the wings, watching the show from the side, you get to see *everything*, warts and all. The division between performers and technicians. The fake... well the fake everything. The kissy-kissy mwah-mwah. The dirty shit. The massive wages for sometimes almost nothing, compared to the almost nothing wages for doing everything. Then the Acid House revolution came and precisely nothing happened. We got gentrified in record time.

In the same way that Tech-Bro 'disrupters' have nothing but scorn for the current businesses they are engaged in destroying, their EDM has no use for musical heritage. It's just another inconvenient thing to be explained-away at conferences with a politicians verve. The history is made to sound 'old' and obstructing essential technological progress. Nothing has changed since Elvis was created to allow white people to be able to take over rock and roll. Nothing. EDM is just white stadium Elvis, gyrating to distract from the fact black culture is being stolen outright. And hey, it's *just* a white face. Much of the time the face had nothing at all to do with any of the musical process. They didn't make the music and they don't mix it. Often black voices and black producers did the work the white frontman took full credit for. It's not new in electronica either, look at pioneering producer Yvonne Turner or Denise Johnson on 'Screamadelica'.

Let us define EDM more closely, as perhaps it is not clear what the distinction really is, and isn't that so very 2020? EDM is, as discussed, what the Americans late to the party have decided is a catch-all term for all genres of electronic music. What is less clear to an outside observer is that to us on the inside who do not subscribe to their re-branding, it is also a new genre of its own. One that is specifically very large, new, and frankly not-very-pleasant American stadium trance. Frequently childlike (as in actual nursery rhymes sometimes), poppy, basic, too fast and mastered way too loud, it is what passes for our scene if given steroids and a lobotomy. It is a Michael Bay film in audio form. And, of course, massively bloated with rather large amounts of dollars. This is the crucial part. It is not merely a cultural gentrification, it is very much economical. If that wasn't bad enough, the whole thing is so stale, pale and male that it is almost a travesty. A scene that was almost entirely a racial and sexual minority in the USA is now forced almost entirely underground, and the big money is entirely white and very heterosexual. Ker-Ching! Bought-out again. Appropriated. Capitalised. It's ironic that sound is genuinely used as a military weapon, literally, and now, more surreptitiously is the sword of globalisation. Sounds a bit over-the-top? Maybe. Perhaps not.

Another 90s UK superclub venture that rode high on trance and furry boots before eventually petering out was Birmingham based Godskitchen/Global Gathering. Headman Neil Moffitt ended up in Las Vegas and became essentially a frontman/partner for mega-wealthy Emirati Khadem al Qubaisi, who financed the Hakkasan empire. The Ultra-Rich are no strangers to controversy and colossal global financial adventures. Connections to Hakkasan have been suggested for naughty fugitive billionaire, Malaysian Jho Low. The 'most expensive club ever built' was theirs in Vegas in 2013, the titular giant Hakkasan. Arguably they are the biggest global EDM investors in the world, rolling out huge numbers of venues and restaurants across the planet. They're also one of the companies most happy to pay the massively inflated fees of the biggest EDM DJs. Behind each of these vast pay packets is almost unlimited money. Fuelling an inflation that others simply cannot match, and a general elevation of talent bills that arguably forces all costs upwards for everyone. Look at the rent crisis in Ibiza to see exactly how the arrival of billionaires raises the cost of almost everything. If you dig into the background of American EDM you will almost always see big money. Sometimes highly suspect money. Some might even argue that the EDM scene is an ideal front. A silly, fluffy party that is a perfect distraction, and Vegas is the perfect home for it, being built by gangsters, for gangsters. EDM as kompromat laundromat. The track 'Washing Machine' has never been more appropriate.

How far have we come, and how low did we go? Much of our scene is now quite literally the plaything of billionaires. Like pretty much everything else. Once more we follow the big picture to a tee.

Anyone switching-off here because you are *so* cool and it's not *your* scene that does all this hideous shit, sorry kid, newsflash. I've been personally in the room watching Arab money being invested in some of the coolest venues on the planet. Some of your favourite super hip, scowling DJs dressed as fake Edwardian chimney-sweeps are financed entirely by dirty oil. Where money is concerned, there is no 'cool'. They are some of the first to drop their pants when the big dollar dildos come a-knocking.

One of my DJ friends was very amused once that my killer New Year's gig was in Bournemouth. I like Bournemouth, it reminds me of those rare golden days of endless childhood bucket and spade holidays. It's pretty fancy round there in my mind. Not to her. She was doing New Year's in Dubai. Her powerful and famously rude manager was going too. A ladies outing. I tried to say something about it being a bit hostile towards girls but it was drowned out by a cheery and sarcastic "Enjoy Bournemouth!" as she tittered off to their first-class flights, champagne and a fat fee quadruple to my own.

As I was driving back from the coast the day after I got the call. She'd told the wrong Prince not to come into the booth, her manager had agreed with her. Both were now in jail. Ostensibly for being confident whilst in possession of vaginas. The look I got later did not brook the opportunity of any trace of told-you-so.

Many years later, in December 2019, a festival in Saudi Arabia managed to attract a raft of A-list 'underground' DJs, despite transparently being another strand of Crown Prince Mohammed bin Salman's efforts to improve the image of a country. A regime just lately implicated in the murder and dismemberment of journalist Jamal Khashoggi.

Alongside names you might expect from the EDM world and local DJs from the region, the state-funded event featured NYC House legend Danny Tenaglia, an openly gay man who made his name in the seminal gay clubs of 1990s New York. Ibiza big dogs Marco Carola, Black Coffee, Solomun and Jamie Jones were there. There were even a handful of women on the bill, including Techno doyenne Nicole Moudaber, and the rightly celebrated Korean trailblazer Peggy Gou. Gay, Black and female together, all consciously helping to burnish the reputation of a country where women have their life controlled by a man under the male guardian system. Where women from the day they are born denied the right to vote. A state where homosexual acts are punished with discrimination, fines, public beatings, chemical castration, imprisonment, torture and even death.

It's not like this was secret. The festival was called 'MDL BEAST' for fuck's sake. Just one month before, The Kingdom's security services had released a video officially categorising feminism, homosexuality and atheism as 'extremist' ideas. Amnesty International responded by saying: "It peels away the veneer of progress under Mohammed bin Salman and reveals The Kingdom's true intolerant face which criminalises people's identities, as well as progressive and reformist thoughts and ideas at home."

But a paycheck's a paycheck, right?

INTERLUDE
HERE ENDETH THE LESSON

Most pro DJs will be asked by a mate if they can teach them how to DJ at some point in their life. I've got a ban on it, personally. Having tried once, I've found I just don't have the elephantine patience required. Especially as most people think doing it is piss-easy. Thing is, it absolutely is! But so is running. And not everyone is Usain Bolt. Quag Allurgie's reaction to DJing around the turn of the millennium was that of nearly every other promoter in the UK. "I can do that." Although I think his actual words were:

"Uvspunndudlungarrunddzaysowurdcunnidbeh?"

Which roughly translated as: "I've spent that long around DJs, how hard can it be?"

Thus it befell me to teach him how to DJ. For Quag it wasn't a patient process to take place strategically over the next following years. It had to happen now, and he had to be performing within weeks. He chose his debut to be at GQ Magazine's yearly party. This year to take place at the sadly now closed but very legendary Wag in Soho's Chinatown. Quag was very well connected, but I feared this might be a step too far. Too much stick and not enough carrot. He figured it would be a doddle.

In those days, there was only one way to play records, which was to play records. I patiently (but frankly not very frequently) stood with Quag by some decks and explained the basics. He wasn't a complete novice. As well as being around it since the start he could bash out a few guitar chords in a punky way. Unfortunately, this led to perhaps a touch of over-overconfidence, possibly fuelled by large amounts of confidence, fuelled further by even larger amounts of drugs. Plus we decided that perhaps House and Techno and seamless mixing might not happen day one, so we aimed at a more eclectic flavour of jam.

I'm pretty patient by nature, but teaching anything is a lottery. Like a lot of things, some people take to it naturally. Some, however, take to things like a squid to a tuxedo. Like my mate 'Bootsy'. Bootsy was called Dave initially, but after he asked someone to teach him bass guitar, his name changed for life. It wasn't a mad request. He was a pro drummer in a successful group. Bass was the logical next step.

I sat with him a bit. Explained you need to find your fave tunes with your fave basslines and try to match them. Try easy ones first. I thought I was making progress. He packed himself away for a couple of months and after a whole summer of rumbling from his room he triumphantly emerged saying he was now ready. He had learned the bass guitar. We sat in awed wonder as he proceeded to play like clockwork with his right hand, each note landing correctly. His left however, didn't do anything. It just flubbed about the fretboard like a beached eel. I asked Bootsy (sorry but where I am from, when you get a nickname that is hard-earned, it sticks) if he could hear the modulation of notes that went up and down? Totally blank face. In those moments and subsequent quizzing I learnt that Bootsy, A PROFESSIONAL MUSICIAN, did not hear musical notes. We suddenly noticed all the favourite records of this drummer were records with drums featuring heavily. Music to him was like morse code. A constant stream of almost binary data. Pa-pa-pah pap, pap, pap. No melody at all. Didn't hear it.

I've since discovered over the years that while an extreme case, Bootsy isn't unusual. If there is a spectrum of senses, some people are synesthetes without question. Eternally plagued by their sensitivity. Some, albeit far FAR rarer than many claim, have golden ears and palates. Frankly, millions more hear bugger-all. I have mates who still only really hear the kick drum when they go out. One of my best mates thinks music is rubbish. Yeah, all of it. So there you go. What you assume to be a universal experience in the realm of the senses and emotions is nothing of the sort. As you will find out the hard way when you fall in love.

Meanwhile, back to Quag at The Wag. As the big day came around, I got the inevitable call that I had to drop everything and come to his debut. It wasn't a big ask. I was a regular at The Wag anyway. The GQ party was a pretty hot ticket back then. Why not? His set was early. I popped in.

I saw Quag's missus first. Very glad I was here, she told me. Quag had been throwing up. This touched me. I never saw him as someone nervous about anything. He was visibly terrified in the booth. All sweat and sharp movements held together with flapping hands. He spied me and gesticulated wildly to come into the booth.

I was asked again what this fader across the bottom did and what the knob at the top was for and I sighed, rolled my eyes and my sleeves and once again started to repeat the lessons about crossfaders and gain control…

Pausing to check he was paying attention I looked up at the growing crowd to see Quag, magically at completely the other end of the venue, raising a glass and grinning.

Left me to do the whole set for him.

He's since gone on to actually get paid for playing records, though granted mainly by himself at his own club. Not many can say they had the patience to try teaching Quag Allurgie to DJ.

One day I may even get to finish the job.

CHAPTER 13
THE PYRAMID SCHEME

I call the current crop of DJ top dogs and fat cats 'The 1%'. It's an arbitrary figure in the mathematical sense. There are so many DJs now it's probably more like 0.001% in terms of the general DJ population, but I intentionally choose a comparison with top businessmen because that is often what these guys are. Sorry, it's always guys, and they are nearly always white, but that is slowly changing. These are acts that not only dominate the top billings, they have prominent roles at an industry level too. Like Fortune 500 CEOs, they tend to fail upwards, their name recognition among the wider plebulace seemingly guaranteeing career immortality. They are perpetually wheeled out with their antediluvian suggestions for solving whatever the clubland crisis du jour is despite not making their own music or even selecting their own tracks since the turn of the century.

Fees? Set your faces for stunned. The biggest EDM beasts can get a million dollars for 90 minutes in Las Vegas. Yeah, they can't even be bothered to do the full two hours. A onepercenter regularly charges $150,0000 for a headline festival slot and $30,000 for a superclub set. Even your 'underground' stars ask me to pay them $20,000 when I promote gigs. To which I no longer even answer. Sadly someone very rich, in a place very awful, will certainly pay them this. The trouble with gentrification is once the price is driven up, almost nothing brings it down again and, before you know it, everything is more expensive. From the ticket to the toilet to the bottle of water.

The '1%' type of DJ breaks down further into second and third categories…

To attain 'Legend' status is as much luck as it is skill. DJing really isn't all that hard to learn, but being in the right place at the right time when it all started to explode throughout the 80s and 90s is pure luck. No, you will never be 'A Legend' if you were born too late. Sorry kid.

CHAPTER 13

Being Legendary can be specific to sub-genres and different locations and generations. Legends have nearly always been at it for at least 20 years, some 30 or more. No, you are not a legend if you played in a bumfuck town in a bar for 25 years, and I have met my share who think they are. Legendary status needs to have more than one person agreeing upon it. Ideally, a lot of people. It's a business, and success isn't only measured in hours at the wheel. Unfortunately.

Legends as well as being in the right-time-right-place have put out records and remixes by the dozen and are generally an integral part of something larger. A movement, an equally legendary venue, even an era or a city. Not all are highly handled by top managers and agents, but the reason they have lasted where their peers have not is usually down to very good representation along the way. Legends, however, are often completely unknown to the younger generation. A gap that is only going to widen. Like fairies, Legends die when you stop believing.

The EDM boom, fuelled by social media, reinvigorated major labels and a resurgence of festival culture in the US and indeed across the world, and has been very good at artificially inflating a new star to the top, as we have seen recently with billionaires buying careers. This happens through forms of graft and payola, as well as old fashioned strong-arm management. I call this type 'The Nouveau-Big'. Now and then, for no reason you can fathom, you will see some new moon-faced gurner leering at you from a magazine or inexplicably headlining a major event. These names are elevated to the top through force of money and connections. Most are almost devoid of talent or have made a pact with Satan about appealing strictly to the lowest common denominator. Sometimes you will see them billed above A Legend. This is very wrong. Not all are 'EDM' johnny-come-latelies. Some were lifted by previous big genres like Trance. The principle is the same. They are bangwagoneers. Confined to the genre forever. They are still 1% though due to the vast wages. You cannot take that away. I guess one day, if they don't fuck it up, they might be legendary. Maybe. Perhaps not.

Next down the rung we have the 'International DJ' who travels the world working but don't command the BIG money, although what they get is often very generous. At the lower end, £1000 a club gig, at the upper as much as £10K. They are frequently the second on the bill to 'The 1%', but headliners in their own right across the world. The most successful 'underground' DJs are at this level. Globally known, and highly-paid, despite the loud claims of Teflon credibility. For some reason (yes, we know the reasons and will speak about them later) women rarely get higher than this level and at this height they are very few in number. International DJs are the top DJs you are most likely to see in your town. It is about as high up the food chain as anyone can reasonably expect to get after about 15-20 years hard at the game. An 'International DJ' is as far as working hard can get you without the luck of birth or massive cash investment behind 'The 1%'.

Like actors, only about 10% of all the DJs in the world actually work at it full time. 'Mid-Rangers' are full-time DJs who are very well known but don't have that 'star' quality that means they guarantee a full venue or large ticket price. Often known outside their own land, but not pan-globally, these are the infantry. They can sometimes be lower-level international DJs, often headline themselves, but more usually have a less glamorous timeslot. The Middle is an area in constant flux with DJs coming up from below or dropping down from above. A strong 'Mid-Ranger' can have a good lengthy career and never need the big time. They can often manage themselves, giving them the freedom to play gigs based on quality and their interest, rather than on the numbers. It's a good, honest place to be, a broad church of good and bad gigs with a fair dose of reality. Some of them even have a 'real' job on the side, or interests outside of wages, where their name goes on the bill, or who has the cocaine.

'Veterans' are often DJs from further up this list who have dropped down over the years. They are highly regarded in their own land or are hard-working local heroes. Some are fully committed to the 'underground' and refuse to move higher either through neglect or design. Some 'Veterans' are actually quiet 'Legends' who were too difficult, too humble, too mad, or just too unlucky to get the full legendary status. Or they had the wrong, or no, management. 'Veterans' can also be 'International', and/or 'Mid-Rangers' but have become stuck somewhere beneath their potential and have to be prised and cajoled out of their niche. 'Veterans' are often low down on a bill when they really should not be. What they have gained in skill and experience they sometimes lose in pulling-power and prestige. A humble Vet can have a good, solid career. A troubled ego can be burned badly by the years of being under-appreciated. 'Veterans' are often forced into part-time work due to an increasing lack of demand. Some give up the DJ life completely. Or do the eternal grand retirement/don't-call-it-a-comeback shuffle. A conversation with them can either be a fascinating insight into an alternative narrative of the scene or an embittered lament, depending on how much they feel they've been shafted down the years.

'Hip Kids' are the new up-and-coming names, and can actually be on a par with higher ranks due to our cultural worship of youth, and blind obsession with the new. Only a tiny handful last longer than two or three years before disappearing again. Often this is the next generation simply getting on with the business of being the next big thing. Sometimes they are our saviours. There can be hostility between the new and old guard. Kids just want the Olds to get out of the way. The Olds think Kids aren't doing anything new. It's all about 'ownership'. Both think they own the night. They don't. They rent it off each other without even realising.

'Working DJs' are the small army of DJs who do the weddings, play the bars, cruise ships and corporate events. They might have their own sound system, a van and lights. They will own a microphone and may even use it. They might sometimes be convinced they are a big deal, but the gigs say otherwise. They sometimes bear no resemblance at all to what we understand a DJ to be, but may appear to be the most authentic type of DJ to someone over 60. They most resemble the DJs of yore who spoke between records and made people happy by playing music they expect to hear and already know. Some of these guys are just hard workers who slum it for cash and have a side-career as one of the other DJ types listed here. Personally, I always say that when you've played for years in hostile environments and survived intact, it's a badge of honour. An awful lot of Legends came up through the ranks starting off like this. It's one of the reasons they are legendary. Only a wanker looks down on other DJs. There but for the grace of God etc.

'The Gentlemen Amateur' is a new type: well-heeled 40 and even 50-somethings who have started to call themselves DJs. They have well-paid full-time jobs which funds large record collections and sometimes operate small promotions for mates, once a month or every two. Sometimes just a few times or even once a year. They are similar to period war recreation-enactors. You know, nerds who dress up as soldiers from the past. They are all fixated on the historical, hilarious in their seriousness and believe themselves utterly superior to everyone. Due to having a good income and a closed loop of friends they can pretend to have credibility and authenticity and only do things now and then entirely on their own terms, warm in the bosom of the lie that they are 'for real'. Blissfully ignorant of having to do it for a living and what that entails, and always the most vocal critics of those who do. All done with the social media footprint of a drunken Brontosaurus. Sometimes they were themselves formerly pro DJs who were forced through circumstance, kids or spouses to give it up, get a life, and treat this bullshit like the nonsense it is. However, well-meaning or experienced, they are hobbyists. There's absolutely nothing wrong with having a hobby. They're also, to be brutal, a fucking plague on the biz sometimes. You get to a certain age and you tend to lean more towards the right-wing side of life, get loud opinions and feel you know better. It's old man nonsense.

Compared to horrific 'Plastic DJs' the 'Gentleman Amateurs' are a gift. 'Plastics' can be any age or genre. They usually started within the last five years or sooner. They are in love with the *idea* of being a DJ but have little knowledge of music or what the job actually entails. They generally use the cheapest tech, the internet, and cobble together music from other DJs and use Shazam instead of their ears and experience. It's a new phenomenon as the technology itself is fairly new. Plastic DJs can be your next-door neighbour or they could be superstars. They can be promoters-turned-DJ or even major producers suddenly thrust onto the circuit clutching a cheap DJ controller or pre-recorded set in the hope of consolidating another fat revenue stream. One or two legendary record producers are plastic DJs. What unites them all is a misplaced belief that DJing skills come from labour-saving devices and cutting corners, rather than experience and hard work. There is nothing wrong with tech, all the types of DJ mentioned above use all different types of gear. But it begins and ends with the gear with Plastic DJs. Frequently they can only use certain types of devices and are lost when outside of their comfort zone. Plastic DJs are amateurs who think they are professionals. DJing is an attitude not a technical issue, even though they themselves will always argue it on technical points. Plastics should not ever be confused with...

'The Beginner'. Unlike their counterparts above, 'The Beginner' is not trying to cut corners or 'become a DJ', they just love music. In time they will become good DJs regardless of tech or fashions. They have an understanding of what is ahead of them and recognise there is some humility required. It is in the blood. They have the right stuff.

Even worse than a 'Plastic DJ' is 'The Chancer'. Someone using their looks, tits, biceps, influential parents, silly hat or a gimmick to overshadow the music completely. (Yes, thank you, I use a mask sometimes recently because I have to). If legit DJs are painters or sculptors, 'Chancers' are jugglers or ventriloquists. All they care about is if people are looking at them. Avoid. At all costs.

Which one am I? I've been nearly all of them at some point, although I've never troubled the 1% zone in any financial sense, and few would describe me as a legend, more a horror story. I've never been a chancer but then again if someone hates you enough you can look bad to them whatever you do, however innocent. I wouldn't be qualified to write this book if I'd not been up and down the ladder more than once.

Inevitably, the more Chancers and Plastic DJs are celebrated, the more they undermine the craft itself. The introduction of the 'sync' button to CD decks was a watershed moment, but there are systems now that completely do it all for you. A new app called 'PLSY' is being developed that allows club-goers to vote on which song the DJ should play next during their set. Users can search and select a song from their music libraries for their suggestion, and whichever track receives the majority vote from the crowd will be played next. Eventually, all my types of DJ mentioned above could be extinct.

I actually first heard about fully automated DJing in the late 90s. Some German scientists had an array of sensors in a club that could read the temperature, crowd noise and even could register when hands went in the air. A computer read these 'responses' and would 'choose' the next record accordingly and mix it in. Allegedly it didn't do a bad job, which is highly debatable as it could only play Trance.

There is of course, also a slew of other tech that automates the DJing process. These are hardly red hot news either. Unbelievably, it is now industry standard to not be expected to mix. These arguments are even alarmingly antique. Even Spotify mixes for you now. The difference here is that this fresh tech is now skewed more towards the crowd. In effect, making the DJ finally and entirely obsolete, and fully cementing the concept of what we hold dear as being nothing more than a very large and *very* expensive jukebox wearing inappropriate sportswear.

In essence we are gradually approaching, if not accidentally, the singularity at the murky heart of the whole thing, i.e. 'what is the DJ *for?*' After all, is not the purpose of modern capitalism to be 'disruptive'? Or to be more blunt, to destroy and replace? So if the tunes are chosen by algorithm, or at best because they resemble each other greatly, and then technology mixes them, is all that is left entirely about looking good or loudly displaying some sort of gimmick or a highly PC or edgy image? Is the next step all about removing the DJ entirely from the equation? After all, we are arguably almost at that point. Personally, I wouldn't mind a long holiday.

This does, of course, hinge entirely on the idea of requests or even the opinion of the dancefloor being important. I would argue that they are not. Naturally, I do not think anyone's taste in music but mine matters. Sadly these days that is also what absolutely *everyone* thinks. Possibly always have. Conversely, the *act* of making a request does have value to the person asking. As a DJ, you're a professional, allegedly, and as such, it is your job to listen, nod and smile. Then utterly ignore the track they ask for, unless it is any good and one you were actually about to play, which simply never happens. All they want is to be seen to be in

CHAPTER 13

the booth and talk to you. Being nice costs nothing. All this 'respect the DJ' prissy bollocks is well daft. It's part of the myth that DJs are more important than the music. We are not. A line is being drawn asking if DJs are more vital to the process than those who have paid for the DJ to be there. Then we have to wonder, are people now merely paying to see a minor celebrity pretend to perform, or are they there to listen and dance to an authentic set of skills? All good questions. And ultimately, of course, a request is a question.

Requests can very much get out of hand, however. I mean, I am always quite pleasant and attentive to people who come at me while I am working. I think it is the mark of a professional to be so. No one is perfect, however.

Many years ago, back when people considered the job of the DJ to be able to mix together, live, two or even three records that might not ordinarily go together, I had a few tricks that I might roll out if the vibe was right. One of which was to play a very famous pop record over the top of a very cool dance record. NO WAY! You cry! Well, yes, before you stop reading, I should point out that this was some time before technology allowed people to do mash-ups and re-edits of their own. In fact, at this time, the only way to do it was live with two records. Or in a *very* expensive studio, which no one did because you'd want to spend that large money making an original record. It was very popular when I did do it. People cheered. I felt good. I used to do it regularly at my residency.

Unbeknownst to me and probably entirely coincidentally, another DJ decided to actually make what we called then 'a bootleg'. Which was basically the same pop record with a modern beat under it. Suddenly my party piece was everywhere, at every disco in town.

The last time I did this piece was when a kid came up to the booth and asked very politely, for about the 30th time that night, when I was going to play the bootleg by the other DJ I'd been playing every week for the past year that he loved so much...

I stopped the record that was played, turned to him and screamed:

IT'S NOT A FUCKING BOOTLEG SON! IT'S THE ORIGINAL RECORD PLAYED SIMULTANEOUSLY WITH ANOTHER RECORD.

YOU MIGHT HAVE HEARD OF THE PROCESS... IT IS CALLED DJING!!

I immediately hated myself for it, if only for the look on his little face. I never played the two records again. And afterwards, I was always particularly nice towards people making requests.

Maybe we should all adopt the method pioneered by Kevin Saunderson, original Detroit Techno pioneer and Inner City legend. When he played at a gig a friend helped organise, he insisted on a bottle of tequila and two shot glasses. This is in London's Corsica Studios before it was refurbed, and anyone could just go up to the side of the booth and be right there next to the DJ. It was quite annoying to be fair. Saunderson sits the tequila and the glasses on the booth door, and anytime someone comes up too close, he would grab them, say "SHUT UP!" pour a shot, make them down it, and then say "Good! Now, *fuck off!*".

Perhaps the trouble is a degree of pomposity and lack of respect for each other, individuals in the crowd thinking the DJ is there to be their personal music curator at best or disposable pasty flesh jukebox at worst. While DJs think the people in the crowd are a heaving mass of barbarians who know nothing about music. None of these things are true. Unity was at the heart of the brief beauty that was Acid House. It can be again if we try.

Further to the question of whether the DJ matters at all, is how to tell whether they are actually any good, or whether there are also things to help you spot someone authentic. Here are five things I just made up that a pro DJ spots in other DJs that reveals they are a bit special, rather than merely workmanlike. Not that there is anything at all wrong with getting the job done. And hey, listen! I am not a superior being by any means. I've just been doing it an absurdly long time. That is all. And there are some things you spot in other DJs that perhaps others do not. Good things. Things that shout 'PROFESSIONAL'. You will certainly have your opinions, perhaps a professional has stronger ones that may be of interest. The details are often unclear. Subtle. Small even. But short of sniffing each other's arses, these are the signs that seem to show up often enough in the truly *great*, rather than merely just passably good:

Attitude is everything. It's a broad church, however. It's not merely 'professionalism' which is often merely code for someone who toes the line. It's a strong positivity. I don't mean in the slightly deranged Californian sense. I mean a clear 'can-do' approach to everything. Great DJs are frequently easygoing. Problem solvers, not problem makers. The 'diva' days are long over, ain't nobody got time for that. Or the money to burn on daft caprices. A good attitude often means speaking another language or two. These and other small skills indicate a head that is still learning. Respectful. This is made none-more-clear than the vast droves of ambitious hopefuls decamping to Berlin and then not learning a word of German. Coming back home a few years later wondering why they didn't make it. 'Attitude' is the opposite of entitlement.

Item two: *nothing fazes them*. A proper DJ can use any set-up. Anything. They could make people dance banging two rocks together if it came to it. Sure they have their preferences, demands even, but if push comes to shove it is about them and not the tech. Their technique starts in their heads, not their hands. If you took that DJ and just dropped them in any situation with nothing but the shirt on their back, they don't just manage, they SHINE. This is an important distinction.

A truly great DJ can play with other people's tunes and sound better than their owner. I once saw Derrick Carter play Ralph Lawson's box 'cos Derrick's got lost by the airline and, afterwards, Ralph was blown away. Like: 'I didn't even know that B-side existed'. Another great moment was when I was in the booth with Danny Tenaglia, and we were chatting and laughing, and I saw the CDJ playing was running down with like 20 seconds to spare, he caught my look, and I swear it was almost too fast to see he whipped the next CD in, cued it and mixed it in flawlessly while barely pausing mid-sentence. This kind of calm only really comes from decades in the glare. Live pressure is no pressure at all. This assurance also allows the owner of it to take risks. A dull, timid selector is petrified of standing out. A great DJ stands out as policy.

'Going with the flow' is the third thingy to look out for. A great DJ might have a unique sound but is able to fit into the larger picture effortlessly. They understand the whole. The thing isn't there for them, they are there for it. They don't play pre-arranged sets or parrot by rote. They are able to improvise. Flex. They arrive with everything they need to do whatever is required. Sometimes everything at a gig can be in great disarray. For example...

I once arrived at a huge superclub and the manager had decided to shut down half the venue because 'January'. He had no clue about DJs, the promoter didn't exist, it was 'in-house'. He panicked and started giving *mad* orders. Kids who'd never played outside their bedroom were suddenly in the main room. Legends who cost more than all the other DJs put together were in the side room. Warm-up DJs played last. Carefully set-up tech was taken down. Everything was on its head. People started arguing about billing, threatening to leave, demanding to be paid without performing. Literally, everything that could do wrong went wrong and then got wronger. Thing is, stuff like this happens *all the time*. A pro arrives to all kinds of weird situations. If all you have is your tired schtick that cannot change or an ego that is painfully swollen, it's just a matter of time before you will be unable to deliver in a situation you are being paid for.

Most of all, being loose and fluid is about paying attention. A great DJ walks in a room and knows pretty much immediately what is going on and what needs to happen. That is more than likely because that is about the twelvety-tenth thousandth time they have walked in somewhere. And paying attention leads to...

Number four. 'Subtlety'. This doesn't relate to matters of taste. The most brutal Techno can be delivered with restraint and intelligence. Great DJs understand nuance. They work with the sound crew, not against them. They understand everyone's job in the place. They know not to interfere with security, not to bosh gear in front of cameras and punters. Know how harassed the bar staff can be. Levels are manageable in the booth. There are no red lines. Or white lines. They clean up after themselves as they go. How to frame an issue in diplomatic terms. They use their ears instead of eyes. They are in-step with the arc of the night. They build a set. They don't hammer bangers out when playing early. They feel the crowd's energy. Respond to it. There is *consideration* also. Like knowing that there are other folk working there that want to go home at the end of the night. Or like right now as I am writing this, there is a 'big name DJ' doing a photoshoot opposite my house in Ibiza. He's brought a *huge* sound system just so he can 'get in the mood'. He's currently ruining everyone's day within a ten-mile radius, something he specialises in at the best of times. MEE-OW!

Grace is what I look for most of all. I'm not talking about thin legs, long necks and nice shoes. Although who doesn't like a good shoe? 'Grace' is how you deal with *being* a DJ. Understanding that it's not a crime against humanity for someone to want to talk to you. Being kind. Being able to talk about other DJs with respect. Not getting in a tizzy when advice is given. Holding down the ego.

There was a gig I was doing years ago with a radio and TV star, at the time she was on magazine covers. After the gig, the booth was utterly mobbed. And a bit unpleasant with it. She just stood there for hours not letting any of it get out of hand, said a few words to everyone who wanted them and most amazingly of all, the next day at stupid o'clock in the morning, without making any notes, remembered every single shout-out and demand from the night before. It's all about being an oasis of calm instead of a mad, flappy crisis. And listen, not all the greats have all the above, the holy five. But they are signs, clues perhaps, that someone has *something*. And they are things most people do not consciously observe at all, but perhaps feel. They are just things I see that crop up again and again in the ones that we tend to admire. I wish I could do them all. But having a code to aspire to is certainly something, rather than nothing.

INTERLUDE
THE SHIT CHAUFFEUR

It was now Saturday afternoon in the eternal vortex of Tour Manager and Sticks, and I was the least fucked up, as per. This was entirely relative, you understand. Due to this condition, I was elected to go to the petrol station for supplies, despite being the only one who actually had to carry on and go to work later. Again. My whole life seems to revolve around Esso, BP, Shell and other giant polluters. I've probably spent more times in them than in any hotel, house, flat or residence that I'm actually supposed to live in. I've put more shit snacks from them in me than petroleum in any vehicle. In the heyday of rave, petrol stations were the epicentre of the movement. The place we would meet. The saviour when lost. The significance of them is not to be sniffed at. Despite any kind of shop, outlet or supermarket being closer, when you are fucked-up, for some reason petrol stations are where you go. Something to do with being in a car and it almost being drive-thru. Always open. Safer. Homogenous. Not part of the row of shops on a street, or even a part of the ordinary world entirely. Neutral territory. They are like a space station for lost astronauts and I am the shiny galactic patron saint of Ginsters.

I'm taking a great risk with this tale because up until now I'm fairly well behaved, but on this occasion, I was not. I did something I had rarely done before and never once did again. I got behind the wheel of a car in a poor state. I wasn't staggering, but I'd not been to bed. It was the litany of the eternally stupid to say; "it's really not far". It really wasn't! It was like, less than a mile. What could possibly go right? I got into T-Man's stupidly awesome car, on his behest I might add. On the grounds that; 'it was my turn'. Saturday lunchtime was a bad idea. Despite happening every week since the dawn of time, it is something that constantly surprises me. In part because I am so rarely awake for it, in others because it is so busy. I'm a touch agoraphobic, or I might just not like crowds. Peak times make me anxious. It's one of the reasons I am nocturnal. I've been trained since an early age to see Normals as dangerous. This is their time. Things as perplexing to me as carpentry is to a cat would take place. Football. Shopping. Chatting. Parks and pubs. Weird shit.

Just a hop and a skip away. Five mins there. Five back. 'Preposterous amounts of sugar, cigarettes and empty carbs for my two elderly amigos please, nothing for me thanks' I repeated in my head, so I wouldn't forget. At least I only had to remember what I was going there for. I had to go really 'cos the other two could easily forget why they were going. The last time we sent T-Man out for night supplies, he promptly forgot why he was driving, drove directly home and went to bed. We were still waiting for the booze, mixers and tobacco three days later. I was repeating the list in my head, stationary at the traffic lights when the car was hit with a terrific BOOM! I almost soiled myself.

I looked around frantically. There was no car behind and nothing in front but a red light. I even looked up through the sunroof. To my left on the pavement was some sort of church. I say 'some sort' as it was one of those modern ones that had taken over a building that wasn't a church. All I could see was about 100 African folks, in splendid robes, as if it was a Sunday. Maybe it was a wedding. Then one of them, an authoritarian man of substance clearly, knocked on the window and explained a kid had run into the side of the car. Now I had to drive them to the hospital.

"Wait, what? Who?" was about all I could manage. So he explained once again carefully that one of the kids from the church had run full-on into the car and I needed to take him to hospital. I did hear a kid crying, quite loudly. When I looked in the rear-view mirror to see if I was holding up traffic, I nearly went through the sunroof like it was an ejector seat. I like to think I said something cool and witty but I just squeaked "hare" for some reason. I don't know how they did it without me noticing, but the back seat was packed with African folks in full best regalia. I mean magnificent matching robes, headpieces and accessories. Small child in the middle, bawling like an air raid siren.

"So you take them now, God be with you," said the pastor in the window. For he was clearly in charge, and Jesus was his co-pilot, sadly not mine. I was so freaked out it didn't even occur to me for a second to ask any questions or even get out of the car. I was in a ridiculously fancy vehicle, in broad daylight, with a crying child, possibly seriously injured, and apparently his entire family. Plus I was, at the very least, overtired. Not in my car, either. 'Just popping to the shops'. I was too flipped-over to wonder why none of this was good and why I felt a combination of existential terror and crushing guilt. In a dream, I just started to drive.

I addressed the crew in the back, asking where they wanted to go. How badly hurt was he? Where had he hit? Which hospital? I just got blank looks. One lady addressed the other, recognised one word and said "hospital" back to me.

They didn't speak any English.

Great. The streets were packed with cars. On top of everything else my cunning plan to get to the petrol station involved trying to avoid traffic and taking unfamiliar back streets. Within minutes I was lost. I had absolutely no idea where the nearest hospital was. I drove east. I drove west. North and south. Every turn was bumper to bumper. The kid kept crying. Which did not calm the situation one bit. I tried to catch his eye in the mirror and made a face, which seemed to make him scream and fart simultaneously. He farted so hard you could see actual gas. I could not tell if he had passed wind or chosen a new pope. The folks in the back were chatting amiably in a language I could not place if my life depended on it. No one tried to placate the kid. They kept touching and gesturing to his head, which freaked me out even more as head trauma is what is known in medical circles as 'very bad'. I was starting to freak out. In retrospect, I should have just made for the hospital far away that I knew of, but I figured in my panic it was an emergency and I must get to the nearest one. Time was of the essence with possible brain damage. I had a lightbulb moment. I stopped the car at what can only be described at an angle usually reserved for the police, and sought help. What this entailed was my forming an impromptu roadblock and cars creeping around mine and honking angrily and no one helping at all. Then a cab approached. Thank God! He slowed and wound his window down.

"Listen, I've got an injured kid in here and I have literally no idea where the nearest hospital is. I've got (frantic rummaging) FORTY English pounds here if you can take them to the nearest A&E department."

"Keep your blood money mate," he quipped as he drove off.

Shit.

I think getting out of the car helped. I realised I was on my own with this thing, and that a smaller city hospital was closer than I realised. Well, close on foot. Miles around a city centre loop system. Eventually, I pulled into the part reserved for ambulances and emergency. Grabbed the still bawling kid and ran inside. The family coming after. Still chatting. Suddenly I heard some words of French come from behind.

"Arretez! Vous parlez Francais?"

"Bien Sur! Couramment."

If only I hadn't been so racist as to assume they could only speak one language we might have been talking for the last 90 minutes.

The wait to be seen, of course, was lengthy. Eventually, I learned from the family the kid was crying so much 'cos he'd been told off. As soon as a nurse gave him a lolly, he was fine. His mum was a very devout Christian who had come to the UK to escape religious persecution, she told me, as patiently as she could with my hampered abilities. I should note I can't speak French in any serious sense, but I understand it sufficiently in a crisis and can speak it comically poorly, school-level. The doctor did all the tests humanly possible. He came out eventually.

"There is literally nothing wrong. This is the healthiest kid we've ever had in here."

To say the relief was palpable is an understatement. I eventually, with much ado, got them back not only to the church but to their home. I should have done what Chudleigh did in Ibiza when there was a car incident. He was, and is, a very successful stylist to the stars. He was a bit frazzled as he'd just landed off the back of the Liberty X Dairylea Dunkers tour, which amused me so much I nearly burst. He was ready to unwind with extreme prejudice, and unbeknownst to me was carrying a very large stash. As we approached a tailback, I leaned out of the window and saw it was one of the usual Guarda Civil roadblocks checking every vehicle in that very Spanish way of getting their quota done all on one go.

"Police roadblock, might be a while."

To which The Chud, who was driving, simply undid his seatbelt, put the handbrake on, opened the door and legged-it. Simply ran at a right angle to the road across a newly-ploughed field, churning up dust like a roadrunner to the horizon. Leaving the hire car like the Marie Celeste.

Back at the final dropping-off point with my new friends, I was given many blessings, some of which I may still be able to cash-in one day upstairs. There was, of course, an utterly sobering aspect to the whole thing that essentially purged and re-set me within seconds of it first happening. I'd almost forgotten the rest of the equally intense weekend. I got back to HQ approximately seven hours after I left.

"Where's the cigarettes?" was the reply from Sticks, as if I'd left 10 minutes ago.

I went purple with rage and then took about 30 minutes to explain in great detail why I was empty-handed and for a solid two, possibly three hours, I thought I had killed a child or committed him to being a vegetable for life. Then it dawned on me. The car had been stationary. I was completely innocent. Had been the entire time.

"Is my car alright?" said Tour Manager.

CHAPTER 14
BAD EGGS

While the previous chapter may have pointed to things like grace and professionalism as marking out the ideal DJ, it would be a hideous mistake to assume that the industry actively rewards or indeed encourages these traits in any way whatsoever. Nope, the upper echelons of the DJ game, though undoubtedly containing some very fine individuals, are also a haven for some of the most spoiled, avaricious, devious, indulged and often deranged people you'll find outside of a Tory cabinet. Having been everything from auxiliary tech support to promoter to, yes, OK, pampered DJ, I've seen all sides.

My friend, the promoter, booked a 'new techno' act, a month or so before their highly successful album dropped and became a large hit. To join pioneering Legit Techno Legend and others onto the bill. The new kid headliners' agent then started emailing trying to wangle out of the gig, as 'new techno' had hit the big time and were getting much more money and bigger shows offered, as is the wont of the biz. However, they were under contract, so sudden attempts at "we need a five-star hotel / we need flights for girlfriends" didn't hold water. In the end, a settlement was reached, with them getting a private dressing room loaded with champagne. Bear in mind that this is for a 500 capacity sweaty lo-fi Techno party.

On the night, 'new techno' were less than agreeable to the promoters, like 'you are extremely lucky and privileged to have the chance to book such an illustrious act such as us etc'... but they still pandered and fawned somewhat over Legit Legend, who had just come back from nearly a decade away.

One of the new kids went up to Legend and said:
"So, what do you think of our music?"
Dude replied, "No idea, not heard any".
"Really? *You don't know our stuff?*"

"Mate, I invented techno. Don't need to keep up with the latest fads."
A glorious moment. If not a trifle awkward.

* * *

One of my personal bugbears is acts who perpetuate an online persona of 'love and light' and constant good vibes but in reality are horrific to work with, some borderline psychotic. Nothing but virtue-signally gestures day after day after day but the minute they arrive at the gig they treat everyone around them like shit. You know how if you go on a date and the person you are with is delightful and funny, but the minute the staff come to the table they change completely and treat them like servants? Yeah. That.

My promoter friend was keen to book Acid Hero and managed to persuade him to do a show. Acid Hero's whole social media persona is highly lovey-dovey, his mastering studio is in the backyard of his house, lots of photos showing how his wife and son come in and help etc. Real family guy vibes, and *loads* of POSITIVITY. Booking him is, of course, a pain in the arse. Even though the date was secured months in advance, flights aren't booked until a week beforehand because he keeps umming and ahhing about when he wants to travel - so they're expensive as fuck. The night before the show, an *entirely* different tech spec arrives via email, including very specific mixer etc. One that turns out to be an unbelievable arse-on to hire. In the end, the promoter found an artist who used one and paid them to strip it out of their studio for about four times the cost of normal kit hire.

The day comes, and Acid Hero arrives, driver picks him up at the airport and Promoter goes to the hotel to meet him. His first words are complaints about the taxi driver parking too far away from the terminal. Promoter takes him into his posh apartment that was hired, he looks about sneering "It'll do I guess". Promoter leaves him and goes to prep for the night. When they come back to pick him up for the soundcheck, he has a young Brazilian girl in his apartment. An escort.

He brings her to the soundcheck, where it turns out he hasn't even gotten batteries for half his kit, so Promoter is going about service stations trying to find C size batteries for a 303 and 9v's for pedals. Gets back and Acid Hero is complaining that the sound engineers are idiots. This is at a major venue, one of great reputation. They know their shit. They are far from idiots.

After soundcheck is dinner. The restaurant is a five-minute walk from the venue. Acid Hero refuses to walk, asks for a taxi. The taxi ride is 90 seconds. Promoter still has to sort out getting all the kit ready, so they agree to leave a deposit with the restaurant to cover Acid Hero, and his escort's, meal. In the region of £100. Promoter leaves to sort out some stuff, then comes back to collect him.

"How was your meal?"

Acid Hero, in front of the waiting staff, replies, "It was not great".

The bill came to something like £40, but he still pocketed the change from £100 and did not leave a tip. He's getting £2500 fee plus flights and hotels etc...

When the night kicks off, Support DJ is playing before him. Acid Hero complains loudly when the kid plays a couple of his older tracks as a tribute "WHY IS THE DEEJAY PLAYING MY MUSIC!?". He's backstage and the other acts have left because he's continually being a rather obnoxious dick. By this point, even the escort, who is permanently by his side and has been giving everyone pained glances, now starts actually apologising to people for his behaviour. He is sober throughout, no drink, no drugs. He plays his set, overruns 15 minutes despite several warnings from the stage manager and myself, eventually having his sound cut at the desk, so he strops off stage in a tantrum.

Promoter's wife then takes him and the escort back to his hotel in a taxi. We must mention, he's 6'3" and probably 20+ stone. Wife is five months pregnant, she's 5'2". He gets out of the taxi and just walks into the hotel, Mrs Wife says: "What about your bags?" and he just silently waves at her and the escort to bring them, so these two tiny people lug his flight cases of equipment back into the room. He is, according to my bud, literally the most unpleasant person they have ever booked. The annoying thing though, as is frequently the case, his set was absolutely fucking belting brilliant.

An American Legend was booked for a gig in London. His condition on the single gig and one night trip from the US was that he wanted to bring his wife, so he got two *very* expensive tickets bought for them both.

The driver rang from the airport saying the luggage wouldn't fit in the car, so we had to book someone with a seven-seater. Promoter met them at the hotel, Legend gets out with a dainty day bag, his wife gets out, and then the driver rolls out one of those enormous wheeled hard cases. The kind that a grown man could sit inside. It is hot pink. It stands maybe six feet tall, insane. This is for ONE NIGHT.

They don't want a meal, so the Promoter sticks £100 on the room tab and heads back to the venue. When he gets to the venue, the phone goes. It's the hotel. Mr and Mrs Legend have already maxed out the room tab on fried chicken. £100 worth of fried chicken in 20 minutes. Promoter puts another £50 on the tab over the phone and then gets working prepping for the night. Phone goes again an hour or so later - the hotel needs to charge for laundry services. Promoter is mightily confused:

"*Laundry?* Are you sure?"

"Yes Sir, your guests have put over a dozen items in to be dry cleaned. Dresses, mainly."

His missus had flown over her laundry from America so that the gig would pay for it to be dry cleaned, on a one-night trip to the UK. Amazing.

The most egregious story of this sort of everyday, low-level DJ bad behaviour for me was a certain American Pioneer who always had a rep as someone a little demanding, but on one trip to the UK really outdid himself. As well as the usual imaginary difficulties, drags, petulant demands and daft fees he would *never* get paid at home, during the gig someone let off a firework in the club. It wasn't anything super-dramatic, a species of banger for celebratory purposes. Pioneer immediately stopped everything and started making out like he was injured. The thing had gone off nowhere near him and, more importantly, there were people surrounding him in, and outside, the booth, all apparently unharmed. Everywhere there were people in the packed venue, including techs who were working next to the percussive sound, far closer to it than he was. Then the dramas started. The gig ended immediately.

CHAPTER 14

He was sick. Wounded. Affronted to the core. How could anyone do this to such a legendary figure? He couldn't work. He was traumatised. Just him. No one else. Then the online started. To *pray* for him. For his damaged career, body and soul. Didn't people understand how delicate he was? How much money he was going to lose over his 'recovery'?

Yeah, funnily enough, he was working again couple weeks later. Apparently completely unharmed. I guess Jesus wasn't deaf either.

CHAPTER 15
'SLEBZ 'N' SCHLUBS

I've brushed lightly against the rich and truly famous. It's an odd world. I don't seek it out and I cannot exist in it for long. I need an aqualung and a large iron helmet ideally. The only thing I really envy or love about wealth is *boats*. I love watching boats, smelling boats, getting in boats and getting out of them. I like big ones and little ones, fast or slow. I have since I was a kid. In Ibiza, I'm in boat heaven.

Few years ago, I was sitting on the dock of the bay, like Otis Redding, and had the pleasure of seeing what was, at that time, the largest privately-owned sea-going vessel. It was Tommy Hilfiger's yacht. A monster so large it had TWO helicopters at either end. It was so huge and cumbersome it took two pilot vessels to guide it in and dock. Slightly overshadowed by this was the arrival not long after of Puff Daddy. Or P. Diddy. Or whatever he was then. Hilfiger's vessel was so large and the port so busy, Diddy's glam arrival was something of a damp squib as it was forced to turn around and moor much further away in a dingy corner where the flotsam collected.

At the time, my girlfriend was bang into high fashion. The following night she got an invite plus one to a very posh sounding event at what was at the time Ibiza's only genuinely five-star hotel. A fashion do. As dos go, I do not do well at these things. I am doo-doo. More a don't for me than a do. Uncharacteristically, I like to hug the walls at things like this, like a chronically shy poltergeist.

I'd only been to one other fashion thing. I don't know anything about fashion so I figured I'd go to this Vivienne Westwood event I was invited to one time 'cos you know, I once was a 12-year-old punk. It was in fact a 'smelling' of her new perfume. Which was doubly ridiculous, as years of drug abuse mean I only have half an operational nostril and can't smell anything other than fear and a crowd's disappointment. Anyway, I was sat in the corner of the 'smelling' and Westwood is COLOSSALLY late and everyone is in a high panic, but I'm on the free booze so very happy to merrily watch it unfold. Suddenly the doors crash open and she bustles in, always slightly ahead of her entourage with a wicker basket and headscarf. More Thatcher than Rotten. For some reason, she clocks me immediately in the corner and comes charging over. She seems to speak in capitals. Like a headmistress addressing a simpleton.

"YOU DON'T LIKE IT HERE. I CAN TELL. YOU'RE LIKE ME. I HATE THIS."

I'm a bit star-struck and drunk, so I'm uncharacteristically lost for words.

"SPEAK UP! WHAT'S WRONG WITH YOU?"

I reply that I'm very pleased to meet her and she must be very tired after inventing Punk.

"FUNNY. YOU'RE A FUNNY ONE ARE YOU? WHY ARE YOU HERE? WHAT ABOUT ME NEW FRA-GRANCE?"

Her Northern twang meant she said some words in two parts.

"SPEAK UP! CAT GOT YOUR TONGUE? THE SMELL!? THE FRA-GRANCE?"

I felt a bit oppressed now. Not by her but that I was an interloper. Not merely an outsider but ridiculously so, a charlatan at a perfume launch who can't even smell. I tried desperately to think of some words about smells that were neutral. Positive but meaningless.

"Er... it's er... very warm."

"WARM!? WARM? WHAT DOES THAT EVEN MEAN MAN?"

"It's... also... highly... er... earthy!"

She relaxed a bit.

"EARTHY? EARTHY IS IT? BY 'EARTHY' DO YOU MEAN 'SENSUAL'?"

Highly relieved, I chirruped "Yes!"

"GOOD. IT IS SUPPOSED TO SMELL OF CUNT. SMELLY CUNT. SPECIFICALLY, MY CUNT. GLAD YOU LIKE."

She gestured brusquely at a minion, who slid over and handed me a coat. It wasn't my coat. Maybe it was a very posh cue to leave.

"I LIKE YOU. HAVE A COAT."

And with that, she stormed and bustled off, taking her wicker with her.

So I didn't have high hopes for this Ibiza fashion event. My form with fashion was poor. Once again, it was free booze. I rarely get drunk. There're too many drugs in me for it to happen effectively. But when I get bored and have lots of time, and there are no dealers about... drunk can happen. I'm a loud drunk. Jolly but grating. I hate myself drunk. Another reason it so rarely happens.

It transpired that this was, in fact, Tommy Hilfiger's party. I wasn't aware until I was already far above the yardarm and two sheets to the wind and may other nautical booze analogies. I was suddenly both engaged and delighted. I wanted to talk to Tommy now. Now he interested me. He had a right big boat.

There was a small kerfuffle that denoted 'something was happening' and the event became abuzz that 'Puffy' was here. It wasn't hard to spot. He had about six very large men around him and seemed to move everywhere in a scrum huddle. Tommy Hilfiger, arguably more famous, and certainly more wealthy, had zero security and even fewer hangers-on. I liked that too. I liked Tommy generally. He had a matey name and seemed easy-going. I even had a brief chat about keels with him. He was highly gracious with a random penniless drunkard. Which also scored highly.

My girlfriend was now highly mortified. Annoyed with drunken man and perhaps a little annoyed that, since Westwood years before, I never get star struck and appear to talk with ease to people she would love to talk to if she wasn't shy/sober. I was being ordered to leave. It was just as well because I had started speaking in capitals now too. Or 'shouting' as it is commonly known. One of the other reasons I don't get drunk is I am a textbook 'roaring drunk'. Roaring is highly embarrassing for any creature unless you are an actual lion.

"SORRY, TOMMY. TOMMY! TOMMY! TOMMY FISHFINGER. I HAVE TO GO NOW. SHE'S HAD ENOUGH. LISTEN... DON'T GET LOST ON THE WAY HOME MATE. YOURS IS THE BIGGEST FUCKING BOAT IN THE WORLD! YOU CAN'T MISS IT, IT'S GOT 'TOMMY' WRITTEN IN TEN FOOT HIGH LETTERS ON THE

SIDE... AND TWO FUCKING CHOPPERS ON TOP! DON'T GET ON THE WRONG ONE LAD..."

Then I turned and found I was just a couple of yards away from the rapper...

"PUFFY! SEE YOU MATE. YOU DON'T GET LOST EITHER. PUFFY! BE CAREFUL ON THE WAY HOME TOO..."

At which point all his bouncers hustled together to form a sort of human shield, a phalanx of beef. Which even in my pissed state I knew didn't render them soundproof...

"DON'T GET ON TOMMY FISHFINGER'S BY MISTAKE, YOU TINKER PUFFY. YOU CAN'T MISS YOURS. YOUR BOAT IS THE RENTAL, PARKED IN THE SHIT BIT."

They didn't need any burly men. The missus had me out of there like a fireman in less than 10 seconds.

Long, loooong before this above, I used to write for a socialist paper up North called 'The Other Paper'. I covered music.

At the time, David Bowie was doing Tin Machine. Which everyone hated but I thought was brilliant. I grew up with Bowie, and even Punk couldn't stop me loving him. I tried so hard to get to speak to him at the Tin Machine gig I was covering in Bradford, but there was simply no way.

I managed to get an interview with his guitarist, Reeves Gabrels, the next day though. Sadly, I woke up that day to a coach strike (this being, I think, 1989) and the idea of getting a train was strictly for the rich. Gabrels was living in Kensington at the time. I was back up North for a bit. No way was I going to miss this. I mean, DAVID BOWIE innit.

Mind you, in them days we didn't think twice about hitching. The entrances and exits of every motorway used to have queues of hitchers. The interview was in Kensington at 1pm. It was about 9am and the drive takes about four hours. It didn't look like I'd make it as the clock got to about 10. I was standing at the top of an on-ramp to the M1 somewhere near Sheffield. Just as I was about to give up a bright purple mustang roared past me, down the ramp, came to a screeching stop and very dangerously reversed back up the ramp to me. The window wound down and a jolly African face looked out and bellowed:

"WHERE YOU GOIN FELLOW!?" and I went "London" and he went "WELL, LET'S GOOOO!!"

He averaged about 130mph all the way down, which in them days was pretty darn fast. He was a salesman from Ghana. I forget his name, sadly. We talked all the way about Bowie. He loved him too.

As we met traffic (again, in those ancient days you didn't hit traffic really until the West End, whereas now you can be in a queue coming off the M1) somewhere along Edgware Road we started to crawl. We passed several interesting posters to promote Lou Reed's new album 'New York'. He was apparently appearing in London to promote it. The first UK visit in a long while. The posters were about 1ft wide and about 6ft high, like a strip of wallpaper, and had a life-sized profile full body pic of Lou. And his magnificently horrible mullet. They were unique posters at the time, the first of their kind.

As the car was crawling towards Marble Arch on this sunny lunchtime in June I had to do a double, then a triple take. I nudged the driver and said, "Am I seeing things, or is that Lou Reed walking past a row of posters of himself, wearing almost exactly the same clothes and the most awful haircut ever?"

Driver was like, "HOLY SHIT MY FRIEND IT IS LOU REED" (he shouted everything, he may have been deaf).

On all these occasions when I meet someone famous I always do something monumentally dickheadish. It's a compulsion. This time I leaned out the window and shouted the immortal words:

"Hey, Lou! Are you lost, mate!?"

He turned around and made a beeline for the car. To be fair, the car really stood out. He walked up and in a voice like an annoyed headmaster explained that of course he was lost and did we know where the 'Cum-ber-land' hotel was?" I was like, "it's literally just round the corner mate". He seemed a bit short-sighted actually. He ambled off. It was now about 1.30 in the afternoon, so I thanked my saviour and headed for the tube. As I crossed the eight lanes of Marble Arch, I saw Lou on the other side looking like a cartoon of a lost person looking left, right and left and right again while stood right under a giant CUMBERLAND HOTEL sign.

I just gave Lou Reed directions! Then I realised I had completely lost any opportunity to make something of the moment, even if just as a person rather than a writer. Doylum.

Anyway, I emerged in Kensington with a freshly bought A-Z and found the street for Reeves Gabrels. A very posh street, all red brick facades and big porches. As I approached from a distance, I saw a guy playing guitar on one of the steps. It was Johnny Marr. No, it really was. Again, I just turn into an idiot and went:

"Oh, you're Johnny Marr. Does everyone on this street play guitar? Do you know where Reeves Gabrels lives?"

He just scowled and nodded to the next door. I was beginning to go a bit funny. Anyway, Reeves answered, and he was really nice, and he was impressed I sometimes wrote for a cool London mag and was a musician too of sorts, and we talked for ages, mainly about guitars really. As you'd expect.

So I started to tell him this story about meeting Lou Reed and Johnny Marr on the way but most of all what a fan I was of Bowie and how hard it was not to talk only about Bowie instead of Tin Machine, and how difficult it must be trying to be 'a band' when it's nothing of the sort etc. etc...

"Oh David's on his way over now, you can tell him that yourself it will make him laugh 'cos we are both off to see Lou Reed now at the Palladium."

All I could think of to say was "Is Johnny going too?" and he just looked at me like I was simple.

I thought I was going to burst when Bowie turned up. I'd been waiting all my life for it. I actually felt a bit sick. Like REAL nerves. I was only young. He was smaller than you'd think, thinner and all twinkly and jolly. This was my moment. I had my chance. This was a moment some people dream of. So I said:

"Alright, Dave. I'm just off the shop, do you want anything?"

...and he does talk like he sings, and he does sound a bit like someone doing an impression of him, and he said very melodiously in the voice that sang 'Space Oddity':

"Twenny Bensons... and a packet of crisps."

I ran all the way to the nearest shops. I found an off-license and got a few tinnies as I'd promised Reeves and then went to the elderly Asian lady at the counter:

"Twenty Bensons please! *They'reforDavidBowieyouknow*!"

She looked at me like I was from Mars.

Running back I was dreaming that they would ask me to go along with them, I'd be reunited with Lou and we'd all roar with laughter at how funny I was, and we'd all be great mates.

Got back to the street and I couldn't remember which house it was. They were all identical. I'd left my bag in there too. It was too posh to start knocking on doors, and there were no handy indie guitar legends mooching about to give directions.

I wandered about the street feeling sick. I sat down on a step and waited. Four hours later it was dark, and no one I recognised emerged from any door. My new mates had ditched me.

I woefully found my way back to Brent Cross, southern gateway of the M1, and stuck my thumb out. Nothing stopped for hours. It was rubbish.

Eventually, a small coach stopped for me that was full of people in wheelchairs who'd been taken on a day out, and all their carers were pissed out of their minds. It was a fitting chariot after a really weird day. I finally got back at about 2am.

I very rarely tell this story because I have trouble believing it myself. But I hope it shows the lengths someone will go when Bowie's name is even mentioned.

RIP Dave. I still have your fags and crisps.

CHAPTER 16
ESPIONAGE, SABOTAGE AND TRIAGE

Not only was our band playing for the first time as a unit in front of people, we were doing so straight after Public Enemy. It was a multi-stage festival, so it wasn't unusual for huge acts to be on before lesser ones. Most importantly, it was raining. Rain, believe it or not, is a godsend to artists at festivals. Instead of milling about looking for drugs, buying beads or getting their arse painted, people rush into the big tops to escape the weather. Which always means big crowds having a good time to music.

Chib, our bulldog-like manager at the time was so verbally violent he would often pass through what I describe as the credibility envelope. Any drug beast knows the envelope. When you are so outré, Normals can't quite process what they are seeing or hearing, so it is easier to be completely ignored. Overlooking it being way easier than having to process and then deal with it. This was Chib to a tee. Even walking into a shop to buy a paper with him he'd be so conversationally and routinely utterly obscene that a kind of blank look would descend on people around as if they couldn't quite believe their ears. Most of all, it is required of the English, by her Majesty, to put up shutters and don a mask of placid complacency when faced with the ridiculous and highly improbable.

To be on the end of one of his tirades was a biblical ordeal. He frequently got his way simply by reputation. In order to avoid him turning up, things would happen. Doors would open just so his mouth wouldn't have to. At this time we were the only band in the world playing electronic music live. Quite a claim, you say? By live, I mean *live*. No sequencing. MIDI instruments played without a safety net, by musicians. It's a small distinction to many, but an important one to us. More of that later, as there have been a few bands under my auspices. At this time the band was large. It had to be to sound anything like the ambitious production of the records. Large meant stupidly expensive.

To say we were nervous is an understatement. As well as our session singer, guest star vocalist, and a rapper flown in from LA, there were strings, session players and tons of very expensively hired kit. Rehearsals were short and inadequate due to the costs. The rain started hard and the big top swelled to capacity to see Public Enemy. The biggest tents hold about 4000 crammed-in. So it's a hell of a vibe. Public Enemy had not played in the UK for a long time. The place is rammed. The atmosphere electric. And, as usual, a DJ plays a few tunes, perhaps 20 minutes, between bands setting up. As Public Enemy end their set, we hear a cheery,

"Alright lads? Excuse me, coming through!"

As through us pushes DJ Smellemy. A nickname coined by Quag due to the vast amounts of cologne he used. Smellemy was one of those mainstream big names from the old days with connections to celebrity. He was into fashion shows and sports cars and, as far as we were concerned, not in the least interested in music unless it got him where he wanted to be. I was sanguine at this point. I had a million things to worry about, and not even Smellemy could affect this: a packed tent in torrential rain after one of the coolest bands in the world. Chib disagreed. Loudly.

"*FUCKED!* That CUNT is fucking audio tear gas. WHO THE FUCK put him on? Get me one of the radio wankers NOW!"

He raged off to find an organiser as we huddled, panicked and sweated about our debut gig. In front of a packed and vibey, thrilled crowd. Last minute preparations and totally pointless panic over tiny details ensued. Miles of cables obsessed over. MIDI drum kits fiddled with, positions changed, then put back where they were. Then Chib strode over. Actually, Chib wasn't the striding type, more of a scuttler.

"Look at this, come here..."

I reluctantly came away from my pointless panicking and went over to the place behind the DJ, the best view of the arena.

It was almost empty. In the space of approximately three records, Smellemy had evacuated 4000 people. So awful and inappropriate were his selections that people literally preferred to go out into the pouring rain. I was aghast. I don't think in my life my stomach had dropped so far. As we

CHAPTER 16

gathered to go onstage, he finished up and strode over with his girlfriend. Cheerful as you like,

"All yours, best of luck!"

Chib went several shades of puce. When he was super furious he became almost incoherent with rage.

"GETCHAFUCKYE! YOU'VE FUCKIN' RUINED IT YE SHITE! FKKEN....."

spluttering,

"....FUCKIN SHITE DJ!!"

Smellemy went white, his girlfriend picked up the baton.

"Who do you think you are? You can't address him in that manner! Don't you know who he is?"

"Aye, I know his name. He's *FUCKIN SHITE DJ*, and you can fuck off *GIRLFRIEND OF FUCKIN SHITE DJ!*"

The envelope was passed through. Neither quite believing their ears, they staggered and slipped off in the mud.

Now, to be fair, it's not entirely clear with hindsight whether it was awful music, a small flood down the centre of the tent, another large act starting up in another part of the fest, bad luck, or the wrath of Zeus. Or Poseidon perhaps. I don't blame Smellemy now, at the time I was furious. But it goes to show that anything can happen where large crowds are concerned and the weather is a factor. What did happen was the small amount of press the record company had arranged to be there saw a brand new band play to an empty tent that was packed mere minutes before. That band's fate was sealed. Never put your eggs into a basket you have no control over. If there is fault to be found, it WILL be found, especially if the issue is massive, chaotic and comprehensively catastrophic.

More than once I've finally got that gig at that dream venue and found out the promoter wasn't even there when I played. Discovered later the boss asked the resident what I was like and the resident, being another DJ, was rather economical with the truth about numbers on the dance floor and general reception. Another time I lost a residency when a jealous newbie DJ told the boss I had done/said something completely fictional. Careful of DJs! They will say or do anything to get your slot. I would hazard a guess that nearly 90% of major issues in my career have been down entirely to the gossip and sabotage of other 'fellow' DJs.

Clearly, it is *never* OK to sabotage another DJ. The whole thing is not about you. Or about them. It is about the dancefloor. And no one wants to do anything but the very best for the dancefloor. If you mess with the night, you mess with *everyone's* night.

This doesn't stop DJ treachery, however. Because, of course, the number one problem with all DJs everywhere is ego. If someone genuinely is deluded enough to think the whole night is entirely about them, then taking their exception and umbrage out on every single person in the disco is *nothing* to a giant, staggering ego-beast.

The most common form of sabotage is the big name contractually insisting all the other DJs have the volume turned down until they play. We've all seen it happen, and heard the results. It's tragic and utterly pathetic. Johnny Laptops insisting the whole thing stop while they install all their bobbins, buttons and bells when they should have done it before the doors opened is another common tactic. And if you don't think that climbing all over the DJ currently trying to work and unplugging the track that is playing isn't sabotage, then you clearly haven't had it happen to you often enough.

Then there are more esoteric examples. Like the Space resident who used to delight in running to the club manager whenever any DJ played music he disapproved of. Or the very same rotter standing next to a guest DJ very early in the morning, yawning dramatically while reading a freshly imported copy of The Sun and eating a fried egg sandwich like some sort of buzzkill driving instructor.

A lot of sabotage is down to ignorance, inexperience or stupidity. Like promoters rushing to get you off the decks for playing an a cappella that used to be considered a moment of great beauty during the Acid House years, something they are simply too young to know, instead concluding it is a remix of the vocalist in question. Yeah, fired for playing an a cappella over a beat, otherwise known as 'DJing'.

These days tech is a big part of ego and sabotage. I've experienced DJs who slyly hand over their laptop and sync set-up knowing full well you are about to play a different format, but leave all the various cables and settings for the next DJ to fathom and change. With less than a minute to go. Then leading the booing when the inevitable silence happens.

I've seen a very famous DJ playing an excellent set when a shambling rave zombie, in front of my very eyes, staggered over the main power cable and cut the electricity of the entire event. Later, in those hideous, toxic zones where the 'comments' are, dozens of frothing, bitter wannabes scream how women shouldn't be allowed anywhere near the sets they would LOVE to play, less their vaginas break everything.

You learn to tell the difference between deliberate acts of evil and just A Bad Gig. Some bad gigs look like sabotage if you are paranoid. I recently had a whole night of nonsense at a famous Balearic venue that was so awful it felt like there was a hand behind it. There wasn't, of course. Perceptions can be skewed.

I played at the truly disastrous *second* UK Love Parade in Newcastle. I travelled over 1000 miles to play to an empty arena. In the last hour of my set the place slowly filled and in the final 20 minutes, I had the place jumping and screaming. Then they switched on the broadcast while my last record was on and grandly announced the next DJ to millions of listeners over the whoops of the crowd I had whipped up, over my record and vibe. That wasn't sabotage. That was just when it goes bad. It is very important to be able to tell the difference.

Practical sabotage and character assassination are two sides of the same coin. While real-life small acts of evil are fairly rare, spending every waking hour online and on the phone and even in print attacking, lying and smearing are so commonplace now it may as well be budgeted for when working in the biz. I've heard everything, been called *everything* and accused of things that actually make me wonder how someone even has the capacity to come up with it. This is the real issue we have to face in the Post-Truth era. I always find that until you see for yourself with your own eyes, it's best to have a healthy scepticism about anything anyone says in this industry. But do not despair, if you *don't* have enemies and haters at the door it means you've probably not been doing it right anyway.

Examples? Hard to do without sounding like you are settling scores, but I've had one stalker who has been engaged in a continual and savage character assassination for over 15 years simply because I couldn't provide him with a free holiday in Ibiza. One of the most unpleasant was also Ibiza, it's a *very* small place, so most rapidly ripe and pungent for the lowest chatterings. It was an after-hours, inevitably, and a guy was slumped outside in the baking sun and clearly not in a good way. He was like a pot boiling over. And, of course, being completely ignored. Then he started to spasm. Then froth. Then a large panic ensued.

I came over and could see immediately he was swallowing his own tongue, so I pried his mouth open and got my fingers in a crab-pinch and fished it out. Cleared the airway, plus got some bonus vomit all over me. I asked if anyone had called an ambulance. No. We called one. The dude passed out but was breathing OK now. Thirty minutes later, there was still no ambulance. The party was, like a lot of Ibiza, on a steep slope. With a winding driveway leading down to the main road. In the hammering heat, I'd run up and down this driveway at an almost 45-degree angle looking out for the ambulance. 45 minutes and still nothing. Unusual for a small island. Must be super busy! And it can be all-too hectic for the emergency services in peak season, unfortunately. Managing to get them on the phone again they said the ambulance was having trouble finding the place. Again, standard for Ibiza, so could we look out for them on the road? They were close. I figured they'd never get a stretcher up the crazy slope so I picked the dude up and we started to make our way down the hill, as they were 'very near'.

Did you know the two islands of Ibiza and Formentera are known collectively as 'Las Pitiusas'? Means 'The Pines', based on the ancient Greek. There's nothing but pine trees wherever you look once you get inland. In olden times they covered every surface bar the odd beach. When the needles drop (pun intended), they are of a species that is very long and cylindrical. They act like the wooden rollers they used to use to transport huge stones. In short, on the slope down my feet shot out from under me and both myself and the unconscious dude went down on the rock, hard. He bumped his head, and anyone with a bit of first-aid training or medical background knows that nothing about the human body bleeds quite like the head. Because our brains are so large, all our blood is pumped up there constantly at great pressure. He bled. And to a bunch of wobbly ketamine freaks, this was the end of the world. I was hurt too but that was irrelevant. No time for PR, just picked the dude up again and I got him down the bottom of the slope. Still no ambulance. I saw it in the distance, stopped about half a mile away. I started running.

Lost in translation, they had stopped at a nearby business with the same name as the address I'd given. I hopped in, and we raced up the road a short way. The adults were here. The guy was tended-to. Most of the revellers went back up the hill while I chatted to the ambulance crew and explained he'd probably OD'd, possibly on ketamine, I'd slipped carrying him, and they immediately looked and dismissed the scratch on his head, got a huge beastly syringe out and gave him a shot of adrenaline that *immediately* opened his eyes. Since I first saw him, he'd been unconscious and floppy as a fish fillet. He was confused, but definitely alive. I got out and went back up the hill...

Then it began. Dum-dum DUUUUM.

First of all, factor-in I had a lot of blood and vomit on me. I didn't notice, being somewhat sobered by events, plus a touch distracted. It had poured cold water on the festivities for some but by no means all. Not too long after we left and in the car someone joked about not dropping any more kids on their heads. I laughed. I should add for clarity also; I was only with about three others when I slipped down the slope. There was a group ahead and behind but both out of sight.

24 hours later, I heard the first of the gossip. I'd brutally beaten up an innocent kid at a party. I was used to gossip on Ibiza, and in my naivety, I actually did not connect this new rumour with what had happened the previous morning. Seriously. I just thought 'That's a random one!' and didn't give it another second. Then, as I got into town after sundown, I found people looking at me oddly. Friends. Next I heard that I'd killed someone. Seriously. I walked into one of my regular haunts and someone shouted a greeting along the lines of 'Hey killer!'. I started to ask around and there it was. The rumour was out there. I'd killed a man yesterday.

Variations on this were that the police were after me, it was 'just a matter of time' until I was brought to justice. There were all kinds of variants on this theme and most annoyingly, when you tried to relate the actual tale there was a lot of "Oh yeah, right! Well, you *would* say that" etc. Which was meant as a joke but was quite scary, it suggested the fruity lie was just way, *way* more interesting than what actually happened. Something our current batch of politicians and the sinister think-tanks behind them understand to a decimal place.

I wasn't just upset by this but flummoxed. It wasn't the first time my name had been muddied, and get used to it dear reader, 'cos it very much comes with the job, but it was the certainly the first time I'd seen it happen so fast and so *extreme*. Bear in mind, this was before the internet! Most of this was text and word of mouth. After about four days of it, well, it wasn't so much the lunacy of it all, it was the slightly joyful tone that came packaged along with it that truly enraged. It was pure entertainment for people.

Five days later and it came to a head at another after-hours. Very similar crowd. I also came to understand who the main architects of it all were. Who were all there too. Enjoying the fruits of their labours, greatly. Whispering, gesturing and smirking as if in the corner of a schoolyard. It wasn't merely this incident but around this time in my life that I also started to see more often the dark underbelly of our thing. The whole job was getting less of a honeymoon, been through the workmanlike aspect of living it, and now there was a general darkening. Suffice to say I was displeased. I was thinking of leaving this party. Then there was a small commotion. Walking towards me were three guys, and they were loudly chanting:

"LAST NIGHT A DJ SAVED MY LIFE, LAST NIGHT A DJ SAVED MY LIFE!"

I won't call it singing, but they made a good go of it. I had no idea who they were or what it meant. Then I noticed the guy smiling at me had a small shaved patch on his head and a fresh stitch or two. I would never have recognised him: as a conscious individual, he looked completely different. He was Canadian, as were his buddies, one of them had recognised me and they came over to thank me, ironically right in front of the small group who had been instrumental in the smear campaign. The guy simply said:

"If it wasn't for you, I'd be dead."

It was sweet, I cannot lie. However, do you think the scunners responsible for the gossip then immediately recanted, and sought out redress at every turn? Of course not. Did the hundreds if not thousands who'd heard the lies then miraculously hear the truth? Not a chance. Once it is out there, the damage is done. For life. Character assassination is like any other form of harm. People do it because they have no idea of the consequences, or want to. If you've never been part of a circle jerk of pure hate, you've no clue how it feels. You wouldn't do it ever again if you did, trust me. Or maybe you do it with gusto entirely because it happened to you a lot? Maybe a parent scolded you so much you think it is normal? Who knows? At times, of course, I've only had myself to blame. Innocent? Who the fuck walking, talking and drawing breath is *innocent*?

Again, we follow society at large. Hate is quite a big business. Being roundly hated as a career path is actually a thing now. Yet another unpleasant American invention infecting the world. 'Shock Jocks' have morphed into professional trolls and mountebanks like Alex Jones and Katie Hopkins. There are more than a few DJs who, their star having long faded, spend much of their energy annoying people for attention. Contrarian is one thing, but actual hatred is often the result. Wherever there is a medium, there are professionally negative voices to exploit them. It's not new. The jolly old British have made giving anyone who does better than them a hard time for hundreds of years. They do so love a backlash.

We accept backlashes, particularly in the UK very much as standard. We put on a John Cleese voice and go "RIGHT! that's it! you had your 15 minutes now GO AWAY!" and nobody ever seems to stop and ask *why*? It's like a mass consensus is reached that this song or shoe or shop or shiny shit is *done*. Over. Anything further is an offence. I'm not just talking about myself here, I've pottered along OK over the years, although I confess it interests me greatly. I've been around so long I've lost count of my own passage through moments of approval and then hate. Do it long enough and there is basically always someone who hates you as well as one who very much likes what you do. The backlash is as inevitable as the tide. Newtonian hyperbole. For ever action, there is an equal and slightly hysterical reaction. You are fine if you pootle along in the shadows. But do something as evil as be *popular* and you can bet solid cash money the backlash is just a matter of time, moments even. I rarely think about it these days. However, it just lumbered into view lately with someone I will call DJ X.

I'm pretty indifferent about who is hot and who is not. It's one of the few benefits of age. I liked some DJ X records, I saw him DJ twice. It was alright. End of my very short relationship with him. I understand he may or may not be something to do with something cool in Berlin, and is large in Ibiza. I guess what I mean is I was fairly sure he was 'a cool thing that is doing well'. Then I noticed the backlash creeping in on social media. I started noticing that if he was mentioned it would be followed by that sort of slightly vague and noncommittal disapproval of the type the British are so good at. That sort of 'rather you than me love'. Kinda 'if you say so' reply. So I would directly ask 'is he not good then?' and rarely get any kind of sense other than 'meh'. This clearly contradicted my understanding that DJ X was riding high as someone good at his job. I should add, in my side job I do actually get to do some actual journalism. Sometimes that even requires standing up in court. I tend to find that if there is a slight cloud over a name, but when you ask about it people are coy answering, it's not 'no smoke without fire', it's actually more often that they just don't have any facts. Try it. Next time you hear a bad vibe about someone, put a lamp in their eyes and ask them for exact details. They won't have any 99% of the time. So, I decided to look into it…

I straight up asked folks 'What do people think of DJ X?' on my socials and the response was, without wishing to over-egg the mix, quite chilling. Quite clearly, the main response was that he wasn't just 'over' in terms of being relevant artistically. He was also a bad man. Now I started to get interested. Because I often see that in tandem with hate for someone's artistic output there is an accompanying demonisation. The person

CHAPTER 16

in question isn't just old hat, they are usually somehow personally deficient as well. Case in point: Ed Sheeran. There is a world of awful music out there to hate on. There really is. But it seems to me if someone has the temerity to be both popular and ginger then they may as well walk around with a kick-me sign on their back. No, I don't like his music, but I do think the hate for him is disproportionate. And, yes, I genuinely think people hate redheads. Like gypsies and fatties, gingers are one of the last groups of humans in the world it is OK to be openly hateful about. Point at a redhead and say "oh no, ginger!" and you can be sure someone else will join in, laughing. I guess my point is, it's not enough that you just don't like a bit of insipid charty balladeering, you have to *hate* the person responsible in some deeply personal way these days also.

"DJ X, he's a bit *rapey* isn't he?" was the comment popping up the most. Again, in a very British way making a hideous, nightmarish crime into a slightly cuddly fun-word. "Hey, I'm not calling anyone a rapist, just a bit of a rapist" is the meta-language here. Like you can be 'a bit of a murderer'. It's nonsensical. I should mention at this point that I'd done a bit of light googling and it seemed to me that some of the hate seemed to stem from YouTube videos of DJ X at gigs and especially *afterparties*. Now I've done a LOT of afterparties. For some years it was all I did. While other DJs were grafting on Saturday nights I was on a plane or in a car en-route to one of my events that were all exclusively on Sunday mornings. So to me, these videos didn't contain anything at all unusual other than people seemed to have their phones in front of them a lot. And I guess that is a clue. Absolutely nothing these days goes undocumented and unscrutinised. But still, it seemed, to me anyway, that DJ X's worst 'crime' seems to be having fun where people could see it, be a bit wobbly and sometimes do a bit of a Dad dance. Call the cops! I literally can't think of a DJ worth hearing who DOESN'T do that.

No. There had to be more to it. You see, I know about viral and I know about reputation. Full disclosure, it was myself and a friend who did the Boiler Room pisstake videos. It was us who shredded Ben Klock with the theme from Grandstand. I sometimes make funny videos that can do very well sometimes. So when I see something like say, 'The Harlem

Shake' meme... I KNOW it is created by someone smart, someone pro, someone with a marketing spend. There is no 'organic' when it comes to most of the biggest memes you see. They are crafted. Why mention this? Because in my gut I knew there had to be more to the DJ X thing for it to go south so fast. Plus I am a journalist of sorts these days. Getting to the bottom of things is still what we do, despite what people with a sinister agenda tell you.

The trick is separating the plain old backlash hate, that humming background radiation that is basically just boredom and fashion waiting to be entertained, and distinguishing it from the more insidious, pernicious string-pulling-thing behind the curtain. Because you see, the two always happen together. It is the fairly humdrum hate that comes from being envious of success and popularity that drives it. There is betrayal too, people love something when the thing it is 'theirs', and when it crosses over it can flip people out. They end up despising their former idols. "Sell-out" is sometimes heard. Often it is less dramatic and is just petulance and disposing of the known quantity. We all know what it is like to move-on in a relationship? How many times have you been sat there, agog, as someone you thought loved you turns around to demonise you in order for them to be able to feel OK about dropping you? Happened to everyone at least once right? Sometimes you HAVE to demonise the other. Especially if you are feeling guilty. Get it in first. Demonisation is part of how we feel better about ourselves. In the age of Trump, you could argue it's never been more about stomping on reps and getting 'them' before they get you. So, yeah, you *loved* DJ X when he was 'yours' and super underground. Now he is lording it up in Pacha with all those other slags you hate his guts.

Sounds stupid when you look at it right? I don't think any of us will change when it comes to this sort of knee-jerk stuff. A sort of neurolinguistic programming starts to happen where people just hear the words connected to the name and it sticks. I saw recently that in the 80s and 90s Trump always insisted on the word 'billionaire' in all his press, despite him not being one. It sticks. All this rotten nonsense is accelerating, fast. If I was a scientist, I'd do you a graph about the need for us to dump things faster as more and more stuff is laid out for us to consume. We're not supposed to stay in-love with things in a consumerist society. Everything about us is about disposability. No, what worries most about all this is when it goes *dark*. How does a jolly dad-dancing DJ become a 'rapist'? And so very quickly?

"Creepy" is the other word I heard. It seemed as if people didn't like seeing him do anything except play records. As soon as he appeared away from the decks, dancing or chatting or drinking... it was verboten. "Cheesy" is the other one. I know this one. It always arrives at some point with anyone not playing the game. This was perplexing for me, as I was fairly sure about five minutes ago he was dead cool. Things sure move fast these days. Understand, I am glossing over the mainly artistic gripes from people. You are absolutely allowed to just not like something. Of course, no thread about something like this is complete without the inevitable 'never liked him' types piping up, you know, those superhuman minds who 'always knew he was a wrongun'. It's a given. No. There was something sinister afoot. More than just online hate tourism.

Then I asked directly 'If you weren't there at the place these were filmed, where does the rape accusation come from?' and eventually someone posted a meme to explain. A 'funny' video not unlike one of many I have made, except far less funny and with an added venom I could never have dreamt of. A site called 'People of Boiler Room' (one of many, I might add, that appeared in the wake of my own satirical videos, Lord forgive me if I helped start this nonsense!). They had made a video called 'How DJ X Gets With Girls'. What it does is, through the use of captions and text, impose a new narrative on an existing visual. Essentially re-writing events into a cartoon. It uses trigger words like 'prey' to describe women and imposes new, false meaning upon normal actions. Thus footage of DJ X, off-duty on the sidelines going over to talk to the DJ currently working is now a ruse to get closer to 'prey'. Giant words fill the screen 'explaining' what is happening. Close-ups are artificially added to add emphasis. 'Dialogue' is added in balloons. What it clearly does is take an interaction that happens a thousand times all over the world every weekend, and re-purposes it into pure hate.

What is astounding is that people do not see this as an imposed narrative. They see it as fact. You also can't help but wonder how many people don't even play the video and just accept its title. Ultimately its authors will cry 'It's just for fun, surely nobody takes it *seriously*? It's OBVIOUSLY not real'. I saw this myself when I added sound to Ben Klock. I was astounded that people were commenting on my joke as if it was a real video. I could not make the plonks and the diongs, the 1970s TV themes and the cartoon effects daft or obvious enough it seems. I should add as well, that being an excellent sport, he was filmed playing the music I'd added for real a few days after, mocking us back.

So yeah, I've made fun of DJs too, but there's sending out a message that maybe some people take the whole DJ thing too seriously, sometimes perhaps the music is a bit boring and that the concept of DJs and a handful of dancers being filmed is sometimes not very interesting... and then there is re-framing someone as a sexual predator.

Ironically, I've just come off three years of looking into sexual misconduct in dance music. I've worked with DJ mag, Mixmag and the AEFM to get together a helpline and to try and start looking at changing behaviours in Dance Music. So I've seen genuine sinister, illegal and, in some cases, downright sickening behaviour that is very real and a foul blight on our scene. And no one seems to care much. In this brave, new and barking mad world, even if you expose a fellow DJ as an *actual* rapist, it is you who is doing the 'sabotage' this time. Whistleblowers have been re-cast as villains in the land of upside-down. If the recent documentaries with victims of Michael Jackson or R. Kelly have shown us anything, it is that fans will never accept anything at all contrary to what they have already decided. Indeed, this seems to be the current mindset for every single person on the internet, regarding absolutely everything. So perhaps I am latching onto this case of DJ X in an attempt to fix something. One thing maybe. And I am OK with that.

Maybe seeking the truth of this is my penance for taking the piss out of other DJs, so let me say categorically; I spent two weeks trying to find a single shred of evidence of misconduct and found *nothing*, zero! Other than the 'funny' video, there was not a sausage to suggest a single bad deed. It really doesn't bear much scrutiny at all once you look into it. But we don't look anymore do we? We just pass on rotten nonsense as if it is fact. I tell you what though, I'm not indifferent about him anymore. Next chance I get I'm going to buy one of his tunes and tell people he is great. Purely because it's *way* too early in his career for a backlash. Really.

There's plenty of real badness out there. Why make any up? Compared to the genuine harm that befalls women and vulnerable people in our industry, these matters of individual reputation are relatively unimportant. But I do worry they can act as a sort of camouflage for the *real* predators, creating a spectrum of false equivalency that distracts from the real issues. There are very real stories from real survivors out there, about real abusers. As we will see...

CHAPTER 17
MORE ENDLESS CLAPTRAP ABOUT PLAYING OTHER PEOPLE'S RECORDS

I'm happy as a species of consultant or pundit these days. Apart from myself not having the energy anymore, the tempo of the biz is very different. Fast track careers in a speedy world is the current vogue. Things are so much more, well... *hurried* now. It's all about getting there without paying any dues at all. Climbing up over the corpses of your mates is normalised. A cynic might argue that the huge, global epidemic of plastic DJs over the last 10 years is due, in part, to it being mistaken for being an easy and swift way to the 'top'. Getting up there by any means necessary is the name of the game today. Ambition, raw, gleaming and tasting of polished brass, is far more important lately than style and intellect.

There's something weird about the way people face the DJ, and because I started before this DJ-fetish phenomena, it still feels weird. "What are you looking at?" I wonder at nearly every gig. I even remember when it started to happen. Everyone used to dance with each other. In wee circular groups facing inward, or as couples. They used to cheer if they liked a record. They cheered the record and technically, the person who made it. Then, like a scene out of 'Invasion of the Body Snatchers' they started instead to turn and gawp at me. When they liked a tune they pointed and screeched. It was very odd and remains so. In fact, I now do gigs as 'The Secret DJ' in the pitch black, behind a screen.

I will never forget when I used to go to one of Ibiza's coolest clubs, walking in and, as usual, the gossip was about one of their manufactured crises. Rather cleverly each year there would be a story leaked about how the venue was being oppressed by The Man. Cementing its imagined status as an 'outsider' whilst quietly being just the same ferocious business as everyone else, if not more so. This week 'The Council' had said there could be no DJs performing outside. So the famous terrace had the music from the indoor section of the club piped out to it. I emerged outside to see everyone pointing towards the empty booth. There was no one in it. Yet everyone faced towards and fixed their adoring gaze on the empty air, without exception.

This image always stayed with me. I wondered what those people were doing there if not to dance with each other. I also asked the boss not long after if he'd ever considered putting on DJs who played dynamically, rather than a continuous minimal drone. He explained at great length to me that they could never have anything that peaked musically, or people would get excited, then consequently and inevitably tired. So they would leave. And that would mean less money at the bar. So the musical policy of one of the coolest clubs in the world was based entirely on economics. At the other end of the credibility scale, at the height of the Las Vegas party boom, sophisticated accounting technology would chart drink sales against musical BPM, structure, playlist etc. to determine which superstar DJs 'performed' best in terms of drinks sales. Fees would be determined accordingly. When faced with this, you can't help but wonder where music itself fits in at all. All that matters is the appearance of cool. Which is simply another form of empty spectacle. In artistic terms, if not economic.

'Cool' cares little about whether people are happy or not. Scowling, head-down, crow-faced Techno goths hammering a crowd of equally uniform sourpusses is the ideal. Indeed, I would go as far as to say some of our coolest venues are sometimes almost entirely devoid of atmosphere. I've walked through some and the amount of people jammed in there together almost silently is quite eerie. The music is loud, of course, but the crowd are not. Cool people don't like to be seen enjoying themselves. I was once taken-aside by the owner of one of London's most iconic venues and quietly asked to have less of a good time, as it 'wasn't the sort of thing they do here'. Memorably, some of their staff once came on holiday with us and spent the entire time on the remote island wondering suspiciously why people were waving at them. Explaining it was something called 'friendliness' was met with total incomprehension. After they refused to watch a video of the newly-released Toy Story 2, on the grounds of "it's a cartoon" we just left them to not-enjoy the rest of the vacation without us. Good people. Friends to this day. *Chronically afflicted with earnestness*, however.

In the spirit of the post-truth age of idiotic polarity, the highly commercial EDM events are the opposite. Full of bouncy, shiny, clappy nappies; boinging about noisily like Tiggers to a soundtrack of Barney the Dinosaur's greatest hits. For sure, EDM is *entirely* about entertainment and spectacle. You can tell if a DJ is an entertainer rather than an educator, 'cos they are fist-pumping at the crowd like they are at a Nuremberg rally, and more thought and preparation has gone into the pyrotechnics than the setlist. The music should have people clawing at the air. You shouldn't need to tell them what to do with hand gestures like some sort of shit puppeteer. I can't talk, I've been known to punch the air and maybe do a tiny little dance when I'm having fun, but you know what I mean. The type who gurn, gesticulate, bask, leap and generally flap around like a recently landed fish. Professional flibbertigibbets.

Both ends of the hip scale are as ludicrously fascistic as each other in their way. Naturally, the truth lies somewhere in the middle of these daft extremes. To be trapped in either is as painful as the other. I know. I've been to both and survived so you don't have to. A true DJ has to be prepared to do the extreme edges and everything in between. You have to ask in each professional situation: what is my function here? Amateurs only see DJing in mono. There is only one setting for part-timers, and that is where they do whatever they want, regardless. Professionals are called upon to DJ in many types of set-ups. Indeed, a travelling DJ often has no idea what they are getting into until they are pushed onstage, blinking their bafflement into the lasers.

So when the talk is about educate/entertain the answer is always "both, my child". Naturally. Because much like a talented teacher facing a mixed class of all abilities, when you are a hell of an educator, you have to be hellishly entertaining for it to work. Sometimes you get to work with gifted children. Sometimes with the problem kids. Understanding all of them deserve your best will be the making of you. And one day, after years of doing all sorts, you will suddenly find that people really start to like your vibe. Your personal brand of art. Your own version of 'no compromise'. Because you've reached that point the valid way. Through graft. Don't get me wrong (and boy, do people love to get it wrong), 90% of my gigs are me doing things my way. To talk in any kind of rational way about two sides of anything seems to be almost impossible currently. The reason why I've been around so long is the other 10%, the trickier ones. The times I had to flex. The times someone had to take one for the team. These are how you get a rep as a professional. You are remembered when you help out. Forgotten easily when you hinder. It's good to be remembered. But make sure it is for the right reasons.

Sadly being remembered has very little to do with your abilities, which is as frustrating as the futility of wishing it otherwise. I've spent many years wondering what the bally-hell I did wrong at a gig not to get invited back only to discover years later that the promoters have a strict policy of never having any DJ twice. It's more common than you think, especially in this age of hyper-fast living and surplus of acts. I once played a major venue in England, arriving there after a very strong Ibiza season, and the venue was chock-full of the same kids who'd seen me on The Island. Uniquely, for the first and maybe last time, the crowd chanted my name when I finished. It was triumphant. Never heard a peep from the club again. Not a word. At a certain level it becomes about business, and a lot of it is about how you move in that business, or your representatives do. Sadly it rarely has anything to do with what music you play.

In a sense, we are talking about being memorable. Remembered for *what* is very, *very* important. For example, a certain venue always speaks of me in slightly awed, hushed tones about the night I did 22 pills and still managed to DJ. They recount the story frequently yet strangely, don't book me. Another very sombre and cool venue speaks highly of my kicking off their yearly fancy dress (I wasn't in fancy dress) but when they tell the story in the press always forget my name, or to book me to play records. And why should they? Once, back when people still had fun, I set fire to a Jimi Hendrix record while it was playing and promptly set the whole club's ceiling on fire too. They did not forget me. Nor did they re-book. It's not merely bad things people remember, however. For a while, I was literally the only touring DJ with Pioneer CDJs and took them in a huge flight case to every gig. This made an impression. I used to cut and scratch a bit back then, and some club promoters were highly impressed as few House DJs did this at the time.

Perception is entirely relative to the beholder, however. For example, I was once called into an Ibiza mega club to fill in for one of the biggest DJs in the world. It was such a vast, dark room that only a handful of people at the front could be relied upon to identify anyone in the booth. Sheer electricity was in the air. Every tune getting huge cheers. Amazing atmosphere. It wasn't until I played exactly the same records in the same room the following night that it was clear that it was nothing to do with me, the music, or indeed anything but the hype and expectation that huge name commanded. The crowd thought I was him. It's all relative how things are perceived and experienced.

These days the market is so saturated with DJs a lot of promoters book you for very odd reasons and are pretty much looking for reasons not to book you again. I find this is true with lots of things. We are so bombarded by information that we've basically become a species of machine for finding fault in things so we can swipe left. *Next!* Hype is a savage beast that is perpetually hungry.

Sadly, I've personally taken many steps to 'tone things down' to avoid this kind of criticism. I used to enjoy playing a fun record at the end of the night only to find the next day it was the only thing people remembered. Doesn't matter that you did an extended six-hour set of un-heard-of newness, you are shit because you had fun at the end for five minutes. I always say "a DJ is only as good as their last record" which is a real shame when you think about it. I used to dance about and smile a lot. I don't as much anymore. I got told off for it once too often.

I'm not so big trousered that there aren't bigger DJs on my bills. I've been a resident and supporting act most of my life. Maybe only five or six DJs can say they have no peer. In fact, even the biggest DJs get trumped now and then into a supporting role, especially when far away from their usual stomping ground. Recently I supported a supercool megastar and the very large venue was programmed well for once, with a great variety of styles. The main guy was very eclectic, the cool supporting acts were all playing precisely the sort of cool shit I like to play. Everything was so very, very coooool. So the venue asked if I'd like to play some of the more obscure 80s pop records? 'Cos frankly, what is the point of trying to compete with the guy everyone is there to see? And I know if I went into three rooms of achingly cool people and music, I wouldn't mind a room that provided a bit of relief from all that relentless hipness. God I miss chill out rooms! Bring all that back, please! Yeah, who remembers programming a venue with a carefully chosen variety of sounds instead of every single room pounding out the same Tech-House records from sub-promoters who couldn't care less what is happening elsewhere in the place? Those were the days.

In short, I was having fun with it that night. And you know what? So did everyone in there, it was a laugh. A highly successful event all-round. Afterwards, inevitably, the online bitching starts. As if that is the only sort of music you can play! You think, 'surely it's abundantly clear that I don't always do this?' but any sort of divergence from the norm is fuel for gossip and hate. The following week the word is out that you were 'cheese'. Lordy! If I had a cent every time someone said I'd been a bit cheesy in a situation where I was being specifically booked to play an accessible vibe, well I'd have about three euros. The point is: when I am being paid the big bucks to headline that main room (and I did, in the very same venue, not long after), baby you WILL get all the far-out cosmic wonders I have to offer. I will play MY way. But sometimes I have to do what I am paid to do in a specific situation. You will fail if you don't flex into what is asked of you. You've seen the Plastic DJs with their heads down in the side room tonking out 135bpm to a handful of oppressed early arrivers as soon as the place opens. Venues without variety and programming empty quicker than those that curate carefully. Yeah, I said 'curate', I will go to hell for it, don't worry. Yes, of course it is almost impossible to have a discussion about this nuance in the age of polarity. "Oh, so you are telling everyone to play shit records is it?". No. Of course not. I'm merely debating that there is always a time and a place, for everything.

And I like to think when I do the job well, I am doing what that gig asks for and I am slipping in a little bit of education too. I am avoiding polarity and attempting a compromise. Because there is *also* a time and a place for NO SURRENDER, as much as there is for eating humble pie and doing what the hell you are told. 'Cos you see, it is always ALWAYS about the crowd. Remember at school how some subjects really bored you because it all seemed pretty obvious and simple? And others were a real pain and truly baffling? Personally, I found arts a walk in the park and maths was like a Martian dialect. Still do, in fact. Schools have to operate at a mean-average of intelligence and ability. Aim too high and some kids will be left behind. Go too slow and some will be bored to tears. It is not too dissimilar in a disco.

That crowd that came for that supercool shiny megabot DJ were pretty sophisto! But not all of them. There were at least a thousand people in there who didn't want to hear obscurities in every room, or not all night anyway. Even some of the sophistos get tired of it now and then. A smart promoter wants to keep all the people that come happy ALL night. So they stay. And play. And pay. The key to that is good programming. And a resident, and indeed guest, is ready for anything. And more importantly, is happy to do whatever is needed. Programming a line-up or a whole venue or festival has also been hijacked by the money. Now it is simply the biggest name available booked to play just before the next biggest name. They are either generic EDM or generic 'new techno' so you can safely assume they will sound so similar it will be impossible to tell them apart without the obligatory pretty face and/or gimmick attached.

The same names at every event playing the same music seems easy to avoid, but that is only the case if you think music has anything to do with the choices being made. Music is now the one thing no one asks about. So to experience one of these events is to enter a generic, culturally gentrified space. Every moment of it artistically is bland and ill-conceived. Art was never part of the process. It is simply the audio version of professional wrestling. Giant fake personalities shouting at each other and not one moment of sport or athleticism. Just spectacle and showbiz. And the same excuses apply. "Oh you still have to be very fit and strong to participate!" Things given as a caveat or excuse when they know it is yawningly empty. Same goes for the mega DJ line-up. "Oh, sync still requires some skill". Or perhaps "sure, very good looking but hey, still a good DJ" is heard more and more often, sounding like excuses rather than reasons.

A properly managed programme is like an excellent twisting film plot or interesting exhibit. Every bit you encounter is intriguing and surprising and makes you want to investigate further. Instead of being trapped in the same room with the same music all night it makes you want to wander around. Take it all in. How many times do you go to a venue, have a quick scout around and find every single room and DJ playing exactly the same music? As well as being artistically unreasonable, it makes no economic sense to me. Bored people get tired. Interested and excited people stay longer. One is static, and the other has a flow of bodies moving through the place. Without exception every well-programmed event I have been to makes money and crucially, is a success that brings people back. Lazy promoting makes short-term money. You don't build a rapport with people if you are a faceless machine for making cash. No art = no soul, obviously.

It's fickle as the wind is all this stuff about getting re-booked. A booker having a bad day won't like anything they hear from you, or anyone. Ultimately the character of the promoter is all. A good, professional and clued up organiser will always see the value in what happens at their event, and be aware at all times of what goes on under their roof. Ignore empty gossip. However, some will look on in quiet satisfaction, while others will be utterly disgusted by everything you do or say. It's so hard to call. Best just let things be. You can only do your best and hope it reached the right ears.

Part of the global rise of the English-speaking idiot is the elevating of style over substance at the cost of all else. People are generally silent in the face of intelligence. Antagonistic even. Stupid no longer apologises. If you are not understood, it is *your* fault. If the limits of the listener's comprehension is reached, the problem is not theirs. It is yours. This is very apparent in the disco, funnily enough.

In the past, people used to ask me all the time "what is this record?" sometimes *highly* reluctantly, their machismo preventing them from being seen not to know everything. Now no one asks me about records. Half because now they are all 'experts' and experts don't ask, they tell. Half because they don't have to ask, they can Shazam it. At a recent international music convention I counted 11 DJs who were so incredibly good at it that they didn't even need headphones while they played. Sync and prearranged sets were doing the work. The DJ's job was more akin to some sort of conductor or magician's assistant. Waving their hands about like an interpreter for the deaf, a rich irony, if not a little harsh.

This rise in 'easy-tech' doesn't merely apply to music. Labour-saving devices are everywhere, although particularly in our scene. It was and always will be driven by technology, and to a slightly lesser degree, sex. Musical devices for people who can't play any instruments. Software for people who can't produce. Apps for people who can't mix. Information in place of knowledge. Luggage for people who refuse to lift anything. More apps for people who don't know what music to play, and another for how to get hold of it. Websites for people who don't understand the mastering process. An entire sub-industry is specifically geared towards no actual effort, authority or experience being required to stand in front of people and play music. Think about the process for a minute. The whole thing is automated to such a degree that all you have to do really is spend the prep time deciding what to wear. And the worst part is, this is happening at a *professional* level. It's not even excused by amateurism anymore. Cheating is normalised. And if all that fails, be sexy. Ideally, both.

Sport was the swiftest way to the top when I was a kid. You just had to run fast. Jump higher. Kick a ball better. What you don't realise is, you have to do it better than nearly everyone else in the world. Same with music. Sorry. Not as easy as advertised! It really doesn't help that society seems to be engineering almost everything so that only the very prettiest get the breaks. Think about that. There are two talented athletes at a quantum career junction and the prettier one will be chosen. What that has to do with sport is absolutely zero, but everything to do with business. Even more insane is that DJs and producers only seem to prosper now if they are inoffensively shapely and blandly good-looking. One of the enduring pillars Dance Music was built upon was that it was *never* about 'showbiz'. Faceless nerds could succeed and be judged purely on music, not their body. Indeed, we started this thing so that we could get rid of that nonsense. Now we actually have model-level credible DJs bemoaning that no one takes them seriously due to their staggering beauty. It's almost obscene.

I am certain many people ask themselves, is it *only* possible to succeed today if you are pretty? While highly egocentric and stage-managed rock and pop was all about image and sex, Acid House was about providing an alternative to the 1980s right-wing assault on culture and youth. An antidote to hairspray, money and hype. It was about coming together in a very dark warehouse and dropping all the bullshit that was sprayed in our faces every single day by voracious marketing and propaganda. Lights off. Ego parked. Hands in the air.

The Punk/DIY ethos was that if you were poor, out in the sticks, too young, too ugly, too unpopular or just plain too geeky to get by; with not much money and the patience to read a boring Japanese or German manual you might just be able to make some music. This music was then played by mostly anonymous DJs in very dark warehouses to people who didn't know who you were or what your music was called, or where to get it. You didn't need the approval of the mainstream. You didn't need the music business. You didn't even need to be *seen*. Indeed, as mentioned previously, at the beginning of the boom in discos and electronic music, many DJ booths were hidden or sometimes, in a different room entirely to the dance floor. Producers chose futuristic names to hide behind. Some wore masks, both physical and metaphorical.

Sure, things change. It's natural. It's becoming very clear lately however that while pretty is par-for-the-course for the horrific sequinned sledgehammer that is EDM, so-called 'underground' acts are now clearly being managed, packaged and sold to us using exactly the same techniques as the mainstream. There is no difference whatsoever in the process. Only the colours on the box are different. It seems now more than ever that even that slight difference is being completely eroded until very little remains to separate the very uncool from the painfully hip. It is almost as if the emperor's new clothes have finally triumphed for their imaginary tailor. Has 'cool' ultimately been revealed as a con?

I call this point where cool is revealed to be meaningless 'the idiot singularity'. There are one, if not two, generations of dancers who absolutely and completely understand this. No one knows better than the kids brought up on it how futile and ridiculous it has all become. How comprehensively vapid and devoid of meaning culture can be. We have truly reached the borderlands of sanity. A place where up is down, the leader of the free world is a tangerine dildo in the shape of Forrest Gump and nothing is true except the inevitability of lies. Where only those who won the pretty lottery deserve love.

If we have passed through the idiot singularity and there can be no return, let's at least remind ourselves of the burning purpose at the heart of what we do. To fight wrong, if only by our absence. To protest, if only with our apathy. To celebrate who we truly are, not who they want us to be.

To listen, hard.

To close our eyes to the noise.

Open our hearts a tiny crack.

Let in a sliver of light.

* * *

When you think about it, we get the idols we deserve. So perhaps it is appropriate that the DJ is the new totem, an avatar for this age. I've mentioned before that maybe we get *exactly* the entertainment that fits the era. The jangling shaman of the Trumpian era is the DJ/Producer and has been reduced to a jester. No longer a quiet, modest authority, but a fake showpony. An empty cheerleader. Flinging glitter, lasers, volume and pyro at our faces to cover up the gaps in thinking. As long as our industry is promoting spectacle over art, it will only ever attract vacuous, Plastic DJs trying to fast-track past the skill and experience required to do it properly.

There's really no point naming names. Look at any recent underground star and nine times out of 10 they are pretty as a picture. With model looks and with often even more fashionista presentation than any professional model could ever hope for. Male or female, trans or CIS, LGBTQ+ or not. The tyrannical requirements of sexy spare no one, regardless of orientation. Show us the one or two glorious exceptions to the rule and we can show you hundreds of contrary examples as a rebuttal. Ask anyone in the industry and they will look at you as if you are deranged. 'OF COURSE we choose to work people who are pretty, are you mad?'. The Americanisation of the planet has led to a no-questions-asked acceptance of some highly uncomfortable new norms. The rise of the cult of the individual. The spectacle overtaking the substance. The photoshoots, the glitter, the lasers, the O2 cannons, the confetti, the dreamy eyes, the radiant teeth, the supine positions, the messianic poses, the slightly parted lips and the pursuit of physical perfection… what the fuck has gone wrong with us?

The tyranny of beauty is absolutely unrelenting and utterly depressing, and it permeates society globally. The social media-led obsession with the self and a plastic version of fame has poisoned our scene to the core. You thought cocaine ruined the dancefloor? It's got nothing on this. The problem with celebrity is now *everyone* has a version of it, thus radically devaluing it to a point not far from zero. When everyone thinks they are famous, how on earth is it possible for the term to have any meaning? Our industry mistakenly thinks that in order to rise above the noise, every single thing about their 'product' has to be unrealistically perfect… including the music as well as the faces and bodies. It's not hyperbole to connect nearly every single one of these new 'underground' dolls with posing behind a device that pumps out drab, dishwater-dull Tech-House or 'techno'. Utterly flawless thanks to 'sync'. Victoriously cool and relevant thanks to its ubiquity. Triumphantly unthreatening and completely, relentlessly *boring*.

It's so easy to point and laugh at someone like Guetta, Aoki, Hilton or the Zoolander prince of EDM, Bob Sinclar. It is what they do. None of them are claiming to be curing cancer. What grates is when the 'underground' is talking so very seriously and at great, monotonous length about 'diversity' and 'inclusivity' and sneers at the commercial elements of the business while merrily doing exactly the same as the overground, but wearing black leggings with the face of a caveman with toothache. One minute hand-wringing about women being excluded, the next minute working exclusively with faces that conform tightly to the beauty myth of the American übermensch.

The industry never understands that to promote this sort of plasticity is highly counterproductive. It is exactly the people who are individualistic, probably bullied at school for looking odd, and subsequently worked very hard on being genuinely talented who rise above it all to succeed in the long term. If global gentrification, homogenisation and the cultural sterilising of all we love is inevitable we MUST fight it by supporting the real deal. We can't be fooled. We respond to authenticity immediately and positively. We are suspicious and guarded when fed plastic particles. Sure, many can't tell the difference, the industry relies on it. However, longevity is entirely about those who instinctively *know*, informing those who don't, over a period of time.

I doff my imaginary top hat and vigorously applaud the anonymous. What have faces and bodies got to do with sound anyway? Why do we say we are going to 'see' a DJ. Why face the booth at all? Why even have any lights on? We understand marketing. We get capitalism. We just thought that we gamely fought the Acid House wars to escape all that blithering, waffling ego-nonsense from the mainstream music world. We didn't sign up for a crowd more obsessed with filming themselves than dancing. We didn't think we'd be pouting, preening, bench-pressing and squatting our way to the 'top'. Our scene was supposed to be an ESCAPE from the oppressive reality of commercialism. It was supposed to be the antidote to being forced to compare ourselves to impossible standards of physical beauty and health. A place of refuge from the bombardment of grasping corporate doublethink. A warm nerd-cavern. A cheery geek enclosure. Our happy little twat-paddock. A getaway from the very worst and ripest of the world's fresh shite, not its smelly product ambassador. It was supposed to be about unity and the death of the ego, not a murky never-ending celebration of the preening narcissist.

I can't help but recollect the 'advice' of American EDM Pop personality 'DJ Khaled' to a kid on Twitter, to paraphrase him, that a 'support slot' was an opportunity to hammer out as much energy as possible and get noticed. Literally the absolute opposite of what a warm-up set should be. Or 'DJ Carnage' allegedly putting 10,000 dollars in confetti cannons and literally shooting money at the crowd, because cake is no longer enough. Do you remember when Kentucky Fried Chicken had a cartoon Colonel Sanders 'do a set' at a huge, swollen festival? What has ANY of that got to do with Acid House? Nothing at all. Zero. What has spectacle got to do with creativity? That's right. Now we are getting it. The application of large amounts of money, almost no thinking, and MAXIMUM SHOWBIZ is 'entertainment' rather than artistry. And hey, I'm all for entertaining people as long as it is done with some panache. Some art involved somewhere in the process. Without it? What? Eventually, nothing is left but empty spectacle. Waving at money. Saluting the machine at a slightly fascistic noise rally.

I have to ask: is it even possible to make future music in the digital age? Because tomorrow is already here. Part of the vision of Techno in the 1980s was to paint a picture of the future using sound. There was also a drive to connect the electronic technology to a simple, handy narrative. Essentially 'electronic = futuristic'. Artists such as Drexciya, LFO, Jeff Mills and Underground Resistance openly spoke of Science Fiction as a main influence, and created entire worlds and characters to inhabit their dreams of tomorrow.

So now the future previously and widely described has very much arrived, what does it mean to be 'techno' today? If the form was a child of the 1980s, it was equally as naive, glossy and deluded as a huge Dynasty shoulder pad. In an age of financial aspiration and the even more cheerful 90s, glittering visions of the future were all part of the dream. Obligatory even. However, nothing ages faster than an imagined future. Doors do not hiss open like in the 1960s Star Trek, they glide noiselessly. Our banks of controls are not made of large, coloured bulbs but of light itself. We've not made our designs and functions chunky and blocky, rather they are thin and organic. We always get the details of the future wrong because in the real world they are arrived at universally, not unilaterally.

Even earlier, sometime in the 1950s, the Situationist International movement of thinkers in France and further afield were refining the ideas of Surrealism and Dada into something great thinker Guy Debord would eventually refine into a manifesto in 1967. In the 'Society of the Spectacle', he put forward many ideas that now dominate our planet. That substance would be immaterial. That the image would rule over thought. That only populism would matter. That lying would be the norm and honesty laughed at. That art would mimic consumerism so closely they would eventually be the same. They rejected the idea that late-stage capitalism's apparent successes could ever outweigh the dysfunction and degradation of everyday life that it simultaneously inflicted. Buy the book. It's quite disturbing how accurate the predictions were. It's not an easy read. Then again, that's part of the problem, isn't it? People are only prepared to be entertained, rather than engaged intellectually. We are chronically confusing stimulation with titillation. To be engaged feels too much like school and not enough like play. We've become a planet of infants.

Situationism led, in part, to the Paris uprising in 1968. A genuine moment in history and societal change. Art taking its rightful place as a prime mover in people's lives. Thinking leading to direct action and genuine revolution. Now we could not be further from this scenario. We have achieved the opposite. A plastic society with a vacuum where there used to be joy, a black hole where thinking used to be. Nothing but opinionated answers where there used to be questions.

This move away from substance towards style can be traced very clearly in our art forms, of which Techno is certainly one. Whereas Techno pioneers such as Drexciya invented highly complex backstories, narratives and themes for their work, now it is entirely about the individual and their ego. As devoid of meaning as anything in our current society. Only more so due to the absurd amount of seriousness and faux-gravitas it awards itself. Is there anything more ridiculous than the studied pose, perma-frown and messianic movements of someone essentially miming to innocuous sync? Compared to the spiky three-deck workouts like those from Jeff Mills or Carl Cox, what dares to call itself Techno currently borders on the obscene. Almost a parody.

One of the thrills of Techno was that sonically it pushed the envelope on how we experience sound. Techno was where the new sonics lived and played. It was an extreme place. A testing ground. A place created by new technology. If sonics have a life outside of music, Techno is the crossover point, much like Drum & Bass came to be. Eventually, the acoustic laboratory that used to be Techno was replaced by Dubstep and its children. Extreme genres where the noises matter more than notes. The central tenet at the heart of producing music has not moved very far from trying to marry music to machine, arguably this is its purpose. There is a burning question, an elephant in the room with all of this. Where else is there left to go sonically?

What has changed unexpectedly is that technology is now far more about enabling users rather than pushing sonics themselves. Its priority is to be easy to use, rather than functionally extreme and challenging. Being 'easy' is killing creativity. Everywhere. Yes, it is arguably making everything more available. Certainly, it is putting music in the hands of everyone, which can only be good. However re-branding EDM, Tech-House and fairly nondescript music as 'Techno' is wrong. Stealing the seriousness of the name to match the blackness of your clothing is astonishingly ridiculous, and makes anyone who does look utterly plastic, which is the *opposite* of the authenticity they seek. Techno has always been serious music for serious listeners, *scientific* even. Not a gothic version of EDM. Emo-tech crows take note:

When you start making and playing actual Techno, then and *only* then do you earn any use of the word Techno itself. You cannot take it, it can only be bestowed. It is not a new and fancy hat, it is an art form.

All worries about labels and genres aside, I hope it is becoming apparent that globalisation is homogenisation, and we cannot avoid discussing it if we wish to survive it rolling over us. There is almost no difference now between the allegedly coolest and the most unrepentantly commercial. If America has openly lumped us all together as 'EDM', how can we fight everything we do becoming exactly the same as every other bland load of shite that dares to pass for art? Who do we turn to? What recourse is there, and where the devil is it?

CHAPTER 18
THROTTLING IT TO DEATH WITH LOVE

In the DJ and production world right now, a class of well-heeled fetishists is arising to display their superiority with their large collections of antiques. This is actually changing how we value music. It's almost as if it doesn't matter if the lyrics put a lump in your throat as long as the wax is costly and rare. It's like the persuasiveness of the rhythms are irrelevant if they weren't recorded in analogue. Ancient rack modules never made the vocal delivery more evocative, nor does the format raise the hairs on the back of your neck at the breakdown. There is a schism forming of have-and-have-nots that is deeply unhealthy. The value is changing from artistic to economic. We are no longer placing value on the content but on the carrier. On the objects, not the artistry. A similar thing happened to painting in the 1950s and 60s. A *market* emerged where previously there was none. And nothing was the same ever again.

These people seem to be in love with THINGS, rather than the art these gadgets are actually designed to make. In the same way that vinyl-only freaks sometimes forget to care whether the music on the wax is actually any good or not, the worship of equipment neglects the function and purpose of the gadgets, indeed why they exist at all, only that they do. It's like falling in love with a cold loom, instead of the nice warm jumper. It's an industry of course, and the purpose of it is to sell you things, especially the rise of very cute little toys that are specifically entry-*entry*-level audio tech. Fisher-Price plastic diversions especially aimed at those who have no intention of a career in music. Nothing wrong with that either. If you are having fun, fun is fine. It's just often these days, people associate possession of the objects with actually being a musician. Owning a telescope does not make you an astronomer.

I can definitely say it is not just possible but never been easier to get started with almost nothing in the way of tech. I know this because I started with almost nothing. You just need to stop looking at it in terms of devices and start seeing it as a collection of mental and physical skills, rather than pricey gadgets.

Much depends on how you view musicianship itself. There is certainly a rise in making music as a collage, put together in a reverse-engineered manner. By that, I mean using the equipment and other people's tunes to stitch together something. People obsessed with the equipment let the gear make the music, entirely. They themselves are merely a type of observer. A sort of audio janitor or diode-whisperer. I put down the rise in fetishising analogue gear to this method. In effect, the machines give the ideas. Composers do it the other way around, write in their heads, and come to the studio as a way of making their ideas happen. Somewhere in the middle is perhaps where to aim. Leaning too heavily on gadgets is a bit like using a phrasebook when in a foreign land. You get by, but never really learn the language. And once you put the book away, the language is gone.

You've seen people head-to-toe in lycra and on carbon fibre cycles that cost thousands having trouble keeping up with a kid on a clunky mountain bike wearing work boots and overalls. Or Dads with brand-new Italian motorbikes who can barely fit into their uncreased fresh leathers, or folks with giant drum kits who never play along to anyone other than themselves in their spare room? It's OK to have a hobby! In fact, I'd argue there was a time when people happily classed themselves as hobbyists but now they demand to be seen as pros. Trying to buy your way into something doesn't help you get there. It's a method for avoiding the work that needs to go into getting good at it. You can look a bit daft, in fact, when you have more kit than ability. Half of the classic dance tracks we revere were made on the most basic of gear. If I am being brutal about it, you really don't need anything other than a laptop. It's perfectly possible to release a tune using nothing else. May I even be so bold as to suggest the racks and racks of modular and analogue are merely there as a front, a wood and metal suit of clothes with rotary buttons and a crown made of cables, worn extravagantly to provide fake credibility and mock gravitas? Too far? OK. I'll wind it back a bit.

All that matters really is how many tunes you have completed, not how many vintage rack modules were used in the process. By the time you have made 20 or 30 tracks that gained some approval from your peers, you might perhaps then be ready to expand into some nice tech. Making ideas happen can be done hitting some mud with sticks and shouting if that is all you have access to. Expecting the kit to make the tunes for you is the number one immediate schoolboy error of any would-be producer. Buy the tech when it becomes necessary. You need to learn to compose first. You already have all the tools you need stuck to the sides of your head and wriggling at the ends of your arms, the rest is just upgrades.

What we do is continually being dominated by the middle classes, and often the middle-aged. It could be argued cogently that perhaps the rise in fetishising the equipment is a direct reaction from the Gatekeeper-mindset to add an extra mythical barrier to the hoards of Ableton-enabled newbies. Essentially cash money is fast becoming the only way to make it happen for you as a career.

The days of pressing your own acetate and pressing it once again into the hand of an A&R guy, or selling your mixtapes on a stall in Camden market as ways of breaking into the game are long gone. A borrowed reggae system, a door on some beer crates, a smoke machine and a strobe used to be enough to make a thousand people happy in a single stroke. I once made a whole album with an Atari, a sampler and a DAT machine. Some of you reading will have to google those words. Most people can't even afford to live in a major city anymore. Thus the exodus to the more reasonable rents of somewhere like Berlin. It's like the Western obsession with their houses is spreading into other areas. Fetishising objects is artificially inflating their monetary value as simply *things*, whilst simultaneously dropping the arse out of how highly we regard the artistic content these tools help to make. Music itself has never been so cheaply sold. So poorly valued. Yet conversely, the physical objects have never cost more.

And if you go to Ibiza, and elsewhere, you will find very very large clubs as well as very small cooler ones who will not pay for a DJ's costs, and offer a fee so low you would be staggered looking at the magnitude of the names accepting pay-to-play. Almost as shocked at the sheer numbers of people shovelling money across the bars and box offices. In many places, far too many, the DJ doesn't get paid at all. As in the rest of society, someone very rich is making an awful lot of money, while simultaneously saying they 'can't afford' to pay anyone. This is exacerbated by inflated fees for big names and their ridiculous demands. Widening the gap between reality and insanity. I've seen a Dolby ATMOS directional sound system flown in from another country sit there, switched-off, its engineers charging overtime for doing nothing because the act who asked for it didn't know how to use it. I've seen FX units, sequencers, turntables and vintage rotary mixers ordered in, and then left to one side while the DJ who demanded it all plays off his USB stick on the warm-up DJ's controller, just like everyone else.

As mentioned, for a while, I played entirely live. And by that, I mean musicians performing electronic music with MIDI instruments in realtime. Each gig cost something in the region of 10,000 euros. Cost *me* that, not the record company. Spot the mistake. And not one cent of that money went on bum-hamsters, rare preserves, spats, leopards or glitter. It went on five flights, five hotel rooms, five wages, and the transport and hiring of a shit ton of high-end musical and recording equipment. Each subsequent gig didn't stop me shooting cash out of my blowhole like a barking moneywhale either. Suffice to say, there ended up only being four gigs for that band.

The epiphany came on the fourth, when we appeared with Danish producer Trentemøller, also billed as a live act. He strolled in with a backpack and four haircuts on one head and was 'live' from a laptop in the booth on his own. He walked away that night with as much money as I lost. I was definitely getting it wrong somewhere. Especially with kids coming up and asking things like 'hey, what were those drum-shaped things?' and you'd have to answer 'well... drums'. To the crowd, it just didn't seem to matter if it was a dude doing almost nothing, or five experts and one amateur sweating kittens doing something almost unique on the planet. No difference to this crowd at all. Both were something to look at and dance to. I needed a re-think. Clearly.

Also: which promoter wants to deal with the complexity of what a live act has to offer when he can just pay one person? One minute you are seeing ridiculous vanity and excess, the next someone basically pressing play. No wonder everyone is confused. The point? Only my decades of work in the industry allowed me to be able to afford to even rehearse that band, never mind take it on the road. It would be impossible today for someone just starting out. It would need funding. And record companies just don't do that anymore. To start now, you need a backer.

The cost of taking your career from the bedroom to the disco is fast becoming totally unsustainable. It is less and less about having a shining passion for the art and, we are told persistently by Gatekeepers, more and more about the equipment, the vinyl, the VIP, the social media following, Vegas, the analogue, Berlin, the modular, Ibiza, the vinyl, the vinyl, THE VINYL. Ironically it has never been easier to start, nor has it been harder to thrive.

Really though? What does it take? Well, you definitely need a manager and a decent-sized bit of seed money to break through currently. Wondering how a lot of these people you never heard of are suddenly everywhere in your face? Dear reader, they paid to get there. If you need the Bank of Mummy and Daddy just to BE in a capital city, imagine the investment it takes to move there and establish a name? And in all this stew why NOT pay to play? The 'law' of supply and demand is heavily in favour of the venues, promoters and industry. There is nothing but a constant stream of people stood behind you not only willing to do it cheaper, behind them even more will work for free.... then on top of that are the queue-jumpers willing to *pay*. As if the line to get a gig is the line outside a club, and bribing the list is the only way in.

In Ibiza, we have seen this impact for real in economic terms. Rich people playing at being DJs and VIP yacht-faced bigpants have driven the rents up so high that none of our workers can afford to live there, a housing bubble has appeared. Ironically, everyone is stood around in Ibiza wondering where that kid is with their cocktail when the kid doesn't exist. Couple of thirsty millionaires are probably still standing there covered in dust from last year. Much like acting, presenting, dance or any performing arts... if underprivileged people are finding it harder and harder to afford to go to connected schools and universities, it is the privileged who are finding the path to the DJ booth a cakewalk. Scratch the surface of many new performers and you will reveal a showbiz parent, a billionaire backer or in one or two cases, a straight-up silver spoon socialite slumming it for kicks. Most obscene of all are billionaires buying DJ/Producer careers for themselves, whilst simultaneously using the day job to eviscerate communities that helped build the scene.

In the 1970s, my family used to go on holiday once a year. We couldn't afford overseas. Few could. We would get up at something hugely mad like 4am. The only time of the year we would do so. All would pile into an ancient car in our jammies, creaking at the seams with luggage, kids and daft things that would never be used. They had things like shops, furniture and food where we were going, but part of the paranoia of people who don't travel much is that they must take everything with them like a tortoise, married to a prejudice that wherever they are going must be backward and highly primitive. Then we'd drive, for the UK, what was a truly unreasonable time and distance to one of the most southern points, where due to its geography, it only rained every other day. We once got to stay in a fairly humble but *beachside* house. It was like being in a TV show. We'd never seen anything like it. There were things like *palm trees*! There was a little shop that sold fishing nets on a pole and a few comics. It was heaven. We'd make friends with other families on holiday. Tearful farewells after two weeks that had seemed somehow to last forever. A once-in-a-lifetime taste of the good life.

This tiny strip of land is called 'Sandbanks'. Today, it is entirely the province of billionaires, multi-millionaires and obscenely overpaid sports stars. Many of the old houses that faced the sea are gone and replaced by truly vulgar villas, mansions, and horrific mock-art deco monstrosities. The little shop is now a restaurant you couldn't even afford a starter in. It is, in effect, now off-limits to those who cannot afford it. Just one example of hundreds of areas in the UK, thousands globally. The effects of gentrification currently can be seen most glaringly in my current home of Ibiza.

Any resident of a tourist zone understands the boom/bust seasonal cycle, and even the richest spots suffer mightily from this beastly rhythm. This inflates an already unrealistic economy into a frenzy of high prices and hay-making, following a mass exodus and shuttering off-season. From festival frenzy to tumbleweed every year. Add a plague of billionaires into the mix and it's ultra-gentrification that borders on the biblical. Trebles all round for those in power who've been shepherding Ibiza towards the new Saint Tropez. An overpriced, tepid, alcohol-free lager for anyone unfortunate enough to be born here of school-leaving age who have graduated into a full-scale housing crisis and cannot expect to do much more than join a nation of butlers. Unless, of course, born into the wealth. Worst hit of all, the Spanish seasonal workers from the mainland who fully expect to be able to work in their own country and find it impossible to afford. Small business are hammered by sky-high taxation and social security payments. Sole traders AKA 'autonomo' paying some of the highest tax in the world while our local fat cats buy up entire buildings to house their imported workers on the cheap. Drawing all the employment away from the independents and into the mega hotels.

Of course, try telling anyone offered several thousand euros a week for the use of their house as a holiday let *not* to take the money. The panorama from the summit of our stately castle 'Dalt Vila', at night off-season, displays an entire city mostly in the dark. Property owners happily mothball a building for 8-10 months of the year rather than engage with the highly difficult Spanish government and their pesky laws protecting tenants and demanding annoying taxes. Year-round tenants are now expected to pack up and leave for the summer and come back afterwards as if something so insane is perfectly normal. Indeed, the rise of Airbnb (now banned here) recently saw a slew of insanity that included a tent in someone's garden going for 700 euros a month. Air-conditioning not included, nor indeed available. A type of 'hot box' usually reserved as torture for prisoners of war.

A small island with a great deal of money breeds horrific inequality. The powerful Matutes family carry much of the brunt of the backlash. Paterfamilias Abel Matutes is an ex Spanish Foreign Minister, no less. This rep is not helped by them owning pretty much everything, and they recently moved from mostly hotels into super discos. Every single other music venue on the island suffering under heavily punitive restrictions for sound, publicity and opening hours, while their own mega-venue pumps out open-air racket all day and much of the evening.

None of the family have horns and a tail, and are, almost single-handedly, responsible for much of the island's positive renewal. However, anyone not born 'Ibicenco' to one of the top families soon learns however, that there is one rule of law for them, another entirely for everyone else. The term for the wealthy locals as 'The Disco Mafia' is perhaps unfair as they are merely rich, rather than corrupt. However, that money and influence can open or close almost any door they choose. Breeding much discontent. Not dissimilar to the UK, overcrowding and inequality are fermenting hate and extremism. Most of which highly misplaced. One day, I woke up in Ibiza to some very familiar-looking extremism online and discovered the very same backers of the British and American far-right had opened up shop here in paradise with the 'Vox' party. All the same sloganeering and hate, just this time in Spanish. You could not convince any of the locals taken with this shiny new political party that they were being conned. Or that the very same people had done it already in the UK and USA. Foreigners like me aren't allowed to tell them what to think. Or it would appear, to warn either. Good Lord, they didn't even try changing the memes, slogans or wordings. They just translated them. A clue to how little the far-right think of us.

The global trend towards maximum profits for minimum wages is simply unsustainable in places with such a ridiculously high cost of living, such as here in the Balearics. Already our workers are renting bunk beds and mattresses on floors like the Emirates. How does it affect our jolly discos? Quite simply, it means only a very few can now afford to exist. An effective monopoly ensues. Think it only goes for the big ones? Nope, the small ones are also owned by the mega rich and pay almost nothing to their DJs. And when there is no one left to serve a proper expresso martini, the money will simply and quite literally weigh anchor and sail off into our famous sunset...

Ibiza, London and other music capitals are squeezing out their homegrown talent and youth. Closed-down clubs, greedy developers and underfunded councils have sterilised city centres. This bad policy has led to a brain-drain and exodus. And if you think this only a problem for up-and-comers, only last season I was expected to pay my flights and taxis to appear at a very cool night in Ibiza, the cost of getting there crushing the 150 euros on offer. Just the taxis there and back comes to 80 euros. All vanity and showbiz aside, it is just not safe to deny someone a taxi in the small hours when no other method of transport is available, especially for women workers. If you take it up with them, you are 'difficult' and 'a problem'. And their total bemusement with your objections is quite real. They have just had a whole season of well-off, often amateur, middle-aged DJs pay to play music there, and the amateur DJs loved it because it isn't their job, it was a holiday. People now offer their 'services as a DJ' as a part of their yearly get-away or access to a festival. Understand when I say 'privilege' it doesn't just mean billionaires. It means the Dadrockers and Balearic Silverbacks with nice jobs and houses who 'do a bit of DJing' on the side. Hobbyists are killing our thing, suffocating it with their fierce and genuine love.

And, quite frankly, they aren't doing themselves any favours. Shortcuts tend to backfire in the long run. Ever wondered why so many bookings in our supposedly youth-led culture are dominated by middle-aged DJs? Why a generation that came up in the last century have such staying power, while so many younger models burn out? Maybe they've lasted because they cut their teeth at a time when dance music wasn't such a business, when hard work itself was often enough to build a career on. Carl Cox got his break rigging up sound systems in Streatham. East Berliner Paul van Dyk built his first set of decks himself using his carpentry skills. You couldn't buy your way to the top because the industry infrastructure didn't exist yet. Though the apparent meritocracy of Acid House may have favoured a demographic that was in the main confident, metropolitan, male and white, the lack of real financial barriers meant more diversity, more opportunity for the dedicated, the hustlers, the POOR. None of them got anywhere playing for free. They couldn't afford to.

In the face of a crash in value, we must fight the global epidemic of pay-to-play. Because if it costs you in any way to play music, you are paying to perform. Why is it just the DJs who are expected to not merely perform for nothing, but *pay*? Do the bar staff work all night for exponential bartending profile-building? Do security stand in the cold and deal with stupidity and violence for the appreciation of their peers? Ultimately, and sadly, the main problem with DJs playing for free is DJ's playing for free. It is something only we can fix. Balance in The Force is about loving what you do and honouring the music, without mistakenly making it all about yourself and inanimate objects. Herein lies the question and its answer.

Truly if anything describes the arc of postwar and postmodern society more acutely, it is Acid House. Started as a revolution, co-opted into the mainstream and eventually belched out as an agent of the system. Few things are more effective at transcending borders, language barriers and culture than this thing we do. It is desired all over the globe, earns billions and now, thirty-plus years strong, is now utterly bland and interchangeable. It is the cultural version of fast food. Indeed, many of the biggest players in Vegas and Ibiza are already franchised globally. If fast food is the cheapest meal that contains almost no nutrition, yet is marketed so hard it is by far the most popular foodstuff amongst those too young to know better, then EDM is surely the sonic version of this business plan. And make no bones about it, it is both a business and a careful plan. Gentrification is the method by which the rich absorb everything. Land. Culture. Trade. You name it.

I remember a documentary I watched about some very nice, well-heeled folks sailing around the world. I love boats. I forget where it was they were docked, but a local kid tried to steal part of this fancy visiting boat in a tiny dugout canoe. It was all fairly innocuous, but when the woman involved went into a tirade about 'how can people do this?' she reminded me of the Americans after 9/11 who were genuinely flummoxed as to WHY. They had the 'what' fully covered. The 'when' was clear. Not a sausage otherwise. I can help. You sailed a fucking luxury yacht into a place where kids have hand-carved canoes and *fuck-all* else, mate. They drove planes into your building because you have been killing indiscriminately in the Middle East for 50 years, mate. It's not for fun why these things happen. It's isn't accidental or because there is 'evil' at work. When you meddle and stomp around the globe, it has effects and consequences you weren't expecting, mate.

The techniques of gentrification haven't changed for hundreds, if not thousands, of years. Arrive, dazzle, bribe, trade, absorb. There is little difference in outlook between settlers offering natives beads for land as there is today with startup billionaires getting all the revenue from our music. And you know how they say the devil has all the best tunes? That's now absolutely true thanks to streaming; however, the church has always owned all the best venues. Until now. A venue is utterly meaningless when empty. Meaningless has no value. Things with no value are very quickly bought-up by the rapacious beasts at the wheel, especially during COVID-19. The pandemic is a fire sale for the über rich.

The devil, not happy with the complete discography, now wants every bit of bricks and mortar on the planet. And when he gets them, he's got the lot. Finally. And, without question, he will own *everything* one day if we let him.

INTERLUDE
LOST LIKE A FOX

It was very rare T-Man got into a car, or indeed got out of bed, without matters becoming very eventful. It wasn't that he was a bad driver, on the contrary, he was very modest and careful behind the wheel, as well as generous with his time, wheels, money and possessions. It was just that things, odd things, gravitated to him. I wish I had some science for you. That somehow being weird means more weird things happen at you. There has to be an explanation from someone very clever. In the same way that mortality follows a kind of 'W' shape on the graph, where newborns frequently do not make it, then dips, then there is a wee peak in the 20s when everyone is reckless and stupid, then rises again for old age... so there must be some ratio for how being a maniac leads to maniacal events in your life, even if you do not initiate them.

For example, on one of the many visits to a petrol station at silly o'clock, he was driving innocently along, stopped at some lights, whereupon someone shunted his car lightly and promptly drove off. He frantically wrestled with the glove-box and various nooks to find something to write the offending car's number plate on (T-Man was covered in notes, writing on hands, pocketbooks and bits of paper as he forgot almost everything, all the time) but could not find anything. Repeating the digits of the plate to himself wildly, he found a pen, which promptly did not work, and a banana. He etched the digits on the banana. Then got out of the car to inspect the damage and saw, luckily, very little except that his own number plate had fallen off. He stooped to collect it just as another car zoomed up, slowed down, an arm came out of an opened door and scooped up the number plate mere inches from his hand and zoomed off, leaving him utterly bewildered.

The tricky part came when he took the banana to the Police station.

"I have in my hand a banana with a number plate written on it!"

The desk sergeant person just looked at him flatly, as they tend to. No reaction at all... and promptly left to go backstage. She came back with two of her colleagues and asked him to recount the whole story. They then proceeded to laugh uncontrollably. Transpired that the offending vehicle had a fake plate anyway.

Or the time I had a gig in Manchester, long before his single, solitary day of employment as an actual tour manager. We arranged to meet in the city centre. In the early years of mobile phones. I was in my car. He in his. A new car I'd not seen before. I was on the phone to him trying to give him directions. One of his loop compulsions was to say:

"What's dead cool and hangs up on wankers?" and immediately hang up the phone, as often as possible.

He'd do this while I was trying to give him directions. Then immediately call back, annoyed that he was lost. It was as weird as the time a lady stopped me in Ibiza to ask for directions and then told me off for mansplaining. About the fourth time he rang, I was repeatedly telling him he couldn't miss the hotel, it was a huge gothic pile in the centre of town.

"I'm there, you idiot!" he yelled. "I can see it on my right."

It was on my right too. Then I looked at the row of cars in front at the one at the traffic lights had a familiar shock of Albert Einstein hair in the driver's seat. Minus any and all mathematical genius.

"I'm behind you, you fool!"

"Oh no, he isn't!" he couldn't let a pantomime joke, or indeed any opportunity for a gag, pass without comment. I'd had enough, I got out of the car and marched ahead and knocked on his window. He did a comic spasm that included a triple-take, spilling everything while a small cloud of detritus exploded around him. He wound the window down. I shouted over the honking traffic behind;

"You're lost, as usual, you poltroon. Right in front of our destination!"

"LOST LIKE A FOX!" he bellowed and slammed on the accelerator. Screeching off into the night for added effect. He then immediately got lost even further, and ended-up circling the city for the next four hours. In the intervening time the gig we drove there for came and went, and by the time he found us again it was time to leave.

He had an ongoing hate/hate relationship with satellite navigation. Like all gadgets, he had to have it. And be the first. However, he was continually the most lost driver I've ever experienced. Yes, that's right, navigation is also an essential part of being a tour manager. Part of this disastrous relationship with directions was him giving up any and all evidence in front off his eyes and doing whatever the lady said (of course, he set it to a female voice) despite not planning anything in advance or the voice telling him to do something clearly idiotic. All this was compounded by the stimulants stopping him processing any and all advice or instructions.

This was writ-large once as we left one of my gigs at the Millennium Dome in London. Geography fans will know the Dome is on a peninsula, one that is so hard to get to via public transport on weekends it has been catastrophic for some businesses there. As we left, very early in the morning, I told T-Man I would get in a car with a friend, as I planned on getting home this century. He merely waggled and huffed and proudly announced he'd be back well before we were. As we drove off the peninsula heading south, I turned to the rest of the people in the car.

"Watch this, he will turn left."

Right on cue, his indicators flashed left. We pulled up next to him. He grinned and made gestures like it was a race and pointed at his watch. As the lights changed, he screeched-off. Left. We turned right ay a stately pace, back into the rest of London.

"What's left then?" someone asked.

"France."

He then proceeded to drive around London's orbital motorway four times. Arriving resolutely in second place at our destination about nine hours later than I did. He didn't do anything by halves. Although, as he would point out frequently and joyfully, at least he didn't kill any innocent African children.

CHAPTER 19
OLD MAN YELLS AT CLOUD

I got told off recently that my first book wasn't 'insider enough' and that they expected more in the way of exposé. All I could think to reply was, 'wasn't injecting myself in the arse with our diabetic dog's needles exposé enough?' But it made me think. The problem with revealing the inner workings of an industry is that the industry *really* doesn't like it. That is because industries operate an alternate reality that has to exist for them to function. It's like the fluffy and highly false bonhomie that actors display for each other. It's hilarious watching from the outside. But necessary for them to work and reach the emotional places the job demands. In order to make a connection to the rest of the cast they have to pretend, in reality, that they are closer to each other than actual real life and logistical experience would suggest.

The armed forces operate almost entirely on a machinery of brutality breaking down your individuality and because everyone takes the shouting, moustaches and leaping about deadly seriously, it only looks daft when you aren't inside the performance, doing it yourself. You may fail now to be remotely surprised at all, but the music industry is jam-packed with things you just aren't allowed to talk about. These fictions make the wheels turn. And like actors, a pro DJ's performance doesn't end when they step off-stage. "Amazing set-up," we've all forced out through a gritted teeth to the promoter, not wishing to lose any future bookings, despite the fact that the monitors were honking, the sound tech was an elderly displeased bulldog with the face of a recently sacked undertaker and the lack of drinks dryer than your Mum's opinion of your career. Social media, in particular, demands 100 small lies a week. About being buzzed-up for something massively unbuzzworthy. Smiling and saying nothing to the sexist or racist promoter. Avoiding harsh truths and politics online. Being beige for cash.

To be fair, a lot of it comes naturally to us. Most DJs – well, those who didn't get their break via Soundcloud before the arrival of puberty – have some experience of the blagging culture that permeates dance music. I spent much of the early 90s poncing around London pretending to the security staff at fancy venues to be 'one of the Happy Mondays' or 'the bass player from Inspiral Carpets' because to Londoners anyone without a London accent and wearing baggy pants might very easily be that person. Maybe I was? I was a cheerful bumpkin, happy as a petrol-sniffing pig jockey (not a joke, where I'm from, my mate used to sniff petrol and then ride around on a pig for shits and giggles).

Despite the issues and threats to our culture from everything from pay to play to gentrifying councils and actively hostile governments, our industry is simply not yet capable of organising itself into something approaching an adult player on the global stage. To effectively lobby at a political level, we need unity, and there simply is none. Not anymore. Everyone at best is deeply competitive or engaged in actual sabotage at worst. We are institutionally sexist, racist and greedy and most of all, lobbying requires *money*. Vast amounts of it. We have a lot of it collectively. Billions. No one will pitch a penny in financially, however, while the industry is *way* too juvenile. They don't care or truly understand the processes involved in lobbying governments, or the huge sums that requires. It's like herding cats. On top of all that, look at the self-appointed utterly toothless 'official' bodies we've thrown together. Vehicles for more lip service. Completely ineffective after decades of opportunity. It's just not a serious enough industry, despite the vast sums earned. And to say any word of this is met with a total brick wall at best, demonisation of the critical voice at worst. Most of all, like Hollywood, our business is riddled with serious drug use that is utterly denied at every turn. It uses-up and spits-out people top to bottom and doesn't give their corpse so much as a second glance as it steps over. And that is just when things have been highly positive and successful.

And nowhere can you see the industry more red in tooth and claw than at a dance music conference. I've done a lot of music industry conferences over the years. They used to be WAY more fun - but then again, so did I. My view back then, and not just mine, was that they were basically a jolly. A very *very* expensive tear-up. This would mean getting up at the crack of 2pm, totally avoiding anything remotely businesslike and only going to the dancing bits in order to behave in a very childish manner. At USA conferences, the locals would be utterly appalled at us, literally hiding the drugs and booze and openly asking what was the purpose of us even coming if we didn't do any business? I can only answer in retrospect that they now have EDM and we have Techno. Case closed, I think. I've since completely turned around. I have a different and more positive view of conferences now. While little gets done, it's better to talk than not at all. The Ibiza live show part of the International Music Summit conference is literally opposite my house in the castle. Mates queue to use my toilet. I issue brown wristbands for the privilege. I not only attend the talks at conferences these days, I even get something out of some of them. The closest I get to the old days is watching a random man giving a keynote lecture to a wall on ketamine. Yes, before you ask, he was on the drug *and* it was the topic of his discourse.

After a few dozen conferences under your belt, a pattern emerges, an imagined anthropological spectrum upon which most attendees can be placed. I mean, you've seen 'The Gunslinger', from handshake to pocket to putting a business card in your hand in less than three seconds. And then POOF! They are gone. To them, it's a simple game of how many cards they can give away; then sit back, cross their fingers and hope someone calls them. This is like going angling and shouting at the water to give you some fish. Sometimes a Gunslinger is actually a Relic (see below) who has just woken up and feels guilty.

'The Stat Machine' is a personal favourite. Statto will corner you and you will very much wish they hadn't. They always seem to have a job that you didn't know existed in dance music. 'Oh, you are a data analyst! Wow, I didn't even know we had them'. They will proudly tell you that blockchain is the future of everything, streaming is *brilliant*, and actually say things like 'music is just numbers really' without any trace of irony or shame. Sometimes they will be there to champion a new device or idea like a mad inventor: "Have you seen this!? It's a box that holds MP3s! It's like a virtual record box!" "So it is a… hard drive, then?". You can tell a Stat Machine a mile off as they are always on their own, dress like they are still at school and look a bit loopy around the eyes.

'The Relic' still thinks it is still the 90s. Everything should be free for The Relic because he is so VERY VERY IMPORTANT, EVERYBODY and gets very, *very* loudly annoyed when everything isn't gratis. He is staggering drunk by lunchtime, or still awake from yesterday, thinks the lectures are strictly for other people and is basically there to get hammered on an expense account. He will have his shirt off at some point and bellows famous people's names across the room as if he knows them, even though they are not even there. He will still be at the hotel a week after everyone else has gone, cry-wanking between troughs of comedown.

'The Enthusiast' is one of those total weirdos who have breakfast meetings. No, they really do! These fizzing Patrick Batemans would have a meeting whilst running alongside you if you let them. They think everything is awesome to a deranged degree and look on in horror as 'The Relic' staggers by. They are in bed by 9pm, vegan, and they DJ sometimes off a laptop with a tiny vest on 'for fun'. Stat Machines love meeting an Enthusiast 'cos one will actually listen to their mad ideas and probably give them money. Enthusiasts think EDM is *brilliant*, everyone is 'nice' and only stop smiling to put on their serious face at lectures or to fire someone. They scare me to death. Essentially, you could run the whole industry off Enthusiasts and Stattos and just give everyone else the rest of their lives off.

'The Sophisticate' is at every conference. This one is aloof from *everything*. They hate every minute of conferences but go anyway, arrive as late as possible, go into talks for five minutes or sometimes pop up at the end to loudly ask very difficult and combative questions like, "Yes, BUT what is the *point* of what you said?" to establish that they very much think the whole thing is a waste of their valuable time. The scene is an ARTFORM, not a *business* and all these awful business-type people are ruining everything, rather than actually keeping it alive. Yes, they used to be and/or are currently a DJ.

You find exactly what you are looking for when you go to any industry conference. It's very much like visiting a famous capital city. You get the city you are expecting. If you only want to see the obvious hits, monuments or shops… and miss anything at all authentic or valuable; just get drunk and sit on the tour bus. Or you can get serious and go deep. For every interminable, awkward and self-congratulatory ramble at conferences, there are hours of genuine and fascinating insight. You will get out of it what you put in. Most of all, if you are serious about what you do, you really need to be in a room with other people as serious as you are. It's really that simple.

I'm not very businesslike, but one could argue that some of the biggest DJs resemble entrepreneurs far more than artists. It's a tough one for me to discuss, 'cos I'm a DJ and Producer first and foremost and not much of a 'player'. The closest I have come to doing business is scoring some laxatives off a bloke called Mooncalf, or complaining to my agent that the hotel wallpaper is too weird, but in my defence, I did once run a record label, and a radio station.

I've done enough business to tell me I'm terrible at it. When I set up my label, dear old Tour Manager dubbed me "The Betamax Kid" as by this point even he was illegally downloading his hand-cranked steam hornpipes off the internet for free, exactly when I started a label expecting people to pay for music. A suitable name, because I have form. I enthusiastically start on most things just as they are becoming obsolete. I was a drummer just as drum machines were taking off. I was in bands just when DJing was getting big. I was a writer for specialist magazines just as the internet came along as the world's biggest and totally free-of-charge specialist magazine. I started a label that after years of graft started to peak just as Spotify came along. I wrote a book at exactly the same time people stopped reading. Seriously, don't take my advice on *anything*.

What was funny about running a label was that I don't think DJs quite understand just what sort of metrics you get back from the online promo system as a label owner. In short? *Everything*. We know when you say "Urg, not for me" that you haven't pressed play. We know when you say "Love it!" that you've listened to four seconds of the intro. We know when you've said "downloading for Richie" and not downloaded jacking shit for anybody. If I was to react to any of this nonsense and respond to them of course it would burst a bubble that would pretty much end the label on the spot. Same goes for websites. The IP owners often know exactly how many identities the trolls have. Who is pretending to be a fan of themselves. Who voted for themselves in that poll. Who has an imaginary agent. Where you live...

Then there are the *really* big myths. That we all make lots of money. That no one cheats regularly 'live' and in the studio with automation, miming and ghost-producing. The lies about stats, numbers, friends, charts and followers. These things are problems with society at large of course. 'Fair play' is an ancient notion, confined to the dustbin in favour of the bubbly 'fake it 'til you make it' and other slightly sinister sayings that don't bear much scrutiny at all when you actually stop to look at them and what they really suggest. Thankfully, faker hares are forever trapped in the revolving door that is confusing energy with results. They think if they flap about doing as much pretending as possible it will pay off. And it might. For a short while. Meanwhile, the tortoises who bothered to make the record themselves, talking to a genuine amount of real followers online, and have the confidence to make mistakes... they are the ones still around when the lights come on and the fakers are shown up for what they are. And one piece of advice I can definitely impart with absolute sincerity is if there is one skill you need to possess more than any other in this game, it is simply knowing when not to say anything at all.

It can seem like lies, polite fictions and coded language keep the music industry spinning. The entire bizarre inverted master-and-servant relationship between agent and artist is pretty much based on the DJ pretending very loudly that they don't touch the dirty, filthy end of the shitty stick they call the music business...then their representative claiming loudly that they can't do anything without the say-so of their impossible diva charges. An eternal waltz of bad-cop-worse-cop between manager/agent/act, each pretending to the world that the other one is the truly *difficult* one and everything would be so much easier if the other one didn't exist. It's part of the code we use. We are rarely direct, in fact direct people are very unpopular. Any hint of challenging the lies is *very* much frowned upon.

And *real* damage is done when these polite fictions/massive lies turn into a code of silence. The management who ignore their artists' mental and physical health and wellbeing and the artists themselves who until recently have been reluctant and/or programmed not to talk about it. The predators who operate with impunity in clubland's dark places and get away with it through their celebrity or power or because, well, it's just too awkward, career-killing, or potentially libellous to bring up. The reps who refuse to say no or hold up a mirror to their artist's behaviour until, filled with self-importance and delusion, said artist bursts, spectacularly and publicly, like a jazzy balloon full of bad giblets.

As well as shutting-up, we like to use code. Those agreed-upon phrases that are loaded with greasy meaning but completely innocent when taken apart. It's an ancient art, especially in England. That thing about language being used as the first weapon. 'Good day to you' being Victorian for 'fuck off'. Or 'hello?' meaning 'what the fuck are you doing?'. We have our own set in the biz. Such as:

'Fresh' - I am rather old and don't know what this is, but I need to say I like it.

'Refreshingly honest' - Oh shit! *you can't say that*!

'Dance Music Legend' - Massive pensioner.

'Diminutive' - Total shortarse.

'Difficult' - Just will not do what they are told.

'Addicted to painkillers' - Total crackhead.

'Outspoken' - Caution! May have a brain. Possibly deranged.

'Challenging' - Absolute fucking nightmare mate.

'Maverick' - Didn't do what we told them, but got away with it.

'Eccentric' - Too clever for us, must be mentally ill.

'Veteran' - Really very old.

'Uplifting' - Total dairy product.

'Ladies man' - Wants locking up and/or chemically neutering.

'Have you got anything good?' - Have you got anything good?

'Energetic' - Sounds like power tools.

'Is there a dub?' - You've totally fucking ruined it.

CHAPTER 19

'It's very dynamic' - The fact that this contained music disturbed me greatly.

'Send me your guest list' - I don't care what you play, you have been booked to bring people!

'Really looking forward to...' - The promoter made me write this...

'The market has changed a lot' - I'm paying you half what you got last year. No, my income stays the same.

'You're very eclectic' - You frightened my wife.

'I just make music for myself and if anyone else likes it, it's a bonus' - I am a penis.

'It's not for me' - It makes me sick out of my ears.

'Are you still making music?' - Fuck me! Are you still *alive*?

CHAPTER 20
NOT SOMETHING TO JOKE ABOUT

However irritating it is at the time, DJ diva behaviour is relatively harmless, except maybe to their reputation. But it is a spectrum, with a dark diminishing scale. The culture of stardom, indulgence, sycophancy and enabling that forms the 'DJ Bubble' has the potential to unleash and/or camouflage some truly awful behaviour. Especially combined with a late-night industry that beneath its utopian message is barely ahead, if not sometimes behind, wider society in its attitudes to gender. I think I glossed over some of the worst behaviour in book one. I'm OK with it now. Let's talk frankly about sexual assault.

House DJ and the man behind Subliminal Records, Erick Morillo, long had one of the worst reputations in our scene. While nothing illegal came to light until recently, he was a self-confessed 'ladies man' - always a term that sets ten bells a-ringing. Unconfirmed rumours abounded all over the world. It recently caught up with him in his homeland when he was arrested for sexual battery in Miami, he then died just days before he was due in court to answer to a positive DNA match. He's not the only one who was out there. Not by a long chalk. I've got friends in the biz, young women, who had to spend many Sundays driving DJs around to visit brothels. Forcing them to be enablers, and if they object, they don't stay employed for long. I've been on tour with some DJs who literally have a sex worker ready when they arrive in town, with another arranged for later. These are just the *legal* version of a tragic bleakness that permeates the culture run by rich old men.

I know of one DJ who has eluded rape charges but has a string of other victims too scared to come forward. He spends most of his days on the internet telling everyone he is not a rapist and will attempt to destroy anyone who says otherwise. His dwindling fame provides a small gang of followers who leap on any accuser, abusing his position during and after the assaults. This is key to the nature of abuse. It's not just physical.

CHAPTER 20

Abuse is about the use and misuse of power. It is having more money and profile than your victims. Using privilege as a weapon. Using lawyers and money to silence, attack or pay-off. The reason there's been no 'Me Too' in the music biz to speak of is simply, in my opinion, because it is far, FAR more rife than anywhere else. The industry is so complicit is embarrasses me even to mention it. I mean, for Christ's sake, Erick Morillo was once booked to do a conference panel titled 'Safe from Harm'! I had to spend two days on the phone with colleagues and organisers just to get someone to even consider the lunacy of it. And what I said to them, as I said recently to angry white straight men on the internet was this: if you think the 'playboy' and carefully marketed 'ladies man' image is OK, that a DJ makes his career on objectifying women, puts them naked in giant champagne glasses at his gigs and generally uses them in a very calculated manner to boost his own image, and then after paying for that crafted marketing, proceeds to fuck their way around the word... if you are OK with that, I can't even start to talk to you.

Women work throughout all levels of Dance Music. Photographers, agents, artist liaisons, managers, DJs, label bosses, promoters, producers... and yet often are treated, *still*, as if they are merely there to make up the numbers. Or are part of the 'fun'. Quite apart from the alarming stories of abuse from male DJs, promoters and managers on the road towards members of the public and fans, it's the problem of equality and safety in the workplace we need to start with. Hopefully then moving outwards to a more mature attitude across the board with how women are treated in Dance Music.

For women DJs, just going on tour can be a hazardous nightmare. Many promoters seem to book a female DJ pretty much based on how they look, and how likely they think their chances with them are. As you will see below, finally across the internet and the late-arriving media we are now hearing stories like these from women across the board. It can no longer be managed by a complicit industry or chatted-away at conferences.

Full disclosure here, in the last ten years as my reputation as someone who speaks out grew, and proportionally the demand for my DJ services dwindled, I moved sideways into journalism. Sure, writing mostly about music, but sometimes politics and a bit of cinema. I'm no Watergate-cracker or top sleuth. But I did spend about six months solid investigating sexual abuse in my industry full-time and generally spent three years on it. 28 brave women got in touch and frankly, the stories were chilling. In the end, only a handful could be legally broadcast. This was due to various factors, such as who gave their approval and which stories had enough clear evidence. I then published the stories in a magazine. I think as many people as possible should hear them. When they first came out I was slammed, mainly by male DJs, many of them quite preposterously trying to tell me that a) they'd never seen any attacks (and if they hadn't seen any, they must not have happened) and b) the whole thing was actually 'impossible' because our scene is 'peace and love'. Yeah. Bullshit right? I will shut up now. Listen to these words, verbatim, from real women...

'The Parisienne'
"I used to go out alone in clubs for many years. I really like moving from clubs to clubs to hear some artists, and to be free if I decide to go home. My legendarily frosty behaviour in clubs helps me a lot to feel safe, to always keep the control of some situations. Just in case. I always play it safe.

I had to go work in Lyon to take some pics (live and portraits) of a famous South American DJ, who is part of a big record label. I missed this DJ two days before in Marseille, he was playing in a club where I knew the promoters. The deal was that he had to pay my train tickets and my hotel to Lyon.

I met him then on a boat with his manager, he was running late and had to perform live 15 minutes after. In this boat I met some very nice people (boys and girls) from Lyon, who gave me their phone numbers if I wanted to join them in an afterparty. After the live show, the promoter told us to leave the venue very quickly, and as there was no backstage area. I couldn't take my pics there. The DJ asked me to go with them to the hotel for some portrait shots instead.

We arrived at the hotel, despite the deal, they said that they wouldn't pay for a room for me now. Also, the hotel was suddenly full. I was quite angry, then the DJ asked me to stay with his manager for half an hour in his room because he had to be alone to make a Skype call with his wife first, and after that he would find a solution.

I shouldn't have come to his room. I guess the actresses felt the same too for Weinstein. And that's what people (other DJs) told me. Because yes, it's ALWAYS our fault. But when you are here for WORK, and when the guys knew I've already taken some pics of other DJs from their label, how I could imagine that the manager would try to rape me?

I was very lucky because the other rooms heard me screaming. Screaming "NO!". A lot of times.

"NO! STOP!"

I thank all the other rooms who called reception. I thank the receptionist of the hotel to have called the room and taken action. And I thank the kind local man I met earlier on the boat to have come five minutes later after my call to bring me to a safe place.

I was in shock, I cried and had an anxiety attack all night long.

I've never published the pics of the gig. I don't ever want to see them again."

AKA 'Soul DJ'

"I knew this DJ a while; he has been part of the scene since the start, as he likes to tell everyone at any opportunity. He was accused of rape formally and had a really awful rep before that too but I just didn't believe it, especially when he got off the charge. It's easy with hindsight but [although] none of my friends or family liked him, I spent quite a bit of time with him until I finally stepped away. I paid for nearly everything when we were together. Something I hear happened to the others. I now know there are many others he abused like me.

The police are almost powerless with 'conjugal rape'. That is his thing. The others and myself were fooled into relationships and gradually the violence and perversity are upped and upped. I won't go too much into the details of what he does but suffice to say it is *not* consensual. I have made numerous complaints to the police regarding him. They have assured me if I made a complaint about his sexual preference they would take me seriously and investigate. I haven't done this mainly as it means I will have to put myself through more trauma and I just want to forget I was even with him to be honest I am in a new relationship and although my boyfriend has promised me if I want to he will support me, I am not sure I am able to handle the stress at the moment. After all, he got away with it before so often.

He has such a terrible reputation and is so paranoid he spends most of his time stalking Facebook and Twitter to see what people are saying about him. His whole life is wrapped up in that keyboard thinking everyone is out to get him. This was long before he crumbled and made everyone aware that he is very unhinged. He was always blaming the women before me, I was too blind to see the signs. When we were together he made me block my friends and people in the industry who were 'against' him. It was so embarrassing. They never asked me to work with them again, which was awful.

He has had fake social media accounts and uses them to monitor and threaten people. He also has spent the last few years slagging me off and telling lies about me all over social media and to anyone who wanted to listen. He uses his small gang of fans to outnumber and surround victims. Abusing his position. I worked in the biz myself a bit but after he blackened my name with anyone he could. In my normal job he got the police to call my work to give me a 'harassment warning'. How he kept finding me I don't know. But stalking is illegal. This is after police gave him a verbal warning about his abuse over social media regarding me. He is a manipulative, narcissistic bully who has got away with it for too long, I'm doing this so one day so others will know, and be able to steer clear of him."

AKA 'The Londoner'
"To be honest it's easier to come up with a time something sexist DIDN'T happen. There are so many I don't know where to start really. As well as the big ones that are nasty and dangerous there are the constant small ones. Like a sort of background noise that is always there. Being quizzed all the time. Being talked over. Pressure to be glam. As if how you look has anything to do with what comes out of the speakers.

There are different types of pressures for different jobs in the industry. I think female agents and managers have to be like ten times more

CHAPTER 20

aggressive and hard than men, and some have told me it is horrible for them 'cos it isn't really how they are. Or want to work, ideally. And, of course, if you are tough and woman you are a 'bitch' and worse. But if it is a man they're just good at your job.

I once arrived at a gig and it was one of the early days in my career of air travel being a novelty, so also a little scary in itself. We don't all get minders and tour managers. You are a long way from home, arriving in the middle of the night. So I got through customs and the promoter is there and he is like really standing out in like sunglasses at midnight, and you can see before he even opens his trap he loves himself. Some people only interact with you in 'come-on' mode. This was one. From the get-go he is turning on the charm. Clearly on drugs too. And you know, it's late and you've already done a thousand miles and a gig the night before.

So in the car he is making loads of innuendo and it is hard to know what to do because if you are too cold men can get aggressive and it is even riskier to pretend to respond, so you are in this sort of limbo of yes and no answers and "uh-huh" and "mmm" and trying to sound like you are listening but also project disinterest. I think all women know what I am talking about. I won't repeat what he was coming out with but it was not very nice. And it is scary on a motorway at night with no other cars about.

By the time we get into town he keeps talking about what a good time I am going to have and you just want to say "look, I'm here to work mate" and then he starts asking personal questions like if am married and all that and you are like "oh Lord here we go!". So the first direct proposition is in the car. Really shit one too, like "how's about it?" and waggling his eyebrows like he is 15 or something. So you just laugh it off. What else can you do? This is the person who is supposed to be paying you, your 'employer'.

So instead of dropping me and picking me up he is 'helping me check in'. As if any decent hotel doesn't have multi-lingual staff. Then he's 'helping with the bags'. So then I get to the lift and it starts to get real. It's a confined space and he is staring me out. Then he presses the emergency stop and I just go rigid. I couldn't even tell you what he was saying I was so petrified but it was a variation of the earlier come-on. I started pressing buttons on the lift and that seemed to break the tension so he started it up again. In hindsight he knew those buttons too well. He'd done it before.

Then he tried it on again outside the door. Saying how he'd booked me because he'd fallen in love with me. Basically booking me because of photographs. I was in bits by this point. Couldn't get in the room fast enough and slammed the door in his face. Been propositioned three times before I'd even got in the hotel room. Had to be some sort of record. Can you imagine how you feel as a performer when you've basically just been told what you do is irrelevant, all that matters is what you look like?

Luckily someone else came to pick me up. My confidence was shot by this point. I played like shit that night. What kind of professional hammers an artist's confidence like that and then expects them to deliver? He ran the night with this business partner who did the journey to the gig from the hotel. I just said as diplomatically as I could "I ain't getting in a car with your mate again" and he just laughed like 'oh yeah, he is a bit of a lad that one'.

This is the real problem right there. Acceptance.

One last thing. I can't stand 'female DJ' we are just DJs, thanks."

* * *

Maybe something's never been quite right about 'rock 'n' roll behaviour'. If it's done with a certain style, wit, or perhaps even innocence it can sometimes be acceptable. I think I got away with my own stupidity because it was mainly bumbling around. There is a rule of thumb that harming *yourself* for fun is fine, but we *don't* draw the public into it. Plus there is something about the 'groupie' side of it that has never been anything but strange. Sinister even. Dance Music is merely a branch of the music industry in general, but for some reason we seem to do a really cheesy, shoddy version of 'sexy' compared to our peers. We still, to this day, see 'sexy laydeez' used in a highly 1970s way to promote 21st century events and enterprises. It is writ large most of all in Ibiza with its 'sexy' shows in clubs and lately, even restaurants. What scantily clad go-go dancers have to do with Techno is still a mystery to me.

At the top of this pervy pyramid are inevitably, the DJs. Everyone must point in the direction of the booth for a reason. It's not even like it's a band. It's one guy. Nearly always a guy of course, until recently. There is something drearily obvious and inevitable that they should be boning their way around the world. Almost as if their penis is the purpose of it all, rather than music, dance and unity. I mean there is certainly a subtle and constant enabling approval, even *aspiration* that for men to be a DJ is to be some sort of non-stop sex tourist. It is something that *really* needs to stop. People make mistakes. Regrettable things happen to people of all sexes and persuasions. However, abuse is *not* a mistake, it is a *mindset*. Abusers have a modus operandi that appears in nearly every interaction they have. You've seen a species of them online. Incapable of interacting with a woman without a sexual insinuation. Popping up on the threads of women they have never met, constantly. Liking every post and photograph and "lukin gud babes" on socials doesn't make you a sexual abuser, just a large dickhead. But it helps to understand there is a mindset here being enabled by a permissiveness that does not actually engage anyone's permission at all.

In terms of our industry, its working environment, it is a basic human right to be free of fear. This transcends anything parochial, it is a fundamental. Part of the problem with a business being about a party is people finding it hard to tell the difference between those who are employed by the fiesta and those who are attendees. What I hope to address is to work towards helping people grasp the difference. If you are a man working in the biz, and you encounter a woman working too, the rules of the party do not apply. The rules of the workplace do. This applies regardless of orientation. In order for our society to progress we need to clear house and address sexual misconduct at all levels. It's happening in government and it's happening throughout the entertainment industries, of which Dance Music is undeniably a part.

Ultimately is all this horror not the *opposite* of what we are supposed to be about? Acid House was supposed to be about acceptance and everything that is good about the world. It enrages me when certain DJs with the worst reputation for predatory sexual violence talk online about peace and love. It shames ALL of us when we allow this to happen.

Indeed, it was a recent online documentary with millionaire 'ladies men' DJs talking about their *feelings* and re-framing themselves as victims of a lifestyle that sparked this raging anger with me in the first place.

If you want to understand just how complicit in wrongdoing and ineffectual as a serious body our industry is, look no further than how it handled the 'revelations' of its most notorious alleged sexual predator. Big name after big name openly paid tribute to Morillo and many of them did not even attempt to pretend he was innocent. They merely performed an extremely Trumpian leap of logic by saying things along the lines of 'despite his reputation...' or versions of 'say what you like about him...' and then launching into a tearful eulogy and showing pics of Morillo grinning his wealthy privilege, arm in arm with them. There was a clear underlying message of 'yes, we knew, and here we are saying quite clearly that we don't care'. Sure it may be, in some cases, unwitting and as tone-deaf as a bat using its own head as a pencil sharpener, but whether intentional or not, it is still brutally savage for a victim to watch unfold. These messages served not only as a frankly obscene gesture, they managed to double as a really, *really* rubbish tribute.

If you ever can be bothered to look into what is wrong with the dance music industry, I will quite simply tell you this, go look at how the death of Morillo was dealt with. Give it a google. You will see everything you need to know in the posts that remain even after so many were taken down. From denial top to bottom, approval sometimes even, to the frankly bizarre 'live streamed funeral', to attacking victims and critical voices... it is all there, glaring its hideousness at you.

Our industry *has* to stand up in order to continue to be relevant to an ever-quickening social evolution. Enabling wrongness, hiding it, pretending it doesn't exist or, worst of all, paying loud ineffectual lip-service is simply not the answer. In fact, all these things encourage it. Professional Omertà is a plague. Not just in our game but throughout society. 'Whistleblowers' are bad, they'll tell you. Shutting up is good. It's 'professional' to never rock the boat.

No.

Bzzzzt.

WRONG.

CHAPTER 21
DON'T CALL US, WE'LL CALL YOU

If there are defining factors in any career, industry or indeed in life itself, they don't come bigger than rejection. If music is simply the binary state of notes and space, then anyone who understands the spaces truly understands *music*, then it can be said this is true for positives and negatives. If you don't understand the lows and only deal in the highs, you cease to hear melody. There is a lot of pressure these days to only deal in positivity. Longevity in the DJ game requires an innate ability to handle negativity, perhaps more than any other skill.

Being in the creative industries means getting a rejection pie in the face every single day, at least if you are doing it right. Anyone who is out there with their bits out on the board is waiting for the chop. And let me tell you, it never, *ever* stops. At best you can hope for a peak decade where a lot goes your way but trust me, that will end. Everything ends. If you survive in the biz long enough, you will return to that point at the start where no one wanted to know you.

As a DJ, rejection is the grease that lubes your machine. If you actually believe that you are so wonderful that the first person you approach is going to slip on their own juices in the rush to give you everything, you have lost it before you even began. *Expect* rejection. It really REALLY isn't personal. There's so much crap out there you would not believe it. *Really*. It is immense. Most people think they are DJs now. Huge numbers are deadly serious about it. People are constantly bombarded by promos and invites just like you are. They have too much social media to engage with, just like you do. There's simply too much noise and information out there. Your tiny wee self against such volume means it's very *likely* you will be rejected automatically. People swipe left now, on almost everything, all the time. As a reflex. They only respond to the very hyped and are pretty jaded about that as well.

And it works both ways. When you are rejecting, be nice. I famously can't be arsed with dickheads online. I'll block anyone at the drop of a hat. Mostly because I have a couple of serious stalkers who often pop up with fake accounts, so I err on the side of caution and block as soon as someone gets nasty. I'd be lying if I said I regret blocking anyone. However, I'm prepared to pay the price. Every now and then someone will send me a screenshot of a group of rejected fans, loons and stalkers all having a lovely tea party hating on me with fierceness that is like the sun. You'd be shocked at some of the stuff they come out with. If you can't handle that sort of negativity, you had best never reject anyone.

Not answering emails is a 'thing' now. The dating world calls it 'ghosting'. If you absolutely want to make an enemy of someone for life, this is a great way to go about it. Nothing says 'you are of no consequence to me' better than completely ignoring someone. Because other people do it to you, you start to think it is fine, then normal, then something you should be doing to look important. Let me explain something very clearly: in the music business the people at the top, and by that I mean the real top, are nice as pie. They really are. They engage, are polite and available. It's the mid-range that have all the attitude. But when you are dealing with an average Joe who can't even deign to reply, you may as well give up right there. The message they are sending is not that they are very important and special, it is saying they are an amateur. Someone to be avoided.

How you deal with rejection is key to how you appear to others. Not merely by dint of response but by example. I once got swamped by promos (as you do) and the quickest way to stop some was just to press 'spam' on Gmail. One of the rejected label's reactions was to then follow me for two weeks on every single form of social media to tell anyone who would listen that I was a very large cunt. This was not a good look for anyone concerned.

It can be personal. I don't approach friends for biz anymore, they won't appreciate being put on the spot and no one lately will automatically work with you just because you know them. This rejection can come between friends and be deadly toxic. I advise caution with how you react to promos too. Most of all, we must learn to have grace in the booth. I've had people utterly ruin the night for me and, consequently the rest of the club, with a nasty comment that was absolutely designed to get a reaction. Fortunately, this generally only works on me lately if I am exhausted. A thick skin is essential to survive. Most of all, this topic puts me in mind of a photo of myself in the dance press some 20+ years ago. I must have been in Ibiza, and inexplicably, I had my top off. Something that very rarely happens unless I am about to die of heatstroke or have just been in a car accident.

The photo was captioned very simply with the immortal legend:
"The Secret DJ: Shit Tits."

* * *

I frequently say to anyone who will listen (my dog, mainly) that the number one tenet at the heart of playing records is *confidence*. Like a lot of performing, or sports, or business... look hard enough at it and in the middle you will see a plucky little nut of confidence, the essential key to dealing with all that rejection. What is standing up in front of lots of people in a stance of musical authority but a large show of self-assurance?

It won't be a surprise to anyone who's read the first book but I've certainly never been immune from the odd crisis of confidence. My issues with it were tied to health. I was generally unfit, unwell and unmotivated, so this had an impact on how I perceived myself. Being a DJ by its very nature puts you out front and sometimes feeling horribly exposed. The ever-changing scene can intimidate too. I know I find all the impossibly good-looking latest junior DJs and their new toys quite oppressive sometimes. I know I look out at the dance floor and sometimes think "what the hell are you all looking at?" Just staring at the DJ brandishing a device is a relatively new thing for me. That carries a lot of weight on its own, as does my greatly overworked pelvis.

I always have and always will try to play future music, but sometimes the DJ before is basically playing records from the 90s, or another is purely genre-driven whereas I am not. Sometimes I stick out like a giant throbbing arse because I don't mime to a seamlessly synched mix. Just playing a breakbeat can be an act of cultural terrorism in a sterilised world. The pressures are many and often odd.

Age is a factor. I was too stupid when I was very young to *not* be scared. I had the overreaching overconfidence that is automatically bestowed on us at the start of life. You certainly miss it when it is gone. An even deeper irony is that it was overconfidence that became my nemesis and ended up eroding what genuine gumption was there very quickly. I thought I knew it all. I felt that because I was always working, I must therefore be doing all the right things. I wasn't. I was becoming a caricature of myself. A lazy impersonator of me. I was moderately high up in the general pecking order, ergo, everything I did must be correct. BZZZZ. WRONG AGAIN!

It took several years of being drastically incorrect and out-of-touch for anything to change. Even more time to recognise the issues and stop blaming other people. We so very rarely look hard at our own part in our downfalls.

Solutions? Well, easier said than done, but I for one stopped resting on laurels and playing the same, easily-found music that was stopping me from being unique. I made a conscious decision to go to a place where I really cared. This, perhaps unsurprisingly, is a zone outside of genres, styles and trends.

This meant a few things. Because society and, to a lesser extent myself, had stopped valuing what we do, I decided to *add* value to it. So I stopped doing cheap, bad gigs even though it meant having no money. And often that meant zero cash. Zip. Not a sausage for long periods. I also started to do something I'd not done in a long time and *prepared*. I never used to prepare for gigs. After busy periods where you legitimately don't have time, eventually, you just tell yourself you don't have to. Incorrect. You really do.

The ritual of preparation helped me rebuild my shattered confidence back up. I was ready. I knew what I was going to do and what was at my disposal. It didn't have to be a fixed set! God forbid, no! But I had that readiness that comes from spending time thinking about it. I also stopped being arrogant and started doing things like read trade papers and mags and websites. How many people do you know who reel out the old "oh god I haven't read Xmag for years" with a large theatrical sigh? Because they are far FAR too important to show an interest in what is going on out there. Far too special to show curiosity in what different people with new, fresh tastes and ideas are into. When you stagnate, it erodes your confidence. Sure on the outside everything is fine… the nature of the subconscious is such that you don't know what is going on inside, until it is too late and it has manifested itself as something odd on the outside. The combination of looking out for myself physically as well as re-training and re-investing in the job brought me back from the brink and back into the middle of things.

Show me a DJ, or indeed anyone who works in a spotlight, and says they aren't nervous beforehand and I will show you a barefaced liar. For a long time, I thought in my conscious brain that for me, it was almost mundane. Didn't 'feel' nervous at all. However, why is it that I have to go to the toilet about three times immediately before? And why do I have anxiety dreams about equipment not working? I've seen DJs who are genuinely nice as pie become highly irritable and neurotic before a gig. I've seen more than a few ashen-faced big names throw up. These are seasoned pros. I know one who can't perform without a fistful of valium and if you knew the irony of his macho stage name you'd be staggered.

The addictions I myself have suffered have always been related to isolation and emotion. I have self-medicated because I spend so much time on my own. Also, while we are at it, let's be clear that alcohol is very much a large part of the group of 'substances'. The attempts to work on your comedown in the week with downers, to combat the weekend's uppers, are one of the biggest traps to getting into a full-time destructive cycle.

It is about experiencing something that is habitual as well as emotional. I've been through it. As well as a need for a 'crutch' for the stress of the situation, the very situation itself now requires it. A Pavlovian response starts to happen. A vicious circle where the body and brain recognises a specific situation and immediately demands the stimulants associated with it. It starts with an emotional need, in fact, a state of panic is the best way to describe it, and a quick fix for that is depressants. Especially, alcohol. Then when you discover you are *always* nervous stepping into the booth, then you need 'medicating' every time. This is a form of addiction known as 'associative learning'.

For some people, the *only* way is prohibition. It is the hardest method. In our modern polarised society, things are very much now 'either/or'. I recommend a more nuanced approach myself. It is about 'reduction'. Scaling back. I call the process 'achievable evils'. Tell yourself there is nothing wrong with a loosener. But know when to stop. The real pitfall here is getting in the zone and then unwittingly hammering yourself while you are playing. And Lord knows I've been there. You barely feel a thing while the endorphins are pumping in the booth, but getting off your nut impacts on your work. It hits you like a ton of bricks afterwards too. The adrenaline holds off the effects and you feel superhuman. For a while. If the 'problem' is you just need a wee kick for your ship to shove off, it's not the end of the world. It's a small issue, relatively easily solved. It's sailing off into the night with no compass and rudder that is definitely foolhardy.

The problem with being off your tits when you perform is that YOU think you are stone-cold awesome, it's just few in the audience agree.

I've been fortunate in a way never to have been particularly cool or hip, I just can't exist easily in places like that. I see right through it. Find it daft. Always have. I don't begrudge those splashing about in it. There are way worse things to be obsessed with. There's just so much else out there in the world. So much! Too much very interesting other things to deny.

The problem with our scene, one of many issues sadly, is that it is empirically about, and run by, obsessives. Fetishists. Anyone who isn't as crazed about things as they are is immediately labelled inauthentic and incorrect. At its heart is a macho competitiveness that is more akin to sport than music. This grip that fanboys have on the planet is stifling everything good. We make things in order *not* to offend them now, and art is very much *supposed* to offend, quite fundamentally.

At a certain age, your brain chemistry starts to dry up. You become reactionary, bitter and mean. If you had a long and wearisome journey in any business, that unique journey influences greatly upon your decision process. Perhaps just before you hung-up your headphones and started to look for a desk and a salary in the industry you were pushing 40 and the bookings were drying up? Trapped in a genre that is dying-out, perhaps? When you try to play different stuff the crowds at the genre nights you were booked at, well, the crowd don't like change much. You don't recognise anyone in the clubs anymore, and pretty much when you've tried to 'get a proper job', it is now way WAY too late in life. Is it possible to reinvent yourself?

We are talking about second chances here. This is a bigger issue than merely genre. Although I would always say to anyone who cares that if you hitch yourself to the bandwagon, you *will* go down with the bandwagon... there are other factors at play too. Lots of things can make you feel like you are approaching the twilight years of your game. For me, one of the things I noticed greatly was being very isolated after many years of support from friends. After a while, your peeps can get left behind, especially if you don't nurture them. You can end up very far away, figuratively, physically and emotionally.

There should be a lovely long German word for when your mates are either too old or too jaded to come to your gigs anymore. I wouldn't expect them to now either, they'd already gone *way* past the call of duty the millionth time I asked them. Social media doesn't help. Suddenly you aren't asking anyone nice and personally any more, and here's a tip: you are playing records in Moscow, or Istanbul, or Auckland... why then send social media invites to everyone in London? Do you think we'll all go out and buy a plane ticket? If you yourself stop caring about personal contact, why should anyone care in return? Before you can say "rewind!" you are on your own, and the fun can go out of almost anything when you are a party of one. Support networks are vital.

Second chances can seem like something you need to whittle down to a single issue. It's common to relate it to a change of genre. "If only I changed the music I play, everything will be fine." Basing your career on releasing records makes it much easier to slip sideways. You may slough off a few old fans along the way, but time would do that anyway. There are more diverse worlds to explore.

But it isn't simply about having put all your eggs in the Trance basket or sitting around on the Dub step too long that can bring on the ennui we describe. Second chances are also about testing who you are in a very fundamental way. Are you a fighter or a passenger? Because newsflash! *Every* job gets hard and dries up. It was never going to be a doddle or a doss permanently. There is no fame utopia at the end of the rainbow, just more work. There is no free lunch or bluebirds of happiness. All the top dogs go through your issues too. Looking like swans on top but little legs going like the clappers underneath the waters is par for the course. What you are being presented with is a simple choice. Are you serious? Because until you are ready to have nothing left except the drive to make things happen, you aren't ready to play the game. Losing what you have and starting again isn't a mistake, it's an inevitability. It's no different to marriage. Expecting it to be sunshine and happiness all the time and pulling the cord the minute anything goes wrong is a recipe for disaster and a rather costly divorce.

In my experience, you are only as strong as the last three or four times you had to pack it up and press 'reset'. Second chances are a beautiful thing. An opportunity. You will get to see who you really are. You know how I *know* I am a DJ? Apart from the DJing-related anxiety dreams? I *know* with a searing conviction I am a DJ because I hit rock bottom several times and did not give an inch. I chose to have literally *nothing* and continue. It was very, very hard. But it steeled me. Gave me armour against envy and hate. Gave me conviction and confidence. Made me take the whole thing *very* seriously when I had to. We've talked many times in these pages about understanding the value of what you do and who you are. You can only truly understand this when you bottom out and push through. Changing what you play is the least of it. Making it through the tunnel and into the light means changing *everything* up. You have to do what it takes to re-energise you. I could give you a list but really it boils down to something really simple; a decision hard as diamond and precise as a laser. Ask yourself this. Am I a DJ? If the answer is 'yes', then nothing will ever stop you being one. Nothing.

A long time ago, when I'd dried up a little, I made myself a new policy. For years I never played solo. For arguably the peak of my career, for something like seven years, I always elected to play alongside another DJ. I know many DJs fear this. Although it has somewhat come back into vogue recently, so less fearsome lately perhaps. But I know for a fact many are scared of it because I have asked them, or it has been presented to them, and they have reeled back in terror.

A lot of times these days the answer to nearly every question about DJs somehow seems to contain the word 'ego'. An awful lot of Eastern religions and philosophies, and a fair few Western ones, are about achieving some sort of peace through quelling the ego, especially one out of control. Now don't get me wrong, I'm about a spiritual as a lump of plasticine left on a windowsill on a hot day, but it's clear that rampant ME ME ME is behind a lot of issues in the world, both general and personal.

DJs against sharing a set most frequently speak to me in terms of 'losing their identity'. It is their schtick. Their jam. Their vibe maaaan. What-they-do. This will *not* disappear when they work alongside another DJ. No more than the ability and style of a tennis player will vanish when they play a set of mixed doubles. In fact, it will become far clearer to everyone who they are, including themselves. Perhaps for the first time.

Back-to-back is not new. Indeed I spent a fair few years doing it with many *many* DJs when it was almost unheard of. So I am eminently qualified for this one on the grounds that I have had to bribe, bully and generally convince many other DJs both large and small over the years that it is both safe, fun and generally a jolly good idea. My sales pitch went along the lines of: "What you usually get is one DJ doing their 'thing', which often can be fairly inflexible and unchanging. When you go B2B you suddenly have to think quite hard about what you are doing, and it tends to end up with two professionals working hard in original and challenging circumstances instead of one going through the motions, which can only be a good thing, right?"

Most of all, this is a good thing for the dancefloor. The expectations of the crowd changes greatly when there are two DJs up there. People become less expectant of a dishwater-dull seamless and endless drone and far more accepting of a changeable, esoteric and binary vibe that adds a frisson of 'whatever next?' to the mix. Quite literally to the mix, in fact. So much of what we do is about acceptance and anticipation. It's never been about how good you are at playing other people's records. It's about hype, vibe and gossip. It's about reputation. The floor either allows or demands. Usually the latter. DJ Harvey is a great example. He frequently plays crackers and random stuff that any other DJ would be boo-ed off for. The crowd not only allows it, they expect and demand it. The vibe is sizzling in the room before he plays a single beat or bar. Carl Cox has a venue in a frenzy before he even arrives in the building. Any DJ who thinks that this phenomenon is about them, or any other, is lost already. It is the people who make this call. It is they who make this happen. You are merely another participant.

A back-to-back session immediately speaks of something special, something different. Something exciting. The only thing that as a DJ you need to be scared of is the reason why you think it will be anything but spectacular and fun. If you are a plastic DJ who can only use one type of format or equipment and plays a set that cannot change then yes. Absolutely you should be nervous, in fact, you probably shouldn't do it for maybe ten years further down the line. B2B is all about improvisation, creativity, experience and flexibility. It quite literally separates the pro from the plastic. The ability to arrive and play not just easily but creatively with a stranger is perhaps the apogee of the skills of a professional DJ. Much like a true musician can arrive in almost any situation and not merely perform, but excel.

Don't worry if you can't. It will come with time. It is certainly something to aspire to. As for tips? In a sense, B2B is something you cannot prepare for. It is experience, confidence and professional courtesy all rolled into one. And yes, scary because it absolutely exposes both your weaknesses and strengths. It is the true test of whether you are about the self or about the dancefloor. This is clear when you do it with someone trying for the first time or still raw at it. They cut your tunes off. They lean in, hog and twiddle when none is needed. They are reluctant to leave and over-keen to arrive in a mix. Some just decide your tune is shit and cut it off almost as soon as it starts, which sounds hideous to everyone except them. Many simply cannot operate without their sync'd and heavily prepped set. Then again, some are naturals. I've broken more than my fair share of other DJ's B2B cherries and some have utterly and immediately *shone*. True pros who took to it like a duck to water. And take it from me, when it works it SO works. Fluid, naturally jamming. True flow.

The opposite of ego, in this case, is *duo*.

CHAPTER 22
CHASING THE DOPAMINE

On 20th April 2018, dance music had its own 'Princess of Hearts' moment, with the death of painfully-young EDM star 'Avicii'. Tim Bergling was just 28. Youthful casualties are not so unusual in our highly hedonistic industry. What was different this time was that the descent of the kid was so clearly documented in an expensive Netflix documentary just six months before.

Suddenly there was a global 'wellbeing' microscope trained on us, and with it came a whole new level of mainstream political correctness and terminology. Social media, magazines and industry conferences began to hum with conversations about 'wellness' and brow-furrowing about equality, diversity and ill health. I think that's excellent, actually, and *long* overdue. But it's also massively ironic considering the ruthless realities of the music business, a business that is worth an estimated £5.7 billion a year globally. Let's be frank also, once the conferences are over, not a lot happens. The wellness retreats are not cheap either, a tidy sum is made. Indeed, it is estimated that the 'wellness' industry now outstrips nightclub profits in Ibiza.

It's not the 90s anymore. Dance music was built back then on foundations of drugs, partying, sleeplessness and excess. Now two generations of selfie-taking young go-getters scratch their heads at why anyone would want to be so out of their mind when there is such good money to be made. The original ethos of dance music as a highly vocal protest movement is long, *long* since lost in the cheerfully chattering ding of happy cash registers. We now face a paradox, a corporate conundrum usually reserved for conglomerates: how to tackle, or be seen to tackle, clearly awful and negative issues that seem hopelessly institutionalised without actually examining our own culpability? How do we mourn dead young acts without digging too carefully into what pushed them to that end?

Watch in awe as millionaire DJs boo-hoo about how hard it's been for them, they wave goodnight as they waft off to their mansions, to sleep like babies on the heaped skulls of teenage laptop DJs, drink from a brimming goblet filled with intern tears and rest their weary crown upon pillows stuffed with money. The dance music press can't do much but repeat these sanitised messages, weak as lemon cordial. Meanwhile, poor kids without access to private doctors, yoga gurus or even vegetables struggle with exactly the same problems as superstars, far estranged from the support and solutions that money provides.

A University of Westminster pilot survey of 2,211 self-identifying professional musicians working across a broad swathe of the UK music industry found that:

71.1% of respondents believed they had experienced incidences of anxiety and panic attacks.
68.5% of respondents experienced incidences of depression.

UK Office for National Statistics data (collected between 2010-13) indicated that nearly one in five of us suffers from anxiety and/or depression (aged 16 years +). This research suggests that musicians could be up to three times more likely to suffer from depression compared to the general public. And yet the majority of respondents felt underserved by the available resources:

52.7% found it difficult to get help.
54.8% considered there were gaps in the provision of available help.

These preliminary findings from 2016 suggest that music, and by this we mean working in or having ambitions to work in the music industry, might indeed be making musicians sick. Or at least be contributing towards their levels of mental ill-health. I suspect it's not limited to musicians and the music industry either. Or that the intervening years have in any way improved the situation.

We are not well. As artists, workers or as consumers. We can't change modern society with any ease, but we can certainly scold a highly culpable industry.

CHAPTER 22

DRUGS. Say it loud. No one wants to, not really. Prohibition is clearly not working, nor is any sane adult dialogue at government level. Hypocrisy is the number one problem. Denial a close second. One hand dabbing at crocodile tears while the other accepts huge wedges of wonga from booze and 'energy drinks' firms, cigarettes and most loopy of all, vast farms of 'medicinal' cannabis.

The UK's own drug tsarina is married to one of the world's biggest weed growers for pharmaceutical use, while her own policy dictated there is no medical use possible from it. Only recently has the UK, as always, copied America and even considered looking at the issue. Just staggering isn't it? Our star DJs and industry leaders lie outright about their own consumption. They completely erase it from everything at 'official' level, while popping off to the bathroom for a lifter while the interns get rid of all mentions.

How can you escape or take a break from a machine so dependent on novelty? People don't enter this biz guaranteed with a job for life. You're not even sure of a job for the *summer*. Most clubbers in their twenties don't last more than a few years doing it with any regularity before real life, proper jobs and family drag them back to reality.

In something like three years the industry as a whole can almost completely repopulate. Particularly in the age of interns and zero-hours contracts. Our whole damn thing is geared towards utter disposability, not just the acts themselves. If the industry can't even take itself seriously enough to offer proper employment conditions and wages, how can we expect it to treat anyone's health, mental and physical, with the correct amount of respect?

I don't have all the answers, are not solutions our industry's job? But when the very method of production is a sausage factory designed to squeeze the meat until it squeaks, what hope is there for action or change? At the conferences, and in online documentaries our fattest cats put on their best sad faces and tell us it isn't easy for them either while offering nothing by way of assistance.

Here's a start: Drug use often falls into two rough categories. 'Means of Escape' and 'Celebration'. Many use drugs perfectly recreationally and have few issues, if any. Others seek regular oblivion, which is highly toxic. Most insidious of all, many people do both. But when one of us dies, we speak of mental health issues and 'exhaustion' and completely omit drugs from the equation. Both legal and illicit. Entirely out of fear. It's time to speak up. It's a Gordian Knot of intense complexity that is aching for the sword of Alexander.

Of course, surviving the DJ biz isn't just about staying physically healthy. Maintaining your relationships is also really important. I don't think we could do a whole book and not talk about relationships, particularly how to actually preserve and enjoy one while one of you is almost never there. I don't think gender really comes into it, whatever your orientation the issues are the same. One is separated from the other. The other is either relaxed and cool about it, or it is a major problem. With many degrees of grey in-between. The job of a touring act is not conducive to relationships, that much I can tell you. In fact, the only time I've managed to hold onto anything resembling normality is when going out with another DJ, which believe me is not in any way normal and has a special set of nightmares all of its own.

We'd both end up spent and furious on 'Mauve Wednesdays', every week. We'd both be short-tempered and exhausted, and you'd think there'd be extra amounts of sympathy cutting both ways but somehow there rarely was. There'd be elements of professional jealousy and competitiveness. We'd both be laughably unfit in both body and mind. However, conversely, there was a certain comfort and security, both being in the same game. I wouldn't swap those times for anything though. Perhaps keeping it in the biz is the most effective solution to the dilemma.

When it comes to holding down love in a cold climate, I put it down to these crucial six factors. Distance. Inequality. Insecurity. Envy. Gratitude. Expectation.

These six can apply to most relationships, but are very glaring when you leave home a lot. Let me be clear that lots of people manage to be a DJ and have a normal-ish life, so please do not despair. It takes work, which is perhaps going out of style, but if you look at these main issues, it is a start. Knowing what the problems are is the first step.

CHAPTER 22

Distance isn't merely geographical; it is temporal and emotional too. If you are distant when you are together at home then any separation is only going to exaggerate this gap. It takes confidence in yourself and a certain solidity in what you have together to survive the parting. Only something secure can hold fast. Only a partnership that is insecure worries about cheating, and it is over-simplifying it to say it is all about infidelity. It is a factor, especially if one of you is a dirty DJ dog, but the bigger picture is far more nuanced. The *Insecurity* and *Envy* factors can glaringly exist even if you are both very open sexually. If your partner is not happy in themselves, then your job as a DJ can sometimes only make them feel worse. Also, if you yourself have issues, it will appear pretty obvious that you are very happy about getting away each time you leave for gigs, which is quite a punch in the guts for whoever has to stay at home when you think about it.

If a relationship in Dance Music has significant *Inequality*, distance will amplify this imbalance. You both need your own life and your own sense of self. If one party is living vicariously through the other, it can tip right over. Finding balance in yourself before you partner-up with anyone as wayward as a DJ is key. Of course, it is impractical to expect everyone to be on an equal footing, but observing and acknowledging these things helps you to understand and conquer them.

Some things are painful to behold in DJs. They get up and go to bed pretty much at will. Having to drag yourself up at stupid AM in the morning while they get up at the crack of whatever is pungently harsh. They earn more money twerking about to sync for an hour than you do in a week of genuine grey grind. No one follows a plumber online in the millions. Few professions expect applause for merely doing their job. All these things can chisel-away on the relationship like a constant drip of water on stone. *Envy* has a green face, and it is not a pretty one.

Gratitude is key to survival. A lot of people really do not understand the value of what is right in front of them. Taking everything for granted, thinking it will always be there is a real love-killer. A sort of dopey happiness is just as dangerous as a pessimistic, ungrateful fatalism. When you gloss-over reality and go on auto-pilot you completely stop looking at what you've got. Yet again I say; if you do not value it, absolutely no one else will, that I can guarantee. If your love has no value, then it may as well not exist. You are just living with someone, may as well be a flatmate or friend.

Demands and *Expectations* are the real danger I find. Again, you are taking value away from what you have by constantly telling yourself things aren't up to scratch. Value is in what it is, not what you have been told it is supposed to be. Following expectations come the inevitable demands: do this; be this; what you are is wrong. Never nice things to hear. More than ever, we are existing more and more in an alternate, almost cartoon reality that is created online, lives only in our heads and exists as photographs, videos and social media threads. None of these are real. Computers, phones and most of all *drugs* cripple our sense of what is important and valid. Things that blur the reality of what you've got are *everywhere* but none-more so than in Dance Music.

The strongest of all these constructs is the myth of work. That our career always comes first and above all things, including those we profess to love. All obvious reasons aside about why this is damaging, it meshes with the modern illusion that we no longer inhabit reality. One of the greatest dangers love can face is forming a relationship with someone who has fallen for an *idea* of you. Like for example a job title such as 'Producer' or 'DJ', rather than your true self. This goes both ways when you are together. People too often come at DJs expecting international adventure and 24/7 party time, when, of course, this is the last thing you want at home.

Conversely, DJs often seek a cartoon stability in those they partner and place the entire onus for domesticity on the other party. Both are simultaneously engaging only with hastily drawn, two-dimensional versions of the other. We have to cut through the bullshit of modernity and find out what is true, delving underneath the plastic. *Only* the real counts. We spend enough time miming, faking and pretending as DJs these days, it would be madness to let these fictions infect our love too.

I once went on a date. They are rare but they happen. T-Man used to call my liaisons 'working at the cold meat counter'. The date was quite short, but I liked her. Asked for her number afterwards. After a few days, I got the courage up to call it.

CHAPTER 22

"Hi, thanks for calling!" she piped, cheerfully.

"Yeah, I know! So sorry it took so long. I'm an idiot."

"No! Don't say that. Don't be so hard on yourself."

"Well, you know... anyway, glad to speak to you."

"Sure, good to speak to you too. How are you feeling?"

It went on like this for about 20 minutes, she kept asking how I was feeling, which was getting a bit weird and Californian.

"Hey, listen, I'm fine, *really*. Feeling good! Pretty chipper thanks."

"So why are you calling then?"

"Well, you told me to..."

"No, we never do that, as policy".

"We?"

"Yes, you understand this is the Samaritan's suicide hotline? Right?"

"Oh."

CHAPTER 23
THE PROMISED LAND (MEMBERS-ONLY)

If one of the great things about Acid House was the way it brought the misfits to the fore, this was not an accident. Nightclub culture dates back to the Jazz Age when newspapers of the time were scandalised by the idea of young white debutantes mixing with foreigners and dangerous black men. The modern version came from disco, and disco came from minorities and outcasts. David Mancuso's loft parties in early 70s New York were not just the template for the modern nightclub, they were arguably the first 'safe space', a hangout for the disenfranchised of the city, a family for people whose own families had often disowned them. In the early days of the scene in Chicago, the word 'House' was gay slang for something being absolutely correct. Your shoes were 'House'. Your outfit was 'House'. Your attitude was 'House'. I use the word in its original, purest sense to say the following: it is utterly, absolutely HOUSE to be anti-racist.

But the foundational myths, the origin stories we in the culture love to tell ourselves, whether it's Larry Levan playing the Paradise Garage or rival firms of football hooligans partying together because of ecstasy and Acid House, don't make dance music, or by extension the people in it, immune from the problems that run through society. In fact, they can make us seriously blind to our own faults, wrapped in a duvet of smug fake exceptionalism. Snug as a mug, tugging in their rug.

Working as a DJ or a producer or a promoter or anything in the Dance Music industry does NOT make a person inherently tolerant, open-minded or amenable to the ideals of Acid House than anyone else, no more than playing Joe Smooth's 'Promised Land' makes me Dr Martin Luther King Jr. We've all seen people whose entire career is based on Black, Gay and Latinx music loudly supporting Mad King Trump, cheering Brexit, trying to 'have a discussion' about immigration and cheering deportations and even drownings. I had a very depressing day dealing with racism on the 'Ibiza Local Residents' website recently, which may surprise you that it is as parochial, mean-spirited and hostile as any tinpot little Englander group. Perhaps worse as nearly everyone on it is a foreign immigrant, and there are none more rabid than those desperately trying to prove that they belong. None more hostile to outsiders than those who think they've made it in safely through the door. None quicker to pull up the ladder or raise the drawbridge.

In the Drum & Bass scene, several artists have been called out for far-right views on racial superiority. Yes, the scene created by Grooverider, Goldie, Fabio and A Guy Called Gerald has racists in it. While I'm all for zero tolerance for cretins, sometimes I worry that these individuals not only thrive on the attention, they're a distraction from the bigger issues, like the way the UK press would rather talk about old sitcoms being censored or statues being pulled down than 'stop and search', or systemic racism. After all, it's much easier to grab an internet pitchfork and 'cancel' some douche than face self-reflection on what we could actually do in the real world to make things better. While there are, to be absolutely fair, some DJs actively working on the side of the angels: the Blessed Madonna raising money for Help Refugees, or Yaeji helping trans communities in New York, too often industry engagement begins and ends with social media or a 30-minute conference chat. In the 80s and 90s, there was in the Anti Nazi League. There was Rock Against Racism. Where is our version? Where is 'House Against Racism'? How many DJs are really willing to forego a night's earnings to mobilise for the cause, and how many of their agents are willing to help them pause the gravy train for even a moment?

The original musical sin, of course, dates back to that whitewash behind Elvis and beyond. Even in dance music, the work and creativity of black artists is often still ignored until given 'credibility' by a white artist who gets the credit for 'rediscovering' it: gatekeeping, once again. The rewriting of history to erase minority and female characters from the key roles they played and reassign credit to a handful of 'great [white] men' is as much a feature of dance music as any other culture. Legislation and policing in the UK still prevents black promoters from putting on events for a black crowd with black DJs because of concerns about 'safety' that are as transparently racist as a Victorian anthropology textbook. So often the 'face' that the corporate backers of so many commercial events want to put forward is one that the suits in the boardroom are comfortable with. It must be utterly soul-destroying for cultural originators to be passed over for (often more expensive and far less skilled) milky white sound-a-likes who better fit the brand.

I'm white, although when I fill in forms in the UK, there's often a special box just for me and my kind. I found that growing up in England in the 70s from Irish background gave me a view of xenophobia. The key difference is, all white immigrants have to do is shut up and/or learn a new accent and it all goes away. Clearly, racism is a process that is learned. The one time overt racism raised its ugly head in my childhood, my Dad stamped on it like a snake. It's literally the only time he hit me (for Punk swastikas on a schoolbook). I remember joining in very briefly when everyone around me was being mildly racist aged around 10 and feeling slightly sick after. And never doing it again because it felt all-too-familiar, like something that happened to me at school. There's a massive pull to be the one pointing and laughing and never to be the pointee. Especially if you've experienced being in the middle of the circle. The abused are often the fastest to become the abuser. The root of it is lack of education. No understanding. No experience of it. It's an abstraction. Hate can hijack the desire to fit in very easily.

I've rarely worried about fitting in since those days (hence many in the wider industry looking upon me as they would, say, a wart, or a boil), but a huge problem throughout the industry and the wider world is the denial of any and all critical voices. The modern liars at the wheel and the average internet nitwit share a powerful if not banal weapon to shut down self-reflection and accountability, which is to say criticism is 'not very nice'. Point to the Emperor's naked arse and you are a 'moaner', you are 'arrogant', you are 'mean', and all variations of generally a rather bad person. You are told repeatedly to 'be kind' when it's clear all they want is for you to shut up. Which isn't very kind at all.

They don't engage at all with the topic. It is immediately personal. They don't have the ability to argue the issues, so their riposte is to go at you personally instead. People whom you question or criticise react with a whispering campaign of how terrible you are. Fear enough there to shut anyone but the biggest idiot right up... hang on!

Capitalist culture has put its alien proboscis down everyone's throats, laid an egg and a little Mickey Mouse has burst from everyone's chest demanding 'positivity' at all times with all things. Nothing could be more fascistic. Not only is every doylum, nimrod and dullardo demanding that their insanity is not merely to be tolerated but accepted, everyone has to be exactly like them too. If you are critical of anything, you are somehow suspect. The criticism immediately ignored, but the critic very much noted.

I honestly had trouble as a child understanding some major lessons from history. How civil wars could split families. How people would randomly attack others who wore glasses because; 'intellectuals'. How people could swallow the lie that Jews were some sort of evil cult, and start a world war. As a kid I used to think it was because it was 'the olden days' and people were simpler. Easier led.

I get it now. Nothing is different from the past. I see how evil rises. It rises as stupidity, entitlement and fear. And it rises right now. Everywhere.

People are scared. Fears with a small 'f' as well as major ones. They react to information overload with a shut-down. A cut-off point where they stop believing, stop listening and start protesting by making wild and irrational claims. Corporate divide and rule has made everyone think they are special and important to a degree that is unsustainable. Everyone's personal space, opinion and trajectory is so unrealistically precious to them, it results in them being completely resistant to input, rationality and co-operation. Social media has been great for linking people with similar interests, but it also hugely exacerbates tribalism and polarisation and amplifies the hate and fear that keeps human beings apart. Fuck the 'marketplace of ideas', it'll never, *ever* compare to the 'dancefloor of bringing people together'. I do not think it is a coincidence that during hard times, people rave.

Because while 'some of my best mates are...' is no defence to racism, it's self-evident that partying with people different from you, with music and various carefully chosen intoxicants heating up the melting pot can help vaccinate us from fear and ignorance of 'The Other'. The more expensive or gentrified or 'upscale' or 'exclusive' the party, the more the inequalities of dystopian capitalism seep into our culture, the more restricted the demographic with access to the club becomes, the further away we get from its healing social benefit, its raison d'être, the thing that always made it about more than getting wasted and jiggling around in a loud, dark room. One of the reasons I personally ended up neck-deep in Dub at the 'West Indian Centre' was because the chrome and carpet discos simply wouldn't let our black and brown mates in. Raves ramped this essential mix up even more. I would go so far as to argue that Raves are not only so very wrongly maligned by the hard-right, they are so massively important for a well-rounded society to the point of being obligatory.

How can we fight the racism within Dance Music? Maybe we should start a highly inclusive, anti-establishment party sub-culture. A place where we can be proud of our differences? Wear our weirdness as a badge of honour. All races. All genders. One love. Oh, wait. Maybe it's been done before? It is truly amazing what can be forgotten in just a few decades.

INTERLUDE
STILL HERE

I was completely convinced the next call I'd get from anyone regarding Tour Manager would be concerning his death. The last time I saw him face-to-face neither of us were in great shape, physically, mentally or financially. Some years had passed with no reply at all from him to any forms of communication. We'd both been through decades of dance music nonsense, much of it at the same time and in the same places. As far as capitalism goes, we'd both had a good go at spinning the big wheel, and lost pretty spectacularly. The house always wins. Thing is, I'd never really had any money. Never really mattered to me. He really did. At one point, a millionaire.

I will never forget his empire crashing, as I lived in it for some of the time, and still find some of the dust from it in my clothes. Yes, it may have been my fault, partially. As enabler, if nothing else, no matter how well-meaning. It all went to pot for two main reasons. One: capitalism ate it alive. Two: loads of drugs. Is a theme emerging yet? For years T-Man's main business was almost a monopoly, the only venue in the middle of one of the biggest student campuses in the world. Ancient, crumbly and venerable, as was the venue. It had a cachet in the 1980s as a sort of no-mans-land between the cooler, local Freaks and the more cosmopolitan, braver students. A small neutral zone. A Checkpoint Charlie of intelligence and style in a horrifically normal city. For a while, literally one of the coolest places for hundreds of miles around. Then the council initiated a capital-raising scheme of allowing a slew of city-centre licenses. Gentrification. Suddenly whole streets that were no-go zones for students, places you could literally be killed, suddenly resembled European cafe-society. Hard-boiled locals looked on in horror as their beloved blood-soaked backstreets became shabby-chic haunts for Tarquins and Jemimas from the Home Counties.

Change happened. Tour Manager's monopoly ended rapidly. People previously too scared and also too lacking in local knowledge to go anywhere else suddenly left the safe confines of his venue and reclaimed the streets of a now safe city centre. Old men in pubs looked-on in slow, glacial shock as their locals slowly closed or were re-purposed. Kids would ask for their photo taken with them, humiliating evidence of the 'local character' the estate agents promised. People very easily identifiable as students and Freaks started to look and act the same as Normals. Normals began to adopt the trappings of the counter culture and those on the edges of society started to get a lot more boring and dowdy. Homogenisation is hardcore. It takes no prisoners, not even the inmates' tattoos are safe.

Unfortunately, if you inherit your success, you have precious little idea of how it happened in the first place. You can only try to learn quickly how to maintain it. Tour Manager was literally born in the venue. When it all started to go bad, he did two fatal things. He threw good money after bad, effectively chucking a large bucket of future at the flames of the present, and then he went to bed. The drug cycle of hyperactivity turns at such a rate that it becomes pointless in its intensity, coupled with the inevitable comedowns that last far longer than the ups... it's a recipe for doom when it comes to business. He'd effectively lock himself in his room, quite literally, and refused to come out while those trying to make things work needed leadership. Then he'd emerge, whooping and yelping with borrowed vigour and literally fuck up everything they'd tried to do while he was in his pit. I know a few industry people on this boom-and-bust cycle. Fundamentally incapable of understanding teamwork. Casting adrift staff to do what little they can when the leader's attention wanes, then the boss shouting at them for what work they managed to do while unsupervised. The cycle of an abuser, as many women will recognise.

T-Man was no Napoleon by any means. A good sort at heart. He gamely did everything he could while trapped in the drug life to repair the unrepairable. He liquidated everything and chucked it at the crumbling edifice. It just made it all burn brighter, putting off the end for just a little longer. There is only one proven skill when it comes to beating the house, and that is knowing when to walk away from the table. With the best of intentions, more and more drugs were taken to fuel late-night wacky get-out-of-jail schemes. More bad decisions were left like sad little puddles everywhere for staff to clean-up while the puddle-makers went back to bed for three or four days.

Tour Manager coveted nothing more in the world than a black American Express card. You may have heard of the Black Amex. It is literally without limit. You can roll-up to a car showroom, or buy a house or yacht with it. No questions asked. You can't apply for it. They come to you if you are rich enough. In the midst of the slow dissolving of the small empire, T-Man and his family had built, his venue manager arrived with the post and a terrific hurrah went up.

"HURRAH!" went the hurrah.

"What is it? What's all the noise?" I objected, disturbed by the break in the bleak.

"Finally! Now of all times! There is a God! Imagine this arriving right now and what I do with it. I can…"

Mid-flow, the venue manager reached over, plucked the card out of T-Man's trembling fingers, grasped it with both hands and ripped it messily in two. Quite correctly, of course. The hysterical laughter that followed from all of us was pure, 100%-proof gallows humour.

Not long after they came for his stupidly awesome and extremely beloved car. I had to take T-Man aside and ask in wonder:

"You've lost so much mate, I can't even… I don't know what to say or what to do."

"Don't worry, they are just… things."

Words I will never forget. He had a way sometimes of being incredibly wise completely by accident.

There's nothing more tragic than those sad blank squares dotted on the walls that denote where a picture used to be in a house that is being aggressively emptied. Blind eyes staring out, pleading. Soon everything was gone. Towards the end, T-Man just stopped fighting and just stood around in corridors dejectedly during his few waking moments. Reality was now the dream, and the dreamer unable to arise from the nightmare that was so persistently real.

Sticks was there to help, which in T-Man and Sticks' terms meant taking loads of gear and having daft ideas that made everything worse. Although to his credit, Sticks did come out with the best sentence I'd ever heard come out of a living person when I asked him what he thought the future might hold:

"The fucking fucker's fucking fucked the fucker up."

I was taken aback. I asked him to repeat it.

"The fucking fucker's fucking fucked the fucker up."

"Sticks! You just did a whole sentence using the word fuck!"

"Fucking right!" he replied.

Tour Manager just mooned about. A lost soul. A ghost, pre-haunting his own castle. I'd not seen him like this since he was particularly high and we were walking through the grounds of a stately home and he was badly startled by an albino peacock that leapt out at us from a shrubbery. He seemed to carry that look all the time now. Perpetually plugged-in to a live socket, being electrocuted in super slow motion.

Fast forward a few years later and there he was, in Sticks' dead Dad's old house. On his own. Surrounded by 7ft high pyramids of detritus. Almost unable to talk, which was absolutely the most chilling aspect for me. Someone who literally never shut up or even paid all that much attention to you, suddenly staring at you silently for long periods was pretty unnerving. And there we left him. Certain that while some of us had come together to make sure he was OK financially, the future looked pretty bleak. For both of us.

Well, much as I hate Disney, the ending was not to be as dark as advertised. Since the first book, the sleeper has awoken. After literally years of constantly messaging him with various degrees of false positivity, fury at his non-response, and all manner of tricks and jokes to try to elicit a response, one day my phone pinged with a message from Tour Manager. Just seeing his name made me jump out of my skin.

"Minsk."

Nothing more. A reference to a place we found hilarious. Nothing more was needed. Eventually, I got through to him. No longer a ruin but pretty much back to his normal, highly deranged self, minus any and all drugs. Or money. Or teeth.

He'd got over the decades of our nonsense, dragged himself off the haunted couch, and taken to retirement like an actual citizen. He then regally announced he was coming to Ibiza to see me. He arrived wearing full cricket umpire regalia and his traditional bag full of moderately obscene novelty T-shirts. He refused to laugh and tried not to do so frequently, due to having lost nearly all his teeth due to excessive use of amphetamines. When you take a lot of stimulants and never drink any water your body effectively dries out completely and you just roll around like a shit sultana, becoming rave tumbleweed.

Hard users tend to lose teeth because they stop producing saliva. Indeed it could be argued they stop producing anything at all. For that bodily function to happen properly again, they would have to stop talking, drink water, or eat once in a while. Bone and joint problems happen a lot too because all the lubricants are gone.

Laughter is a brilliant curative. Luckily for Tour Manager and I, that course of treatment continues. Neither of us was fully loaded with the understanding that, like every rugged and experienced traveller, we would find our salty tales met with incredulity by youthful mock sophisticates. We had no idea that the next stage in the rocket separation was simply 'being old' and telling our tales to increasingly disinterested audiences. In the face of the ignorance of our future invisibility, we would at least be able to remind each other of the unbelievable truths. Finding a chuckle became the holy grail, our dry quest to find even a patronising crinkling of the crows' feet to meet our outlandish dispatches from the frontline of stupid.

It was really great to see him alive and kicking but very annoying watching him try not to laugh out of an uncharacteristic vanity. Then I remembered a story from my birthday years ago. We had a party that, as I was always working, was also a gig. One of my good friends is Mr C. An excellent DJ and person, also unafraid of a bit of controversy. I first introduced T-Man to the idea of him when I pulled up outside an old, long demolished chip-shop on Tottenham Court Road in London called 'Mister C's' and constantly asked the staff how the peas were. Were the peas good? The peas are good? I'd heard that there were really really good etc. T-Man didn't understand why the patrons were laughing. Eventually, I got to introduce them to each other in person at my birthday gig at DC10.

Another good friend is the legendary Johnny The Dwarf. So named for obvious reasons. What is less obvious is how to navigate mutual piss-taking with a mate with a disability. The rules are actually fairly simple. Johnny decides. He's a tough guy, Fighting Irish like me. Say the wrong thing too early-on in knowing him, you could easily end up head-butted in the groiny areas. This isn't colourful language, I've seen him do it. Naturally, you don't get to be mates with him long if you don't understand the rules. However, given time, it ends up being endless shortarse gags. Not least of the reasons why is because Johnny starts them, and says he enjoys them if they come from the right source with the right intentions. It wasn't my thing personally, but I observed the phenomena with interest.

* * *

I was taking a break at the entrance, back in the days when it was a much more modestly-sized place. Tour Manager, myself and then Mr C came out for a quick cigarette too. The night was well under way, closer to over than starting. Some taxis pull up and out comes Johnny, along with about 10 of the famous Manumission girls. This happened a lot. Johnny was frequently surrounded by them. He was famously small in only certain areas. He'd had a drink or two, as was his wont, and probably inevitable at that time of the morning. I was very pleased to see him on my birthday, always pleased to see him full-stop. He was not small in temperament either, especially when lubricated. He swaggered up to the door, literally surrounded by professionally beautiful women.

"Alright, you lucky fuckers. Look at all these stunners I've brought."

Mr C piped up, it was his event, Superfreq: "You still have to pay though, mate."

"Hey! I'm Johnny The Fucking Dwarf, you cunt! LOOK at these! You should be paying ME to come in with them."

"I think he has a point there," contributed T-Man.

"Charge me half price at least", Johnny said with a wink and the usual nod to his stature, safe amongst old friends.

"Yeah, it's my birthday, let him in on my list come on," I chimed in.

"OK, but the girls have to pay something."

Johnny was fuming. Put his hands on his hips, glared at Mr C and said,

"Listen, I am not fucking happy."

Mr C looked at him for a moment. Then replied:

"Which one are you then?"

A pause.

Then Johnny let us know it was OK by creasing up laughing.

"I've been a dwarf 34 years, but I have to give it to you, that was a new one."

Tour Manager finally remembered to laugh when I reminded him of this, years later. Teeth or not. After this blast from the past, all bets were off, and it was like the dark times never happened. And in a sense, they never did. The past is long done. Dust. I remarked that all we have now are memories. In his distinctly cheery way he simply countered:

"Time to make some new memories then."

Beaches are for children and tourists. We'd seen all the Ibiza sights a thousand times. We spent a week laughing about all the things that happened. I decided to write a book containing some.

We'd come a long way. We were still alive. It hadn't beaten us yet. If there is still some fight in us, there is hope for everyone. If holy fools like us could survive the machine, anyone can. Which means it can be beaten. Kids with truth and energy have the glowing baton. Everything is in their hands now. If idiots like us can come through the other end, there's no reason at all that the world cannot be changed.

None.

CHAPTER 24
MY 0.004 CENTS

You think billionaires and capitalism have nothing to do with a career in dance music? They are intertwined with EVERY career in *every* industry now. How much do you think the head of Spotify, Daniel Ek, is worth? Well, at the time of writing it was, wait for it, FOUR BILLION dollars. Think about that for a moment. He doesn't make anything. We do. He essentially got a web developer to build him an online delivery system. A system that delivers OUR artworks, which he then collects money from and quite literally gives us less than zero for. Recently he did an interview and said these exact words:

"There is a narrative fallacy here, combined with the fact that, obviously, some artists that used to do well in the past may not do well in this future landscape, where you can't record music once every three to four years and think that is going to be enough. The artists today that are making it realise that it's about creating a continuous engagement with their fans. It's about putting the work in, about the storytelling around the album, and about keeping a continuous dialogue with your fans."

Now if after reading that you have a vein pulsing in your forehead with rage, like me, you may see it as someone who has become vastly wealthy from YOUR art telling you that you need to jolly well buck your ideas up. You may see it as someone who wants even more of your work, and everyone else's, to sell for his own profit. You may see it as one of the architects of destroying an art form and turning talent into 'content' telling you to chop-chop and churn out more for his machine, while hinting that if you don't, you are obsolete. That those who are 'making it' are, by insinuation, fully on-board with his way of thinking, and if you disagree, you are *not* going to make it. And doesn't that one killer word say so much?

'Content'.

Content is a word that I fear did not arrive naturally. It is too conveniently full of meaning. Firstly, that your art does not exist standing alone in the world, it is simply ammunition, luggage or fuel. To impose the new narrative, that 'art is now content', means it simply cannot exist without the *carrier*. There's a second underlying meaning that may or may not be perceived that perhaps you need to shut up and be *content* with what little is now paid you. Hush. We own the game now. We own you.

Do you see yet? This is our industry. In a recent Rolling Stone article, it was massively unsurprising to learn that 90% of Spotify's stream earnings go to 1% of labels and artists. It's not in favour of us in any way other than as a highly disposable resource, at the very best. The financial model is clearly broken. It serves no one but a handful of very powerful figures, both behind the scenes and on the stage. We'd listen to artists if they had any interest in anything but themselves, but they prefer empty virtue-signalling to actual change. Sure, many of them have some sort of personal charitable cause or bugbear but rarely, if ever, is their attention focussed inwards on the machine they serve. There is literally nothing to be gained but everything to lose by questioning the system. Believe me, I know. They are petrified of rocking the boat. Change might involve them reaching into their pockets. After all, isn't that where we keep it?

Devaluation of our art form is, once again, wider and not exclusive to us. Devaluation is happening everywhere very much intentionally. Devaluation starts with language; 'Beats' not music. 'Content', not art. 'Curator' promoting the role of amateur magpie to professional. 'Creator' demoting us to craftsman rather than artist. Familiar? Spread the idea wider. 'Disruption' not destruction. 'Rant' instead of reasoned discourse. 'Liberal' as a pejorative term, rather than absolutely everything that is good in people. Mitigations as control. Crucially, the value only goes down for *us*. The wages of the people drop, the profits for the rich go up. There can't be a single person reading who hasn't seen the average bar of chocolate almost halve in size in their lifetime but quadruple in price, right? Is it too purple to go as far as to say we are being systematically downsized and devalued for higher profit too? As fun-sized humans? I don't think anyone on a 'zero-hours' contract could disagree. This won't be news to them.

"Yeah but no but yeah but AHA! Secret DJ, YOU once worked with MEGA CLUB X, ergo, *shut up*, you big corporate slutty sell-out"...

No, you see, compared to these shambling, planet-sized mega-monsters, the old dogs are just an everyday business. While there may be some very wealthy shareholders, just like every other major venue and label, your average superclub also employs hundreds of people, pays them well, on-time and efficiently, pays its taxes and runs a tight ship that actually protects clubbers while within its walls. It's no more the enemy than say, in the world of retail, Harrods is. It's an institution, but it's just a business. It's not trying to pay anyone numbers under zero, get rid of any and all physical product, outlay, and shut down any and all opposition. Compared to the new globalists, they are just a local disco.

What I am talking about is Libertarian billionaires. Types who by day are developers who cut huge swathes through our venues and culture and then by night have the gall to pretend to be DJs. I'm talking about the BIG money. The sort that has major political and international influence. So much so that they pay nearly zero tax. The sort that are legally untouchable in any sense that we understand. I'm talking about the children of billionaires who decide one day that Daddy's cash is going to put them on a magazine cover carrying headphones they will never once use in anger. Who cheapen our art form by miming and mugging, bringing it down to the level of reality TV shows.

I'm talking about private jets, yachts and personal islands. Influencers and models. Empty, vacuous and grasping. I'm talking about the same attitude that leads to cheating elections and hoodwinking the public being applied to artistic careers. Buying your way in. Oiling the tracks. Clambering over the corpses of your friends to get to the 'top'. Doing as little as possible but paying for maximum effect. Cheating at every turn. Marketing way, *way* harder than working or creating. Again we are engaging in The Spectacle, rather than art. If modern movies are merely set-pieces of action and special effects designed to batter our senses, what is EDM but their audio equivalent?

Dance Music follows world events to the letter, indeed sometimes we even lead when it comes to protest. Or did. Our scene has been slowly gentrified, then outright appropriated by capitalism, much like every other industry and resource on the planet. It is now moulded into a strange golem that stomps around looking very much like every other business but with meaningless sleeve tattoos and a medieval haircut. We have long ceased to be a celebratory protest movement, a glittering refuge for freaks, the downtrodden and the terminally odd. Now we are purely another form of entertainment, as revolutionary as a beige sofa forever on-sale. Our industry has made sure of this, it represents and protects the richest elements of our movement and does little else. Nothing illustrates this better than COVID-19.

During COVID, record companies reported record profits from streaming, while artists literally had not only nothing, but every day were going into further debt. People were being laid-off or asked to accept lower pay but their bosses just get richer and richer. We are being had. Expecting the industry to represent us during the COVID crisis is completely futile. It's just a version of the Victorian philanthropic rescue fantasy. That some shadowy association that doesn't exist in any meaningful form, or union that was never formed, or benevolent God-like billionaire will descend from their crystal mothership to help us when the chips are down. I mean, if you needed any kind of indicator as to how unlikely this is, cast your mind back to, ironically, the 'tour manager appeal', where millionaire DJs were asking us to back their staff who were not working during the lockdown. Granted, it was misunderstood a little online, in essence, the tour managers had a scheme to help themselves and the big names were simply helping to publicise it. But again, the general response was there that the rich should help, because God knows no one else will, least of all the loudest objectors. The drive by Libertarians to dismantle the state worldwide means there will be no assistance anymore, for *anyone* if they succeed, never mind the music biz.

Don't know what I mean by Libertarian? Let me help...

Many think that the right-wing is 'neoliberal' which is the conservatism of Reagan and Thatcher. Sadly, and rather unbelievably, The Right are now far worse. Most of their key figures are now Libertarians. Some of you, I am certain, may actually be baffled at the global Conservative response to things such as COVID-19. Wherever the right-wing is in power, the USA, Brazil, UK etc., there is more death than anywhere else. By some degree. Without question, even when they lie about it. You may think they are stupid. They are not stupid. You may think they are incompetent. They are only incompetent if you think they are in the game of running their country. They are not. They are in the business of dismantling it. If you understand what a Libertarian is, then everything they are currently doing makes perfect sense. Libertarians don't want anything complex. They just want the complete destruction of the state, nation and community. It is the final boss level of ME ME ME. A Libertarian would no more tell anyone what to do in a crisis than they would come to anyone's aid. They also believe that anything at all can be replaced by the market. Seriously. The lot. So things like disasters are to run their course or *maybe* fixed by altruism.

It is no accident that these dangerously selfish ideas about giving other people absolutely nothing came about from people who have everything. I get it. How can someone who needs nothing and has everything truly understand the gifts of The State. How can they comprehend that The Elephant Man would never have had to strip and turn for money if a functioning State existed. How a woman would never be forced to hold out a hand out to a man again. How anyone with a shred of dignity in their soul might be gifted with the choice of going it alone, knowing their country stands by them when the chips are down.

Libertarians often claim "we are not monsters, if we see something terrible we will give it money". If that sounds stupid or, for example, resembles an odd system of relief based on someone rich actually noticing it is happening in the first place, then yeah... you are starting to see. It is the concept of "every person for themselves" taken to an almost sacred level. It is the church of the self. The ultimate expression of every daft idiot you know who cannot see anything beyond the gelatin in their sockets. It covers the world currently with great ease because highly intelligent but empathy-deficient Libertarians can chime and connect with people who can't even spell it but are similarly densely Libertarian to the bone.

CHAPTER 24

Libertarians and Disaster Capitalists are not merely the political and economic side of the same coin, they are beasts of no nation. Libertarians seek the destruction of all states, everywhere. And what is a planet without states and nations but, yes of course; *globalised*. So, for example, if you wonder why it is odd that sinister ultra-rich Americans or British seem to be happily in bed with Russians you have to remember, Libertarians have no country. Only wealth. They are often richer than actual nations. Too big to ally to one, they instead see countries as competitors. Competitors must be crushed. The oversight of governments impedes them greatly. Yet 'patriotism' is the first thing they shout about, very loudly. The ultimate aim is for no accountability to anyone. Which is why they inherently cannot govern. Governance is inherently *all* about accountability to the people. And when Libertarians do lead, it *must* be as a demagogue. Think about this for a second, what on earth has Putin got to do with The Left? What single thing about Russia has anything to do with socialism? He's more right-wing and Libertarian (he's personally a multi-billionaire) than the lot of them put together.

Libertarians are in power in places such as the USA, Brazil and the UK because, quite openly, Steve Bannon, Robert Mercer, Dominic Cummings, Trump, the Koch Brothers, Aaron Banks, Nigel Farage and many, *many* others worked very hard and spent literally billions for those elections to be pushed, rigged, cheated or bought. Aided most ably by the Kingmaker-with-no-nation himself, Rupert Murdoch. They join hands with Hungary, India, Australia, Israel, Japan, Netherlands, Poland, Switzerland, Thailand... the list is depressingly long and growing every year. Libertarians own the world's media outright bar a ridiculously small corner. Beyond irony, in 2017 The Kingmaker himself, Murdoch, sold much of his empire to Disney, but, of course, kept a large interest in it. The Disneyfication of the planet is no longer an ironic concept or cartoon dystopia, but utterly real. Libertarians understand completely a very simple credo:

Promise everything. Do nothing. Wait for the public to forget. Deny it was ever said in the first place.

You do not have to govern if you simply spin perpetually like an evil ballerina. They talk regally about the governance but do not do any unless it serves them personally. The constant chatter is merely a distraction for the only thing they actively do, destroy. Sounds purple? What do you think Uber does to other taxis? Tickle their tummies and take them for tea? It destroys and replaces. It takes a system, breaks it up and then reforms it into a monopoly. They do not pay tax, they do not pay well. They simply do not believe in anything that bears any resemblance to community.

When you understand Libertarianism you will no longer be confused by the strangeness of modernity. It is simply doing what a small group of extremely powerful men and women want. For you to be nothing more than a revenue stream for them. In absolutely every single aspect of life. Don't like it? Fine. There is a VERY easy way out of this jam... become a Libertarian.

And hey, the answer to Libertarian-led globalism is not isolationism, that is precisely what Libertarians want. All of us shut in our tiny little fiefdoms, borders closed, hating each other, fearing 'The Other' whether home or abroad while Libertarian billionaires pretending to be politicians are free to bestride the world like colossi, raking everything in. Pocketing the lot. Literally laughing all the way to the bank.

Angry? Bored? Bad news I'm afraid. The fault isn't cartoon James Bond villains. It's *ours*. Yours and mine. We've also devalued personal responsibility to almost zero. Everything is always someone's else's job, especially when it comes to fixing things and tidying-up. Quite literally, I mean, have you seen parks and fields after festivals now? Never mind the political landscape, the *actual* landscape is also fucked. Devalued personal responsibility is absolutely essential for globalisation. Blaming everyone but yourself is terminally rife throughout society and especially in business, and so rife in politics it is almost comical.

This attitude of zero accountability is absolutely everywhere. The ruling party are awful, therefore it's the opposition party's fault. The news isn't to our liking, so somehow the media is broken. It's as mad as looking in a mirror, thinking you are ugly, and sending the mirror back and demanding a replacement. The problem isn't the BBC, the problem is people not voting. The problem isn't just Spotify not paying musicians.

It is people who use it not wanting to pay anyone either. Your spouse didn't leave you because they are crazy, they left because you are plain awful sometimes. Personal growth is impossible without 'fessing-up and taking personal responsibility. What is entitlement but the absence of any and all responsibility? The two cornerstones of zero consensus and no personal responsibility are meeting Confirmation Bias and the Dunning-Kruger effect to form an unbreakable square foundation of stupid. Our house is now built on sand. We are royally fucked.

And again, what has globalisation, Libertarians and the reign of billionaires got to do with DJs? As well as practical knock-on effects, the ATTITUDE of imperious megalomaniacs is trickling down, but unfortunately, none of the money is, as per the very tired economic myth. Mark me well here; are you starting to think everything in the sets of the biggest earning DJs all sounds the same? You'd be correct because musical homogenisation is simply a cultural version of gentrification. Resolutely and without question. Not only are these issues artistic in nature, they have now become thoroughly moral.

During COVID-19 some of the wealthiest and perhaps, significantly, *newest* DJs were the very first to ignore the possibility of killing old folks, the disabled and the already weakened, and gaily trotted-off to work as soon as was feasibly possible with crowds not socially distanced at all. They were happy for actual *death* to spread so they could make money, despite being the ones who needed to earn the least. They will argue it was all completely above-board, in the countries they travelled to, because, of course, in their own land it was *not* legal.

They will argue that they distanced and wore a mask. But look out into the crowd and all you see is a manky soup peppered with crusty croutons of carriers. The DJs will claim it isn't their responsibility. They will talk like a businessman or politician. They will have a raft of rationalisations ready-made by their 'team'. They will arrive pre-excused and leave with a clear conscience, like any good entrepreneur. The nickname for this scene being 'Business Techno' is not an accident. So we come full circle. Not only is EDM a hollow, ridiculous pantomime impersonation of Acid House, even the 'credible' side is a travesty. A non-stop feast for the richest DJs. An elite 1% that mimics the world-at-large precisely. Unregulated. Unchecked. Devoid of moral integrity. Rampant with greed and utterly, *utterly* selfish.

What has happened with the digital age is essentially a reverse industrial revolution of sorts. We have dismantled the factories in the West, everyone has migrated back out to the countryside and now sits at home weaving on digital looms. Tiny 'artisanal' things are popping up everywhere, and the big stuff outsourced overseas and left to the new industrialists almost single-handed. A dissolution of an economy in-favour of the 1% and the 1% *only*. Possibly the ultimate goal of capitalism is within sight. A society where people are the product, either as data or in the case of bio-tech, even physically. A retardation of thousands of years of progress almost coming full circle back to the Victorian era once more, which was the golden age for the 1%. Any microscopic scrap of goodness was down to the random caprices of a handful of mega-rich philanthropists, many of whom were the cause of all the bad nasty in the first place. Believe me, we do not want that. It was fun for almost no one. It was a disaster for the environment, a catastrophe for the 'third world', in fact, let's be frank, it was shit for almost everyone and everything except a handful of total bastards.

So, I repeat once again, our daft wee dancing business follows the larger picture to the letter. When we no longer represent togetherness and community, we gather only to point ourselves at the money on the stage and applaud its existence. We've allowed the millionaires masquerading as politicians to make what we do illegal unless it takes place in a structure that makes large, sometimes vast amounts of money for a tiny elite. You saw the plague ravers and Nob Squad DJs in August and September 2020, midway through a global pandemic that was killing hundreds of thousands of mainly the most vulnerable, and that is a very conservative estimate in both senses. Despite warnings all over the world of a looming second wave, there they were, merrily doing gigs with no distancing in the crowd whatsoever. A month later, the global headlines are about a massive surge in cases amongst the young. So what can the only reply to this, frankly dreadful behaviour be? That the disease doesn't exist, of course. Can't have killed anyone if I don't believe, right? *Right?*

CHAPTER 24

Not forgetting to mention untold amounts of illegal smaller gatherings in Berlin, London, Ibiza and much further afield. As well as random illegal raves, 'legit' ones have appeared in some countries. Legally allowed, but morally utterly degenerate. The irony is almost palpable, considering our scene's origins. And no wonder kids have started raving illegally again. We've utterly lost touch with them, and they with reality. No example is set unless a truly terrible one. No industry advice or guidance OR indeed from government. No rational voices. Just endless, recklessly off-the-cuff personal opinion online. Which again, is exactly the same as the bigger political picture. Consensus is dead. Regulation and oversight nowhere to be seen. Sane voices demonised. Expertise reviled. All that matters is the self getting exactly what it wants, *now*. A sort of moral hedonism has appeared. An unquenchable gluttony of the soul. A wild west of reason.

I used to insert a caveat when, in light of Avicii, artists are being run into the ground, that when I spoke in the past of 'an industry that wants you dead' I was being a tad purple for effect. I think with the Coronavirus this is perhaps less of an exaggeration that even I could have dreamed of. It doesn't stop with our personal safety. COVID-19 is also, along with the billionaires behind streaming, working to bring the value of our music down even further, if you thought that was even possible. Because being reduced to 0.004 cents per stream just isn't low enough it seems, because value isn't just money. These attempts at properly distanced gigs appear, on the surface, to be background music for a fancy booze picnic. You can certainly dispute that during the pandemic, a gig may be distanced, but getting there and back to it isn't at all.

Is this 'the new normal' we can expect? Budget VIP-mimicking table service and the DJ as muzak? A clear and much, *much* further reduction in value. Sure, I get it. Some businesses are doing anything to try to survive. But how come myself and thousands of other DJs are fine with literally going to the wall rather than putting lives at risk? Seriously, I will personally go bankrupt any day now. And I am TOTALLY fine about it if it means I don't endanger anyone. Because I'm not the only one. If the choice is me losing money, or someone losing their life, how is that even a choice? It's a complete no-brainer. I'm even going to have to give some readers the answer, aren't I? I choose *life* you selfish dimwit. Put the book down and go stand in the corner and think about what you've done.

How do we come back from it? How can we lobby a government that hates us, and they always have, for support at times like this when our industry does not represent us at all, merely itself? Hey, we are by no means short of cash. A multi-billion dollar global business is where we are at lately. But it's simply not capable of thinking about anything other than enriching its top 1%. Sounds familiar right?

All is not lost, however. Perhaps all this is needed? Pandemics often lead to strange changes, some highly welcome. After plagues, a lack of labour can lead to increased wages and rights. It can be the straw that breaks the camel's back and incite genuine restructuring. It is a prism through which we can see truths far more clearly. The spectrum of light that emerges illuminates the dark corners where the very worst people operate with impunity. We get to see people literally choosing their own profit over the actual lives of others. We never see more clearly that during times of great stress, it gives X-ray specs for an entire generation. Openly displaying the practical differences between the self-serving right and the socialist left. The endemic and institutional faults of our systems are held to account during these times. Leading to unrest and direct action. It's about shedding the authoritarian rules of the gatekeepers and engaging in revolution, however mild. You think the Arab Spring, Gilet Jaunes, Chilean riots, Hong Kong protests, Black Lives Matter, Belarus and others all happened sequentially by accident? People all over the world have simply had enough.

Even silly things like discos have an orthodoxy. An establishment. The formation of anything has to have an infrastructure, history and rules, and if those things exist, Gatekeepers must always follow. And what we do should always be the polar opposite of orthodox. Acid House isn't a historical period, it's a state of mind and could not be more current. It is about rediscovering that slightly childlike innocence of the original feeling and wresting it from the hands of the too-cool-for-school hijackers who have made it into an unrecognisable business. A gravy train for them and their mates. The trick is understanding the difference between the real underground, and the thing that has taken its place for profit. Identifying the real thing is quite easy. Underground is not about being cooler-than-thou or *better* than other people, or even really about being 'in-the-know'. It's an unwavering standard that flutters proudly. It's a benchmark of a degree of quality and care that says what is clearly going on here is the pursuit of excellence above all.

I've mentioned the tyranny of cool before, but we have to realise that it's strangling everything to death. Acid House wasn't cool. I'm sorry, but I was there, and it wasn't. It was an organic, grass-roots movement that sprang up all over the UK because people were politically disenfranchised, poor and pissed-off. It wasn't created by a handful of hipsters or arch-marketeers, it was a melting pot of random influences from all over the planet. I meant *look* at it, geeky, dressed-down, awful TERRIBLE 'white people' dancing, music that sometimes sounded like a giant tambourine made of bin lids being chucked into a skip. It's not cool. In fact, I'm sometimes asked who my favourite DJs are, and after telling them I don't think DJing in itself is all that and it's entirely about the party, I tell them for me it's always the ones that clearly don't give a shit about what is cool. Danny Tenaglia. Harvey. Carl Cox. Weatherall. Blessed Madonna. You think any of them scour the internet or style magazines wondering what is hot? You think they use Shazam and then the 'you-might-like-this' algorithm on Beatport? You think they give a tuppenny fuck about what anyone else is doing? You reckon they spend hours trying to make sure every record is indistinguishable from the last one they play? None of them are fashionista types. No, *really*. You may be afflicted with adoration and think they are, but I've met them. They aren't at all. In their own way, they are pretty goofy and utterly genuine. They were the weird kids at school. They are just examples of that old adage that if you really, *truly* do not give a shit about fashions on a very fundamental level, you are automatically cooler than anyone else. You lead, never follow. Be bold. Do not fear. Joining the minimalist in-crowd is just conservatism wearing black. If your plumage is not glittering, you will be eternally camouflaged by your own timidity.

Over time, and especially in a live setting, The Secret DJ has grown conceptually. Call it a justification after the fact if you like, but it started to feel like it could be anybody. That anyone at all can be The Secret DJ. You could be. Which is why we tried (and arguably failed) to do the gigs in the dark behind a screen. Take the ego right out of it. Take the phones and cameras and lights and bangers and The Spectacle and bin the lot off. Blackout. Best music and sound available. Return to the source. Do the NOW take on Acid House. You should try it. You be The Secret DJ next. I'm knackered.

Ultimately this is really not about my advice, my 'wisdom', my jaded, antique and highly coagulated career... or was entirely ever about me at all. It's about *now*. Where we *all* go from here. What we do about it physically in the real world, not what we blither and witter about online. It's all about kids defying the law in warehouses and fields, and always has been. Making tapes and fanzines, or the online equivalent. It's about people in their bedrooms making cosmic wonders and then sneaking them into a set somewhere. It's not ancient VHS tape footage, antique records or even more antique Gatekeepers telling folks what to do, it is owned outright by whoever is doing it *right now*. And it is yours precisely between the moment you start dancing and the moment you wake up after the glow has worn off. Talking about something ain't doing it. It's entirely about *doing it*, and doing it yourself, because, and if I say this often enough it may sink in, literally *no one* is going to do it for you. Make some noise. Give the bastards at the wheel value for money with their law specifically designed to put us down. It doesn't matter what the music is, it simply serves as a siren. A clarion call to the lonely, lost and dispossessed. The kids doing it right now aren't reading dry books, they are living it. Happily breaking the law while I am dreaming in my Balearic castle.

I've quite literally racked my brain for answers for months while writing this. Some sort of roadmap out of this hole is absolutely required but I don't think I am qualified to do it. I've long been consigned to the shelf marked 'nutter with opinions' by the industry. All I can do is warn you. How can we reclaim the world short of physically dragging them out of their gilded bunkers? Is it more and more riot? Have we not developed further than violence? Maybe I have forgotten that what we did in the 80s when presented with evil was to dance right in the devil's face. Wiggle our bits at him and show him just how many of us there are, and how few his agents are in comparison. Maybe the lesson of Acid House has already been learned? That we don't deserve it. That we sold it down the river for cash. That we are getting exactly the governance we deserve. We got the world to this point. By inaction, compliance or design, it almost doesn't matter in the face of the horror of the final result. All it takes for capitalism to take absolutely *everything*, every single last thing that is ours, every small corner that is sacred... is for us to let it.

I was back at home in the mountains recently, come to see my old folks and try help out during the pandemic. It always recharges and reconnects me when I get back to where I am from.

I was walking along a countryside pathway, the young summer grouse were flocking, a big group of them waddling comically along the road. I was walking with high dry stone walls either side. They ran away clucking in high dudgeon from my dog, stuck in the road, navigating with as little option as a narrowboat in a canal. Never thinking. Just running fearfully ahead in the only direction available. Eventually, the dog barked, they remembered they could fly, and the walls became irrelevant. They just needed a big enough scare to find their way out.

When they did, they were beautiful.

ACKNOWLEDGEMENTS

This book is dedicated to Mark Devaney, Prince of Bradford. Who nursed this entire thing since birth, through COVID-19, and has been the prime force keeping the Secret DJ project, and me personally, alive enough to get everything done.

Special thanks to:

My family. Always.
The Cast of Players. Thank you for your stories.
Duncan J.A. Dick. Editor of great quality and gentleman of substance.
Colin Steven. Velocity Press Boss. Thanks for standing up and being counted.
Johnno Burgess and the Bugged Out! crew.
Andy Kayll. Simply the best ears in the biz.
Paul Morrissey and Bozak. Nothing sounds better.
Andy Booth. De facto adult and designated driver. Keeping me out of jail since 1999.
Jon Child. Thanks for keeping the faith.
Danielle Breese. Most excellent intern and keeper of the social media keys.
Brian 'Beezwax' Barrett. Audio ambassador to Ibiza and huevo bueno supremo.
Mr and Mrs Jostler and the mini Jostlers.
Arthur Baker. A constant support over the years.
Lee Brackstone. The midwife, mother and father of this thing.
Duncan Brown. Thanks for your help with Book One, not forgotten!
Paradise Lost, Ibiza. Shivverin' me liver throughout.
Paul, my No.1 Cuz.
Nikki Gordon. Stalwart hero.
Ben Clark and The Soho Agency. Reppin' hard.
Andy Robinson. Thanks for everything and best of luck.
Grayson Shipley and Hugo Quintanilla. Ibiza's finest audio.

Additional sincere thanks to:

Denise Johnson. Rest in Peace comrade.
Bill Brewster
Ivan Smagghe
Richard Norris
David Dunne
Posthuman
Ewan Pearson
Denney
Miguel Campbell
Neville Watson
Justin Robertson
Carl Loben
Manu Ekanayake
Frank and Ruth
Bob Stanley
Annie Nightingale
Marius De Vries
Roisin Murphy
Carl Puttnam
'Business Teshno'
The Quietus and Ed Gillet

La gente de Dalt Vila, en mi corazón siempre.

Particular thanks to Andrew Weatherall for his help at the start. A shining example of how to fuck the whole disgraceful thing right off and do everything your own way. Rest in peace.

A GLOSSARY OF TERMS

3-deck workout - A situation whereby a proper DJ uses synthesis to make something new out of component parts. Almost extinct.
A&R - 'Artist and Repertoire'. A music industry job. A&R are talent scouts, midwives and then handlers. They are the liaisons between the artists and the biz at the lower level, pretty much in charge of things at the top of the A&R tree.
Acid Dad - See 'Balearic Silverback'.
Acid House - A global phenomenon that began in the 1980s and, technically, is still going strong thank you very much.
AFEM - 'Association For Electronic Music'. One of the least ineffective of the industry's self-appointed bodies that seem to pop-up and disappear every few years.
Afterparty - The temple of Bes. The professional wronghole. The inevitability of excess and the fabled wages of sin.
Agent - An earthly representative of that which should be rendered unto Caesar. Never to be confused with someone who represents the interests of a client. Most are afflicted with a rare bone condition which means they can only pick up a telephone when it rings, but cannot pick it up to make a call. No known cure exists.
Ambient - 99% music-free music for slimmers, vegans and magicians.
Amen Break - One of those things you have heard so many times you don't even hear it anymore. Like the voice of your spouse.
Amphetamines - Things you take that make you go faster. Like risks. Actually, yeah, just like a very large risk that absolutely never pays off.
Analogue/Analogue Gear - An imaginary brass and solder duffle coat that ageing nerds wear to let everyone know they are to be avoided.
Back-to-back Set - When two DJs perform simultaneously on the same equipment. Urg. Yeah, that sounds horrible when you put it like that.
Backstage - The holy grail for punters. For professionals, a tiny regional train station's waiting room on a rainy grey day.
Badgerwatch - Televised night-vision fun for lovers of rural vermin.
Balearic - Who the fuck knows?
Balearic Silverback - See 'Rave Dad'. 'Chelsea Pensioner'. 'Dad's Army'.
BBC Radio One - We continue.
BC (Before Clubs) - A packet of crisps and ironing your woggle. Oh no wait, that is 'before cubs'.
Beak - Stuff people who clearly have way too much money put up their nose to let everyone and especially themselves know that they clearly have way too much money.

GLOSSARY OF TERMS

Beatport - A dull supermarket for DJs who can't be arsed anymore.

Bernays, Edward - Worth a google, defo.

Betamax - What happens when you go head-to-head with porn. You lose.

Billing - Not to be confused with beak. A thing DJs will never confess an all-encompassing obsession with.

Blues (clubs) - All over the world, when Black folks want to escape the white man, if only for a few hours, they seek refuge here.

Brighton - Like many geographical cities that are one of the most southern points of a civilisation, all the lunatics end up there, possibly in a botched escape bid, like naughty grounds in a coffee filter.

Bro - A dickhead, usually.

Classically Trained - Something DJs say about themselves for added gravitas, not realising that it really, really has the opposite effect. Seriously mate, if you are that much of a ninja what the fuck are you doing pointing a finger in the air like you really don't care, wearing jeggings and using sync?

Club Promoter - Someone who promotes themselves in a club.

Content - Something that has eluded me all my days.

Cool - The greatest con ever perpetrated.

Corporate - To be embodied, and once whole, to rip-off everything, everywhere, for all time.

Crossfade - When you get so old and angry you literally start to become invisible.

Dead Air - As opposed to being live on-air.

Deep House - See also 'Deep House'. Not to be confused with 'deep house'.

Dekmantel - The item of furniture upon which you display a small collection of dek.

Disco - Not so much a type of music, more a way of thinking.

Diva - French for dickhead.

DJ Booth - A pit that usually houses cocks.

DJ Fee - A truly terrible name for a DJ.

DJ Management - A large misnomer. More of a curse across the aeons than a job.

DJ/Producer - Like a DJ, only worse.

Dolby ATMOS - Too much like hard work for most DJs, it would appear.

Driver - The thing in a speaker that makes all the BLAH come out.

Drug Safe - A small metal cabinet designed to keep idiots and crackheads out, generally full of pens, Bic lighters, lost earrings and sweets. All the proper drugs were pocketed by the bouncer, manager and/or promoter before reaching it.

Drum Machine - A small device where if you depress the keys, you sometimes depress the listener.

Eclectic - A word people use when they don't know what they are on about. See also 'Balearic'.

EDM - The endless honking of the idiot trumpet.

Electronica - A catch-all term for music by people who take themselves extremely seriously.

Experimental - See 'not very good really' and 'I've not finished it yet but… fuckit'.

Fader - Something you slide up and down to make things better. Like a toboggan run, or penis.

Flight Cases - Large boxes designed to make life extremely easy for their contents, and utterly miserable for their handlers.

Genre - Something the makers of 'cool' came up with when they were bored on a wet Wednesday in Bradford.

Ginsters - Food of the Gods. If the Gods are rather chubby and spotty.

Glastonbury - Mud, bindis and gak.

Goths - An ancient tribe of furious Germans who wore black and mercilessly complained their way across Europe.

Grunge - The thick layer of gunk you take home from the dancefloor. See also 'Rave Gravy', 'Trenchfoot' and 'Disco shit'.

Hacienda, The - Never heard of it.

Hipsters - People who only comprehend the shiny surface of individuality, and nothing whatsoever of its inner darkness.

Ice Machine - An expensive, prosaic and fundamental piece of equipment in the hospitality industry. Not to be confused with 'dry ice machine' which is loads more fun.

Industrial - To be of use to the people, rather than a person.

IP Owner - Fuck knows? Did I even use that?

Knuckles, Frankie - A very nice man.

Laptop DJ - Just like a real DJ, only much less so.

Libertarian - The great adversary. Lord of the flies. The turd in the aquarium.

Line-up - The bit just before a nose-up.

Live Set - This thing where musicians play all the notes you hear in real-time, and if their hands, feet and fingers stop, so does the music. Almost extinct. Not to be confused with pressing buttons, unless it is an accordion.

Lost Vagueness - Can't lose it if you never had it.

M1 - England's first motorway, named after a very useful keyboard that hadn't been invented yet.

MIDI/MIDI instruments - Something-something-digital-information-something-something-yawn-zzzzz.

GLOSSARY OF TERMS

Millennium - The massively underwhelming King of all New Years and apocalyptic end-of-days for many promoters and DJs.

Minimal - A refuge for both the least and greatest minds, simultaneously.

Miniscule Of Sound - A tiny tent, a parody of one of the world's biggest clubs. Very similar to a noisy Punch and Judy, which bears no resemblance at all to the actual, full-sized Ministry of Sound. No Sir. Nothing at all like a giant Punch and Judy in the pitch black.

Modular - Pretend science for covetous souls.

Music Biz - A singularity so dense it crushes everything that enters. Especially light.

Music Magazines - A Jurassic Park of paper and ink. Once powerful, now long forgotten, like a Medieval Blacksmiths Guild.

New Beat - A very old beat from the 1980s from the Benelux regions.

New techno - Not to be confused with New Techno. 'techno' with a small 't' is music for folks who think wearing black makes them instantly cool.

New Wave - Punky pop for spunky monkeys.

Normals - Those rarely troubled by individuality.

North, The - A state of mind absent of delusion. A magnetic point you can trust.

Northern Soul - Music, sweet music.

Oldskool - A deeply ironic spelling crisis.

Pirate Radio - A wireless ship that plunders hearts.

Plague Rave/Ravers - A plurality of dickheads.

Progressive Trance - Blimey heck, who put that in??

Public Relations - A misnomer whereby the masses are mentally herded by shepherds of ill intent.

Punk - The last true religion on earth.

Quadra-spazzed - A sizeable mental inconvenience.

Rare Groove - The best and most delicious way to cook and serve a groove.

Resident DJ - One less assailed by the perils of the road.

Shazam - A scoundrel's digital net, made for catching other people's rare butterflies.

Shroom - A very quiet room.

Situationist International - The only citizenship worth pursuing.

Sonar - Dunno, never been.

Soul Boys/Girls - Dancers and chancers.

Sound Engineer/Sound Tech - A collection of grievances held together with tape, holding a torch and all the aces.

Soundsystem - The pillars of the proscenium arch which bestride the portal of the soul.

Space/Space terrace - An old disco. You'd have liked it

Spetsnaz - Bunch of nutters you definitely would not call a nutter.

Spotify - Satan's thorny bell-end.

Stadium Trance - Urg. That sounds awful.

Stage Manager - Those partially responsible.

Summer Of Love - An utterly delightful mass delusion.

Sync [synch] - Mechanical stabiliser wheels for kids that can't ride. Yet.

Tech-bro - Those inheriting meek that you were warned about. A misogynist who made his money in a made-up world.

Tech-House - Audio pastels for the kitchen of the future.

Techno - A place to aspire to.

The Funk - When the spinal column is still attached to the undercarriage.

Tour Manager - Rave Butler to the least deserving.

Trance - Here be monsters.

Villa Party - Pretending to be rich for a bit.

Vintage - For when you are too fancy to say something is second hand.

Vinyl - A by-product of oil that some fetishists covet almost as much.

Vocoder - A device that allows a voice to control a mechanical function. A bit like being married.

Warehouse Party - Like a regular party, but lots of it, in a big shed.

Warm-up Set - An opportunity for a dimwit to shine, or for a real DJ to be humble.

Whizz, Whizzy-water - A right big goblet of hideous.

Wispa Bar - Unnecessarily complicated chocolate.

Working Class - People who used to do all the work but actually got paid properly for it. The overlooked engine of every cultural change.

Yardies - Not to be messed with innit.

HEARTFELT THANKS TO EVERYONE WHO BOUGHT THE BOOK ON PRE-SALE

Michael Ainley, Alistair Aitken, Brian Anderson, Dean Anderson, Luke Anderson, Simon Anderson, Wayne Anderson, Paul Atkinson, Neil Bailey, Ian Bainbridge, Jonathan Ballard, David Barlow, Martin Barraclough, Gemma Baughan, Dylan Beale, Konrad Bednarski, Tim Belcher, Joanne Bennett, Lee Berry, Mark Blee, David Boardman, Van Bolle, Keeley Boon, Eric Borgo, Guglielmo Bottin, Simon Boulind, Simon Bradbury, Alex Brady, Scott Broadhead, Peter Bromley, Simon Brooksbank, Nick Gordon Brown, Steve Brown, Christian Broyd, Ryan J Bruce, Markus Buhmann, Simon Bullock, John Burgess, Rob Calcutt, Theresa Caldwell, Mark Callaghan, John Cameron, Lucy Campbell, Cam Carr, Niall Carroll, David Carter, Michelle Castle, Robert Chadwick, Craig Challis, Timothy Child, Peter Clark, Anna Clements, Peter Collins, Rob Cooper, Jake Conlon, Paul Cossey, Edward Coward, Ricky Cox, Andy Crone, Tanabe Daisuke, Gip Dammone, Andrew Darling, Kenneth Dargan, Darren Davies, Tom Davis, Nick Dawe, Marc J Dean, Tom Vojko Dekanic, Peter Devery, David Docherty, Shaun Dodd, Josh Doherty, Kim Donkersley, Mel Donnellan, Colin Drummond, Andrew Duff, Matthew Duffield, Yvonne Duffield, David Dunne, Michael Dunning, Juss Dymond, Manu Ekanayake, Mark Epstein, Darko Esser, Iain Farrell, James Faulkner, Fraser Fearn, Adam Femia, Lynn Fergusson, Jonny Fieldhouse, Barry Firth, Julian Foddy, Andrew Ford, Gavin Ford, Karen Ford, Tim Forrester, Stuart Forsyth, Michael Foy, Bastien Francois, Bruce Franklin, Sarah Franklin, Oli Freke, Aaron French, Paul French, Rich Furness, Artur Galanski, Laura Gallagher, Michael Gallagher, Mathieu Gendreau, Matthew Giardelli, Gilly, Lynne Girdwood, Alex Gold, Scott Gordon, William Gould, Martin Green, Phil Gregory, Brian Grieve, Stuart Guffogg, Martin Hanna, Rob Hardy, Craig Harrop, Barney Harsent, Keiron Hart, Jon Hearn, JM Henfrey, Kai Hepworth, Damian Herrington, Andy Hickford, Laura Higgins, Keith Hill, Jason Hink, John Hollingworth, Guy Hornsby, John Horsfall, Marc Horsted, Edward Spencer Howarth, Katherine Howell-Jones, Stephen Hunt, Ergin Hussein, Steven Jackson, Paul James, Juli Jane, Shane Johnston, Victoria Jolliffe, Lucie Jones, Owain Jones, Daniel Joseph, Serkan Karaca, Samuel Kehoe, Dan Kelleway, Niall Kelly, Tristan Kelly, Ross Kemp, Gavin Kendal, David Kenning, George F Killgoar III, Melanie Kingston, Kevin Knox, Steffen Korthals, Oliver Lailey, Thomas Leigh, Matthew Lewis, Michael Locco, Cheryl Lomax, N Lumsden, Oisin Lunny, Marjory Luxenberg, Mario Macari, Warren Mann,

Will Marin, George Marrison, Alex Martin, James Masters, Adrian Matheson-Bruce, Gary Matthewson, Lisa Maxim, Neil Mayes, Elizabeth McAulay, James McCauley, Terri McLoughlin, Conor McNicholas, Greg McPake, Gareth Mellor, Stephen Mellor, Robert Merlak, Simon Michell, Mundia Miles, Lee Monaghan, Paul Moran, Wayne Morgan, Darren Morris, Alex Mundy, Tim Murray, Paul Nichols, Will Nicol, Sarah Norton, Sheena O'Brien, Carl Packman, Michael Paley, Wayne Parkes, Tim Parkinson, Matthew Parsons, Rob Parsons, Ceinwen Paynton, Joel Pearson, Curtis Phelan, Paul Pickering, Paul Pinder, Scott Pirie, James Popplewell, Andrew Potterton, Abdul Qayum, Roger Quilliam, Andrew Rafter, Rayees Rashid, Damien Ratcliffe, Richard-Lee Read, Claudia Redmond, Jason Regan, Daniel Reynolds, Fred Robertshaw, Stuart Robinson, Tim Rodwell, Alun Rogers, Rachel Rose, Timo Rotonen, Ben Russell, Anthony Savell, Alistair Sawyerr, Matt Scott, Jeff Scroggin, Konstantin Semionov, Matthew Sever, Ann-Eliza Shapera, David Sheridan, Jeremy Shields, Robert Sillitoe, Mark Simpson, Nikolas Sinkola, Jon Slade, Ashley Slater, Jonathan Slater, Jon Smith, Pierce Smith, Leigh Strydom, Clara Suess, Simon Suviste, Chris Sweet, Steve Tavernor, Karen Taylor, Michael Taylor, Andy Thomas, Andrew Thompson, Simon Thompson, Anders Tollefsen, Rowan Triffitt, Brian Tuck, Gordon Vandal, Matt Walliss, Garry Wakefield, Chris Walker, Ben Walthew, Daniel Walton, Daniel Ward, Graeme Ward, Jan Warner, Roland Warren, Dan Watkins, John Weissinger, Simon Westfield, Dan Willett, Alexander Williams, Mark Williams, Steve Wilmers, Andy Wilson, Stuart Witts, Alex Woodhall, Zoelee Worsley